Tessa Shaw's
ULTIMATE
Home Help

Tessa Shaw's
ULTIMATE
Home
Help

EBURY
PRESS

As always, Peter

First published in Great Britain in 2001

1 3 5 7 9 10 8 6 4 2

Text © Tessa Shaw 2001

First published by Ebury Press
Random House, 20 Vauxhall Bridge Road, 20 Vauxhall Bridge Road,
London SW1V 2SA

Random House Australia (Pty) Limited
20 Alfred Street, Milsons Point, Sydney, New South Wales 2061, Australia

Random House New Zealand Limited
18 Poland Road, Glenfield, Auckland 10, New Zealand

Random House South Africa (Pty) Limited
Endulini, 5a Jubilee Road, Parktown 2193, South Africa

Random House Group Limited Reg. No. 954009

www.randomhouse.co.uk

A CIP catalogue record for this book is available from the British Library.

Editor: Emma Callery
Designer: Dan Newman – Perfect Bound Ltd

ISBN 0 09 187919 1

Papers used by Ebury Press are natural, recyclable products made from wood grown in sustainable forests.

Printed and bound in Mackays of Chatham Ltd, Chatham, Kent

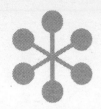

contents

introduction

This book sort of crept up on me. I've been answering people's questions on design and decorating for around four years now and I started to get lots from people who said they had read them, then lost them and they would like a book of them all that they could keep. I began to think there was a wide enough selection of information that it would make a useful reference book. It isn't meant to be comprehensive in every area. I see it as being handy to have on your shelf. I have tried to arrange it in a simple fashion, so that if you are doing up your bathroom, bedroom, kitchen or garden, you can access the section easily. I have also got sections on some of the most popular areas like flooring, furniture and paint, and then a directory at the back to help you find a supplier quickly.

I get asked everything – from where to find a collapsible car parking post to what are my views on art for someone's sitting room. I try to make the ideas and information a cross between practical tips and shortcuts, seeking out companies who offer great services that you never knew existed to offering news on trends in the design and decorating world. I never thought I would be an agony aunt to the decorating world but who am I to turn my back on it?

I hope the information is useful to lots of people but I do also love answering the occasional wacky ones – I once told someone to use hawthorn thorns on his wind-up 78 rpm record player if he couldn't find anything else. Apparently, they work once and then start to splay open. Of course, then I had a letter from someone offering 72 needles that he had and didn't want. That's also the fun bit – people write in and offer help to others with problems. So I get letters offering ceramic draining boards and I match up people. Perhaps I should consider a dating agency too. I've found discontinued tiles and wallpaper for people who need just those extra two tiles or one roll to finish something. There is something quite satisfying about proving all these shops wrong when they say it is impossible to get hold of some item that has been discontinued. I love finding discontinued items, stockists of old parts for electric cookers, making a 1930s' fridge work rather than buying a retro 1930s' fridge. It is something to do with my belief that you should try to recycle things and not just throw it away the first time something breaks down on you. As we all have so little time to spare in tracking down what we need, it is so easy to get into the throwaway frame of mind, but I hope this book goes a little way in drawing together all sorts of information that you might find useful.

Recently I took a broken doorlock to a fantastic ironmonger and asked him for a new one in the same size. The guy looked at it and said it was a beautiful 150-year-old lock and he was going to repair it. He did, charged me £1.50 for doing it and I left feeling yet again I need to try harder. You see, what is a broken old lock to me becomes a work of art to someone interested in that area. So don't throw stuff away without thinking about it carefully.

In the main part of the book I give telephone numbers rather than address as you are more likely to get a result from the telephone. People don't reply to letters these days and if a firm has gone out of business you will find out quickly. It is easier to speak to someone about your needs and get your enquiry answered. I have had great phone chats with incredibly helpful suppliers – many of them are unsung heroes, doing amazing work on everything from restoring antiques mirrors and glass to making up fabulous spiral staircases. The quality of some of the traditional craft people (and I mean from ironwork, basketry, glass, leather upholstery, stone masonry, copper restoration – I could go on) is fantastic, but it is still incredibly difficult to seek these guys out when you want a new spindle turned for your Victorian staircase. In the main, they can't afford to advertise and it is a case of phoning around and seeking them out. It is the sort of knowledge that people acquire over the years but it is difficult to find when you want to fast. I hope this book helps.

I do want it to be fun to browse through, too, and hope that you will pick up all kinds of information you never knew you needed. Whether you like it or not, the chances are we will all be doing some DIY and decorating in the next few years, and it pays to do it properly. With the surge of interest in home and garden design and there are so many products around I hope that I can steer you through some of the better products and trends. Of course, decorating should be about what you want to do in your home but we are always swayed by others. I still believe you should trust your own views – television programmes come and go – but you still have to live in your sitting room that you painted orange on a whim.

✳ **Tessa's tip** When you are using the book, do phone and check prices and colours because I cannot be responsible for any changes that suppliers make to their products. And remember that the numbers here are a good starting point for finding things. Talk to the suppliers – better and better products are being manufactured all the time. Good Luck!

✳ walls and ceilings

With the amount of different paints on the market, it is not surprising that this is one of the areas that you ask me about most. Every company is constantly updating its range with more colours, more textures, better applications, more coverage. It is difficult to know where to start to advise. The most obvious advice is that you need the paint for the job and there is always a specialist paint to suit what you are doing, whether it is indoor or outdoor, an old or modern building, and then there are a number in each category from which to choose. I would always go to a specialist paint shop if I was doing a particular job, rather than just a spot of emulsioning or gloss work. They will guide you as to what you need and what tools to get. Rollers and brushes are made for specific work too and they will make the job much easier for you if you use them.

When you are choosing paint colours, remember that they vary enormously depending on the light source in the room. Before you start, get a cardboard box and paint the whole of the inside and look at how the shadows affect the colour. I have painted my sitting room three types of yellow – none of them worked and it is now green. In my defence, yellow is a particularly hard colour to get right. Get tester pots to try out first but even these will show slightly different colouring to a whole room.

I'm often asked about allergy-free paints – some oil-based ones are very smelly and can give you terrible headaches. There are low volatile organic content (VOC) paints around, again made by specialist companies. Although everyone sells paint, it is difficult to get professional advice in the big superstores so before you buy, ask for help. We all think we understand paint, but the market is so immense, that it pays to ask.

As for wallpapers, you never forget a good or bad one. Most of us have patterns etched on our minds from childhood. It hasn't been so popular in the last few years because it is cheaper to paint a room than to wallpaper; and with the urge to change our rooms every few years, wallpaper gets costly – and you need a decent decorator to put it up. Most aren't. However, there are lots of fabulous wallpapers on the market – right from copies of William Morris natural prints to Wallace and Gromit – so there is something for everyone. Even artists are developing ranges. A tower-black wallpaper is one that comes to mind. If you haven't used wallpaper before, it may pay to try it out on one wall first. It gives a rich, dramatic and warm feel to a room that paint cannot. There are good wallpaper hanging leaflets available and excellent tools on the market to help you. Again, preparation is key. If you have everything ready when you start and have an efficient method, you shouldn't get into trouble. And it is very satisfying to do!

 paint

Q We have lived with the hideous 'spiky' relief paint finish in our hallway for two years but feel the time has come for it to go. The question is, how can we remove it? It seems very solid and no amount of sanding seems to smooth it down. Help!

A You're talking about Artex, I'm sure, and that drippy, swirly plaster work is splattered over many a dodgy wall and ceiling. It's the scourge of many decorators and it's hell to get off. You're right, sanding doesn't work. I've known people take electric drills to it in desperation. If the Artex is really solid and doesn't soften when wet, you could plaster over the whole thing, giving you a smooth surface on which to begin again. Alternatively, colourwash the Artex. I have even seen it covered with tinfoil – the effect was very space-age, very eye-

✳ Tessa's tip If you hate Artex-type coating – that textured icing look that covers so many ceilings and walls – there is now something that will remove it without resorting to a pneumatic drill. Tex Remover made by Action Products will remove both textured coatings and any paint that covers them. It comes as a thick gel, which you apply liberally and leave to work initially on the paint finish. After 40 minutes, remove the wet paint with a scraper. Then apply a further coat and leave for 20 minutes. It will remove the textured ceiling or wall finish. It is a water-based biodegradable product and is non-corrosive. It has no harmful gases and is easy to handle. One litre will cover approximately 2-4 sq m (2 ⅓ -4¾ sq yd) but it does depend on the thickness of the finish. Tex Remover is available by mail order (tel: 01454 228702), and prices start at £17.99 plus p&p for 2.5 litres. Action Products pride themselves on being environmentally friendly, and they also make Paint Remover, which is non-toxic.

catching, and positively sizzling. Even though most people hate it, new houses are often coated with Artex as it doesn't crack like new plaster.

Q I have been trying to obtain the old-fashioned pumice stripping blocks for rubbing down paintwork. Are these still being manufactured?

A Try a company called Pumex on 020 7363 5455. They sell mainly to the wholesale trade, where pumice is used for glass, silver and pewter polishing, but they will put you in touch with a local agent. Expect to pay around £5 for a block – 15cm (6in) long by 7 x 7cm (2³⁄₄ x 2³⁄₄in). Though light, pumice is very tough. Used with a lubricating oil, it mixes well into a powdered paste form for some decorative paint finishes.

Q I am 14 years old and I want to redecorate my bedroom using paint. At the moment it's a disgusting peach colour, but I have to keep my green carpet. What colours will match my carpet and also brighten up the room?

A It's quite good to have one thing in the room that you must retain, as it makes you focus more on the overall colour scheme. So many people start from scratch and end up painting all sorts of clashing colours. I imagine your carpet is the soft green that carpets often come in. First, think of colours you like and then think about how you use the room. You probably have friends round, do homework there and have to wake up and go to sleep in it, so make sure it's a colour you really like. Get yourself a paint chart from one of the big suppliers and see which colours work best with the carpet. I would go for a bright yellow to liven things up. Don't forget to paint your ceiling, which I'm sure is white! Go for the same yellow colour – it's more dramatic. If you are short of cash and want to add drama to the walls try blocks of colour on one wall. Buy a sample pot of paint for this – it's much cheaper. Alternatively, buy some hardboard sections, paint them in bright colours and hang them round the walls like an art exhibition.

Q Some relatives of mine want to redecorate their home, but they are asthmatic and cannot stand the smell of oil-based paints. Do you know of a supplier of odourless paints?

A More and more people are complaining of allergic reactions to paint. All vinyl paints for walls and woodwork are petroleum-based and give off vapours, even after the smell has died down. Very few paints have no odour at all but some have less than others. John Lewis do their own range of low odour, water-based eggshell, gloss and emulsion paints. Another option is to paint walls with a soft distemper. This is vegetable based and has a neutral odour. It comes in light colours and is non-washable, though you can wipe it clean. For woodwork, try linseed oil paint, available in many colours and made with pure turpentine. This 'breathes' and smells only of turpentine. It is slow-drying, so you should allow 24 hours between coats, but it is nine times more flexible than a normal gloss paint so it lasts much longer. If you're unfamiliar with distemper and linseed oil paints, contact Potmolen Paint on 01985 213960 for a free information pack. They sell by mail order and will also send out 250ml sample pots so you can test them for any allergic reaction.

Q **How can we test the gloss paint in my sister's home for dangerous lead content before we start stripping it off?**

A JH Ratcliffe (tel: 01704 537999) do a lead test kit for £14.69 including p&p and VAT. The kit will do 20 tests, and full instructions are supplied with it. B&Q also do a one-off kit for £2.99. If you live in a house built before 1960, the chances are there will be lead pigment in the paint. The local paint may well be under layers of new paintwork and is not harmful unless disturbed. It is the lead dust that comes off when redecorating that can be extremely harmful.

❋ # Tessa's tip

Remember, if you live in an older home (pre-1970), the chances are it has lead gloss paint on the woodwork and you should take serious precautions. Modern paint no longer has a high lead content and isn't a problem. Because of public concern, B&Q has put lead test kits into all its stores, together with a free leaflet on lead paint. If you are about to redecorate an older property, first buy a kit and check. If there is lead paint, wear mask and overalls. Seal the room you are working on with thick polythene and masking tape to stop dust escaping. Make sure everything is out of the room. Don't burn off old paint with a blow torch, don't rub it down with sandpaper and don't vacuum up with an ordinary domestic vacuum. You can buy an alkaline-based poultice from a company called Strippers (tel: 01787 371524), which you paste on and then scrape off and sponge. Lead poisoning is a serious problem and is particularly dangerous for pregnant women and small children. Don't let them near any lead paintwork that is being worked on. However, if you are not redecorating and the paintwork isn't chipped or being gnawed at by children, then there is nothing to worry about.

Q I am always envious when I see DIY experts demonstrating trouble-free decorating with a roller brush. Whenever I've attempted to use a roller and tray, I seem to end up generating a load of paint spray, and, in despair, return to using the brush. I use a foam-type roller and do it carefully, but what am I doing wrong? Would another type of roller perhaps be better? Any suggestions, please.

A The best paint to use with a roller is water-based. You may be having problems if you are using oil-based paint or simply putting too much paint on the roller. There are other types of rollers available for different types of job. A mohair roller is great for large, smooth surfaces, but hopeless for textured ones. A lambswool one or nylon equivalent is more suitable for textured walls. The foam one you are using is fine for both smooth and textured surfaces, although it does start to deteriorate quickly. You can also get patterned foam rollers where the paint picks up only on the raised bit of the roller. I created a great stripy wall effect once by putting two elastic bands on a roller and then painting. Very effective and much cheaper than wallpaper! Don't forget the small rollers for painting tiles, too – they give a smooth, even finish.

Q Effects are often achieved using oil-based paints, acrylic paints etc – I am confused about which paint to use for which job. Paint tins don't have a lot of information for the non-specialist. Any guidelines would be gratefully received.

A I can see you are flummoxed. A very simple guide is that emulsion is water-based and easy to clean off brushes. Oil-based paints are harder to apply, smell horrible and take ages to dry. They are often used for woodwork and also surfaces that need to be wiped down frequently.

However, you can use acrylic paint, which is water based, simple to apply and has far less toxic fumes. The best thing to do is get yourself a book. Try *Kevin McCloud's Decorating Book* and *Jocasta Innes's Paint Magic*.

Q My home is mainly Victorian but part of the house is older, including my sitting room, which has a lower ceiling and two original beams. Currently the walls are boring, white-painted Anaglypta. I would love to paint them in a more dramatic shade but feel I've tied myself down with furnishing colours

(samples enclosed). Should I remove the Anaglypta and/or paint bare walls – which are pretty rough? I would welcome suggestions on a colour scheme.

A I would strip the Anaglypta. You'll probably need to line the walls before you paint but it will give them a finish to complement the room. I would take the yellow from your curtain material and go for that. Try the Dulux Heritage range. They have three ranges: Georgian, Victorian and Edwardian. Call the Heritage Hotline on 01420 23024 for stockists in your area.

Q **I saw something on television recently about a computer service that allows you to try out different colour schemes in a room. Do you know where this service is available?**

A The DIY chain Focus Do It All offers a computer service with which, free of charge, you can try out your favourite room design. The computers are installed in 25 of their shops around the country and by August will probably be in all of them, so there should be one near you. You select a blank room set and get the computer to do the costing, measuring and colour scheming. You can try different wallpapers, borders and paints. Don't worry about your computer skills: all their staff are trained to help you. John Lewis stores round the country also offer a computer service connected to Dulux paint, so you can experiment with what your room would look like in lime and magenta!

 # Tessa's tip

This is a very clever idea from Dulux. Basically they have put their new Discovery range of paints into complete colour scheming packs. Included in the pack are special match patch sticky cards, which you can put directly on your wall to test the colour. They are simple to remove, just peel them off and continue to try all kinds of complementary colours before you buy. It saves on buying the tester pots and Dulux have also helped in that frightening choice of too many colours, with the pre-selection of good toning shades. There are three different ranges – the African, the Oriental and the Urban. The pack also comes with all kinds of handy hints about making rooms look bigger, what colours to go for depending on the way your windows face, and how light looks at different times of the day. They have also put together room sets using clever colour combinations and showed you how to achieve the look. And there are even cashback coupons on the back of the brochure. What more could you want! Call them on 01753 550555. £2.95 at decorating shops.

Q How can we make our porch look more welcoming? It measures 90cm (3ft) wide by 2.4m (8ft) long, has a partly glazed roof and terracotta quarry tiles on the floor. The outer wooden door is fifties' style, painted racing green with a panel of green and orange/red stained glass. The inner door is white.

A For starters, to give consistency to the space, I would paint both doors the same colour. Try a deep red to tone in with the stained glass. Then brighten the walls with a warm terracotta colourwash that will lift the colour of the floor's quarry tiles. Narrow areas can benefit greatly from mirrors to reflect light. Also, consider installing a coloured lantern or swapping the overhead light for uplighters on the walls. Even a different type of light bulb or a change of lampshade can alter the effect dramatically. Try adding a few pictures or wallhangings to jolly things up without too much clutter.

Q I live in a very old cottage with a cellar. I'd like to paint the walls of the cellar even though they're rendered and slightly damp. What paint would you suggest?

A My first question would be, why do you want to paint a damp cellar? If you're just storing things there, then I would advise you not to paint it. You would be better off making sure that any stored items are above floor level and away from walls. If you really want to get to the root of the dampness then be prepared for it to be a pricey job – I was quoted £5,000 to have my damp cellar sorted out. You can use an anti-damp paint that will help prevent mould growing but it won't actually sort out the damp problem. Call International on 01962 711177 for your local stockists.

Q I can think of a thousand fun things to do with luminous paint, but I can't find any of it in the shops. Help!

A Luminous paint used to have a radioactive charge in it, but these days it comes in a much safer form. Plasti-Kote do a range of fluorescent paints in green, yellow and orange (£5.69 for a 400ml tin). You simply spray it on to any surface, including fabrics. Call them on 01223 836400 for details of a local stockist.

Q I have just moved house and have started to redecorate the hall. Off came the ghastly flowery wallpaper and I am now ready to put my idea into effect. I would like to create a warm, rustic farmhouse effect, with burnished orange walls, although not too dark. However, I'm not too sure if I'm intending to go about it in the right way. Would I have to paint the walls in a neutral colour (such as magnolia) and then apply the orange with a sponge? If so, is there a special sort of sponge for the purpose?

A It sounds like you've got the right idea. To get the rustic effect, start with a coat of emulsion (but not magnolia) and then sponge a colourwash over the top. For the orange colour you want, there are some ideal combinations in the Paint Magic range. I suggest Sunny Yellow emulsion with a Cinnamon colourwash, or Bleached Yellow emulsion with Terracotta. Colourwashing is easy: once the emulsion is dry, apply the wash in a figure-of-eight shape with an ordinary, large sponge and then blend and soften the effect with a large, very soft brush. Paint Magic emulsion costs £17.45 for 2.5 litres, colourwash is £16.95 for 1 litre, which is sufficient to cover 30-40 sq m (35-48 sq yd). A sample pot costs £1.95 if you want to try out the effect first. Call the mail-order number, 01225 469966.

Q I would like to use emulsion to paint some walls that are wallpapered at the moment, but can we emulsion if we take the paper off? I am worried because the plaster is old and I would like to avoid having the walls replastered if possible.

A It depends on the final look you want. Of course, you can strip off the wallpaper, but with old walls it has usually been put up for a reason: to give a smooth finish. If you don't mind an uneven result, then take the wallpaper off. Then coat the wall with a primer sealer: this will stabilise any slight powdery finish there might be. Leave it for 48 hours to dry. Then go ahead and emulsion with your chosen paint.

Q We have just bought a house that has extremely bright-coloured walls throughout. We have tried to paint over a red one, but our muted white doesn't cover it. Is there some special paint we could use to get rid of the colours before we start painting everything white?

A I'm afraid all I can really suggest is lots of coats of emulsion. There's nothing else for it – unless you decide to put lining paper up, which would be a lot of work. But painting need not be too much of a trial. Keep going, and you may be surprised after a couple of coats with the finish. If you use a roller, it shouldn't take too long, and emulsion dries pretty quickly so a weekend should be enough to get a room done. Good luck!

walls and ceilings

Q Can you tell me how to make distemper paint? If not, where can I buy it?

A It's quite a performance making distemper paint, but here goes. These amounts should make enough paint for one room. You will need gelatin glue, powdered chalk, a bucket, a double boiler, a whisk and some muslin cloth. Dissolve 340g (12oz) of glue in 1.2 litres (2 pints) of cold water in a container, stir and leave overnight. Put 5.5kg (12lb) of chalk in a bucket and add cold water so that the top of the chalk sits just above the water level. Leave overnight – do not stir. Pour off dirty water from the top of the chalky mix the next day. Then heat, but do not boil, the glue in a double boiler. Add the glue to the chalk, stirring all the time. Any colouring should be mixed with water and added with a whisk at this stage. Sieve the paint through muslin. Wait until it is cool and jellylike before using. When painting, cover a square metre (yard) at a time. Then brush the wall again with a clean brush. Brush marks should become less obvious as the chalk dries. Ingredients can be bought from L Cornelissen & Son on 020 7636 1045. The lazy option is to buy it ready-made from Paul Smoker on 01536 373158. Other suppliers include Paint Magic on 01225 469966 and Potmolen Paint on 01985 213960. Remember that distemper washes off with water, so it's not suitable if you have small children with sticky fingers.

Q What is the best way to paint skirting boards with the carpet still in place?

A I'd buy some thick masking tape and run it around the edges of the carpet to avoid accidents. Alternatively, put down a dust sheet or push a piece of card between the carpet and the skirting board as you paint. You do have to be careful as it's easy to pick up small fibres and dust from the base of the skirting boards – get the vacuum cleaner in there first to lift any dust deposits. Skirting boards look very tacky with gloss-painted hairs.

Q I have tried, unsuccessfully, to paint a wooden dado rail around my lounge/dining room in a shiny metallic gold paint. I have used several gold paints but have never managed to replicate the bright colour that is often seen on dados. The paints I have used tend to discolour easily and never quite live up to my expectations, but to use gold leaf would be prohibitively expensive because of the quantities involved. Can you help?

A Try something called transfer metal leaf, which is a good imitation of gold leaf. Call Stuart Stevenson on 020 7253 1693. A book of 25 leaves, each measuring 14 x 14cm (5½ x 5½in) costs £4.04

and will cover 2.3 sq m (2¾ sq yd), allowing for no wastage. First you will need to use either an acrylic or an oil-based size. The acrylic costs £8.44 for 500ml and the oil-based one, £8.05 for 250ml. Wait until the size is touch dry. The acrylic will take a lot less time than the oil-based one. Then simply place the leaf face down on the dado rail, and peel back the protective paper (just like a transfer). When you've finished, you will need to seal it. For acrylic size, use a water-based acrylic varnish – 236ml costs £6.15 – and ormolu for the oil-based size. This is just like a shellac varnish, and costs £7.20 for 500ml.

Q **Our *en suite* shower room has poor ventilation and the paintwork keeps developing black, mouldy patches that I have to clean off. Can I use a special paint for damp-prone rooms that will resist the growth of mould?**

A Special anti-condensation paint absorbs moisture and contains a fungicide to prevent mould. There are also special bathroom mastics (the plastic used for sealing around showers) which don't go black and horrible. Avoid porous surfaces – use tiles and stylish slatted wood bathmats on the floor. But most important improve your ventilation. It is a lack of airflow that encourages damp, and hence mould. Install an electric ventilator or, if you already have one, get a more powerful one.

Q **The bathroom in our shared house has mould coming through the ceiling and walls. We don't want to spend a fortune doing it up as we hope that we will**

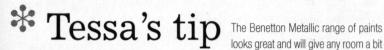

❋ **Tessa's tip** The Benetton Metallic range of paints looks great and will give any room a bit of excitement and interest – it really does have a sparkle in it when it dries. First apply the specified base colour for the Metallic colour you have chosen with a dampened short-pile roller (base colours cost £12.49 for 2.5 litres). The Metallic paint, £17.99 for 2.5 litres, should be applied with a dampened Metallic Effect roller, £6.29. Use even, vertical strokes in the same direction from the bottom to the top of the wall.

Leave for an hour before reapplying. Work in 2-m (2-yd) wide vertical panels and, after each panel, wait two minutes then run the roller, without paint, up the wall again to complete the effect. Benetton Metallic paint comes in a range of 18 colours and is available only from B&Q stores. Tel: 020 8466 4166 for details of your nearest local store.

walls and ceilings

be moving to a new house next year. But how can we tidy up the bathroom while we are here?

A You want Perma-White Mildew-Proof bathroom paint from Zinsser (tel: 020 8866 9977). You need to remove as much mould as you can before you paint, so first buy a fungicide. Paint it on the mould, then wash it off. Repeat this process to clean the surface thoroughly. Once it is dry, paint on the Perma-White. Two coats should stop the mould coming through for five years. The paint is fine for bathroom walls and ceilings and anywhere with high humidity, but don't use it in a shower or directly beside the bath where it will get really soaked. Perma-White costs £12.30 for a US quart (1.3 litres/2 pints).

Q I have used up my supply of natural sponges, for which I have many uses. Can you suggest where I might get some more?

A Try artists' supply shops. They often have all kinds of sizes and shapes, and you can pick up bargains. You can also get them by mail order from E Ploton on 020 8348 2838. This company sells both bleached and unbleached versions, ranging upwards from one that's about the size of a small potato. You don't say why you want the sponges, but if it's for paint effects, the unbleached type are cheaper and just as good for the job. E Ploton also does a fantastic range of gilding materials and other decorative artists' supplies. A good shop to know about!

Q I want to do some stencilling, but most of the stencils I have seen are awful. I'd like to do something a bit different and more dramatic than the usual stuff. Where can I go to get some inspiration?

A I like the stencils by Tony Roche that I found on the Internet. They can be seen at his website: www.tonyroche.co.uk and he can be contacted via e-mail at lemon@tonyroche.co.uk. He has all kinds of stencils including Moroccan, Indian, Victorian, Scandinavian, Egyptian and more modern designs. His stencils are cut from Melinex for durability, and are delivered within 28 days. He can also do specific sizes by arrangement and will work to commission. Prices start from £20. If you feel like trying your hand at making your own stencils, Mylar stencil sheeting and hot stencil-cutting knives are available from good art shops. If you cannot find these tools locally, AS Handover, Unit 37H, Mildmay Grove North, London N1 4RH (tel: 020 7359 4696), can supply them by mail order.

Q We have painted the hallway of our Victorian terraced house cream above and below the dado rail. It looks fine but we feel it lacks a finishing touch. Can you suggest any accessories or added decoration that could create a dramatic entrance? We'd like to stick within a £100 budget.

A Try a more dramatic colour below the dado rail – how about pink, mauve or yellow, colours loved by the Victorians? If you just want added decoration, consider a colourwash with watery emulsion and a Victorian-style stencil on top. For added drama on a budget, an ornate framed mirror is a good bet. It is also worth hunting around junk shops or local auction houses.

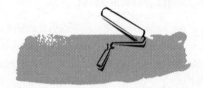

✳ Tessa's tip

There are smelly paints available now from Urchin, which are great fun. Especially designed for children's rooms, they come in great shades (and smells) – Gob Stopper, Jelly Bean, Banana Skin, Chocolate Biscuit, Popcorn, Bubble Gum, Strawberry Jam, Bilberry Pie, Dough Ball, Orange Peel, Peppermint, Paddy, Granny Smith, Coconut and my own favourite – Slime.

Don't worry: your children will not want to eat the paints as an ingredient called Bitrex makes them bitter to the taste. They are completely safe to use with no added lead. The firm does a primer and scrubbable satin that you can use for walls, woodwork and radiators. Prices range from £4 for 125ml to £22 for 2.5 litres.

Call Urchin on 01672 872872. Their mail-order catalogue has lots of other fun products for children – I particularly like the black and white spotted potty.

---

walls and ceilings

wallpaper

Q My problem is removing woodchip wallpaper that has many coats of emulsion on it. I have tried using a steamer, but it removed plaster as well as the woodchip even though I used it for only 30 seconds. Any ideas?

A Removing woodchip wallpaper is a horrible, laborious job, best tackled room by room. A steamer is still the best tool for the job, though you do have to be careful and persistent and expect some plaster to come away in the process. Hire the machine by the day – allow one day per room. If you cannot bear the idea of going through that, try disguising the woodchip with one of the textured paints on the market. These are available in DIY stores and by mail order from specialist outlets, such as Paint Magic on 01225 469966.

Q In the seventies we had the wall around the fireplace in our sitting room decorated with brown Lincrusta wall covering. As this is now dated and rather soiled, could you tell us how the covering might be removed without pulling all the plaster off the wall?

A Before you do anything, let me say that we have just done a *Home Front* feature on Lincrusta, and we all thought it looked fantastic! In case people don't know what it is, Lincrusta is like a linoleum for the walls. It is made of flax, and you can get wall coverings, friezes and borders in it. It comes in a natural colour finish that you can paint or varnish. It is an expensive wall covering, so before you decide to rip it off, remember you may well kick yourself in a year or so when it is high fashion again! If you do want to remove it, I don't think you can avoid taking off the plaster underneath, particularly as yours has been on for nearly 30 years. After only a couple of years on a wall, it would be possible to remove Lincrusta by soaking it with water and scraping it off. Instead, if you are tired of the colour and it is a bit grubby, why not repaint it? You would need to use an oil-based eggshell or gloss paint. Crown Paints make these, to the same recipe used 100 years ago, and you can call them for information on 01254 704951.

Q Where can I buy plain wallpaper borders, similar to those made by Lincrusta some years ago? I am keen to use one as an alternative to plaster coving but all I can find in the shops are patterned ones made of blown vinyl.

A I think you may be out of luck with this one. Lincrusta is an extraordinary embossed natural wallcovering. Crown Berger, the manufacturer, used to make a super, durable border suitable for coving, but hasn't done so for several years. If you want the same effect, you will have to go for a plaster coving instead. Crown Berger continues to produce patterned Lincrusta borders, however, so why not call 01254 704951 for a brochure? It might inspire you to re-think your plans.

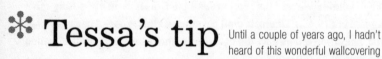

✱ Tessa's tip Until a couple of years ago, I hadn't heard of this wonderful wallcovering called Lincrusta. It comes from the Latin *linum* (linseed oil) and crusta (hard shell) and that is what it is. It was launched in the 1960s from Anaglypta and it was designed to mimic the grand Victorian interiors like moulded plasterwork, carved wood and tooled leather. It basically comes as a creamy thick paper – almost plaster thick – which you can then paint if you so wish. What I like about it is the texture – it goes so well with both modern and traditional looks. The only drawback is the expense – it costs £91 a roll. You do get 10.5 m (11⅓yd) on a roll, but you need to think how to use it most economically. It is also extremely difficult to remove once up which is also a plus point for it as it lasts for years and is easy to wash. If you have the right setting for it, it looks fabulous. It comes in 21 patterns, which include wallcoverings, dado panels, friezes and borders. Call 01254 870137 for your local stockist.

walls and ceilings

Q My sister, who lives in America, has asked me to find a wallpaper border decorated with hedgehogs. The only one I have found is by Crown but it is a little childish. Can you come up with anything else that fits the bill?

A What would grown-up hedgehog wallpaper be like? To be honest, I'm not surprised that the only ones available are aimed at children. Wallpaper specialist Paper Moon (tel: 020 7624 1198), does stock a Mrs Tiggywinkle border – but it has all the other Beatrix Potter characters on it, too. It costs £16.50 plus VAT for a 4.6m (5yd) coil. Has your sister considered stencilling a border? This wouldn't take long to do, and a hedgehog stencil would be very easy to cut out.

Q I have two cats, one of which is very keen on attacking the wallpaper. He has now scratched the paper in every room. I have tried everything to stop him, other than giving him away – which I don't want to do! Obviously, I need to redecorate, so do you know of any substance to treat the walls with or if there is any specific type of wallpaper that will not attract his attention?

A Unfortunately, I don't know what type of wallpaper he has already destroyed! But maybe a shinier one, such as washable vinyl, would fox him – but this might look odd in your sitting room. Why not go for paint instead? It is easier to apply, looks great and your cat may have an aversion to it. Even if he does get his claws out, you can easily retouch it if you keep a spare can handy. Also, have you thought that your cat may be bored? Pet shops sell great poles for cats to scratch on while you are out – and you may find that a toy distracts him from the decor.

Q We've recently moved and are trying to discover the origin of one of the wallpapers in our new home, as we'd like to use some more of it. Is there any organisation that can help us?

A A small company, Baer & Ingram, specialise in stocking other people's wallpapers as well as their own. They can help with tracking down a wallpaper, but they stress that because this is so time consuming it isn't the main part of their business. Send a small piece of your paper to them at 273 Wandsworth Bridge Road, London SW6 2TX. If the wallpaper turns out to be made by Sanderson (one of the biggest manufacturers), they will be able to trace it in their archives.

Q Can you tell me please whether it is still possible to get 'picture' wallpaper, a wallpaper that makes up into scenes of Hawaiian beaches, conservatories, etc? These were quite the rage a few years ago but I can't find anyone who now supplies them.

A Yes, you can still get hold of them. They are known as photomurals. A company called Paper Moon (tel: 020 7624 1198), stocks them. Not only can it supply the Hawaiian beach scene and conservatory view, but it also does Alpine scenes, lake views, a map of the world and woodland, seascape and skyscape scenes. A mural based on the children's cartoon Pinocchio is available, too. Prices range from £70.15 for the smallest mural of 100 x 70cm (39 x 27½in) to £170.38 for the largest, measuring 388 x 270cm (12 x 8¾ft). Carriage charge is £5.50 plus VAT. The murals come as a billboard rather than a traditional roll of wallpaper and can be used very successfully in a doorway, alcove or even to cover an entire wall.

Q My mother has adorned our home with tartan products – carpets, bedding, etc. But she has yet to find any tartan wallpaper. Do you know of any suppliers?

A Paper Moon in London sell the classic Black Watch tartan and other tartans in reds, greens and neutrals. Their papers start at £26 a roll. Call them for mail order and samples on 020 7624 1198. Ralph Lauren also do a range of tartan wallpapers, costing £32 a roll. They are available through Harvey Nichols in London and Leeds: House of Fraser in Glasgow; and also through Designers Guild – call 020 7243 7300 for details of local stockists.

❋ **Tessa's tip** I get asked how to hang wallpaper a lot and, to be honest, it is not easy to give a short, comprehensive answer to this, but a new 12-page guide from the Wallfashion Bureau is just the thing. It tells you which paste to use, how to cut the paper, where to start and finish in a room, how to tackle corners, doors, sockets and windows. It also shows you how to calculate the number of rolls you will need. The booklet is free, so simply send an A6 sae to The Wallfashion Bureau, High Corn Mill, Chapel Hill, Skipton, North Yorkshire BD23 1NL. Wallpaper is definitely being used a lot more now despite it being trickier to use than paint and more expensive. My one criticism is that the pictures the guide shows of people wallpapering make wallpaper look dull and colourless. Let me assure you that there are fabulous wallpapers out there to have fun with.

---

walls and ceilings

Q I'm decorating my son's room with an outer space theme. Once in a magazine, I saw friezes of windows looking out into space, with planets and so on. Do you know where I can buy them?

A Friezeframe (tel: 0151 650 2407), does a range of nine DIY mural kits – paper products that look exactly like freehand paintwork when dry. The themes are: space, deep sea, dinosaurs, teddy bears, trains, woodland, grand prix, clowns and jungles. They come as two-wall kits for £35, or as four-wall kits for £65. Simply paint your room, then stick on the kit's images to build up the picture. Visit their website: www.friezeframe.com

Q My seven-year-old son's bedroom desperately needs redecoration. I fancy trying wallpaper, but I'm not sure what is available for children. Any ideas?

A Most children seem to be Wallace and Gromit fans, and Baer & Ingram (tel: 01373 812552) have now produced a brilliant collection of three wallpapers and two borders featuring these popular characters. (Both cost £9.95 for a 10m/10¾yd roll.) Also, Vymura (tel: 0161 368 8321) do a huge range of children's wallpapers, including my favourite, Thomas the Tank Engine. Prices start at £7.99 for a roll and £6.49 for a border.

Q I'm gradually getting rid of the dull, boring magnolia paint in my house and replacing it with brighter colours. It will soon be the turn of my 18-year-old son's bedroom. He may be going away to university in September. If he does go I would like him to know that the room will always be his when he comes home for weekends. I wanted to have a decorative border around the room, but I haven't seen any that are masculine enough. He is keen on sport and music – is there somewhere I can get stencils designed to order?

A My advice is to let your son paint his own room. He could do the whole thing with a roller in an afternoon. It's great that you want him to feel that the room is his and, as long as he has painted it, it will. If you decide you want to go for individual stencils, get some art books from the library, choose a drawing or design you like, and photocopy it. Enlarge or reduce it to the size you need, transfer the pattern on to a thickish laminated paper or card and cut it out.

Q I've just bought a small flat in London – and I want to do something unusual with my sitting room. Any suggestions?

A It depends on your budget, of course. There are wonderful bold colours available to jazz up the simplest room. If you really want to get people talking, why not have a mural. I have recently seen a dining room with a fantastic Tuscan scene painted over three walls and it was sumptuous. You would never have a grey city day again.

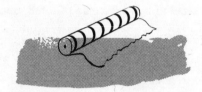

✳ **Tessa's tip** The latest product from Baer & Ingram is a stylish wallpaper called the Naturals collection. It comes in three natural colours – ivory, mango and bamboo – and it is actually a washable vinyl paper with a ribby, textured look. What's more, it looks great painted, too – a simple emulsion makes it look even more sophisticated and cool! It is 53cm (21in) wide, 10.5m (11⅓yd) long and costs £24.50 a roll. Call 01373 812552 for details.

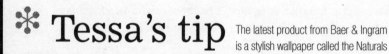

walls and ceilings

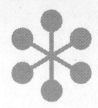

Q The bathroom suite in my new home is in good condition but I dislike the surrounding wall tiles. Is it possible to paint them? If so, what paint do I use and must each tile be painted individually in order to retain the grouting division?

A Tiles can be painted, although you must remember that paint is never going to be as durable as the original ceramic finish. Don't worry about trying to paint tiles individually, simply cover the entire surface including the grout. The job requires an appropriate tile primer, available at most DIY stores. Start by cleaning and drying the tiles, then paint on the primer. A synthetic brush is best for this, as natural bristles leave heavier marks. Let the primer dry for at least 16 hours before applying the top coat.

In bathrooms, a solvent-based paint is the most sensible option for this coat as it will last longer. But if the room does not become too steamy when in use, you might get away with emulsion rather than gloss or eggshell paint. Don't try to varnish the finish. Steam makes water-based varnish go cloudy; solvent-based varnish has a yellowing effect on paint.

To keep the surface in tiptop condition, use a non-abrasive cleaner to avoid scratching it. Also, clean only when the surface is cool – the paint is more stable then and less prone to damage.

Q Where can I find ceramic tile paint? My kitchen tiles are a horrible design but in good condition and I cannot afford to re-tile.

A If your tiles form a worksurface, you will not be able to paint them at all, as continuous use and washing down will cause the paint to peel off. For walls, prepare your surface by cleaning off any grease and dirt, then apply a coat of tile primer using a synthetic brush or roller. Leave to dry for two hours, then sand lightly and apply a coat of tile gloss, changing to a natural bristle brush or roller to give a smooth finish. Give it half a day to dry. When you clean painted tiles, use only liquid products, or you will scratch the paint. Tile primer and gloss are available from DIY superstores, or from International (tel: 01962 711177) at £8.79 for 750ml of primer and £8.99 for gloss. There's a choice of 15 colours.

Q Is it as easy as I've been told to put new tiles on top of old ones in my kitchen? Do I need a special adhesive and are there any other hints you can give me?

A It is extremely easy to put new tiles over old ones. Clean the old ones first. Buy tile adhesive from any DIY supplier and simply place your new tiles over the old ones. Slightly offset the new tiles so that the joins don't match up – this will make for a better grip. But do make sure there is enough space behind any taps for two sets of tiles.

Q My kitchen has recently been extended and I am unable to decide whether to use rough or smooth tiles on the walls. What are the advantages of each type?

A There really is no advantage in using one over the other. The rougher, more textured, handmade tiles tend to be more expensive than the smoother, factory-made ones, but it entirely depends on the sort of look you want to achieve. Go into a good tile shop and just look around at some of the displays, see which appeals to you and which will suit the mood of your new kitchen. I suppose it could be marginally easier to clean smoother tiles, but I have rough ones in my kitchen and they are no problem.

Q This may be a mad idea, but I'm going to have a go at tiling our bathroom. What worries me is how to get neatly round the fiddly bits, such as the sink and shelf units. Please tell me there's a foolproof method.

A I'd really recommend employing an expert, but if you're determined to DIY, practise on areas that won't show, for instance under the sink. Try getting hold of a reference book on how to do it – from your local library if you don't want to buy one. I'll warn you it is not an easy process and even the experts make mistakes. Do remember to buy extra tiles to compensate for your mistakes – you're sure to break some with the nippers used for cutting. Or try mosaic tiling – you can buy end-of-range tiles, usually in fantastic colours and because they are so small, there's no complicated cutting, so it's easy to get a stunning effect.

 We are redecorating the bathroom and we are looking for transfers to stick on to the tiles but we have been unable to find any. Do you know where we might get some?

 I am cautious about recommending tile transfers because I am convinced they will come off, especially in a bathroom. However, Homelux assure me that they do a range of about 150 different designs and they are extremely tough. They do a pretty new range of metallics of leaf designs in chestnut, lime and ash leaves, which would look very sophisticated in a bathroom. They also do funky fish, which is their best seller, mosaics, wall plaques and many more so it depends on the look you want. All you have to do is to clean and wet your tiles, place the transfer in warm water, slide off the backing paper and then place in position. They say that if they are to be used in a shower where they will be getting wet all the time, then they need a coat of clear varnish on them to protect them. They do come with a coating of lacquer on them and as they dry they harden. They are scratch resistant but only gentle cleaning agents with scourers should be used. If you do want to remove them at any time, use nail polish remover and leave it on for a couple of minutes. This breaks through the transfer and allows you to scrape it off. Bleach also has the same effect so don't clean the tiles with bleach unless you want to remove the transfers! Great Mills and Focus Do It All also carry ranges. Call Homebase on 01335 340340 for stockists in your area.

My family and I live in a very pretty 19th-century cottage; all thick walls and small windows. In the seventies, my husband installed an avocado bathroom suite and tiled the walls up to the ceiling. I tried to stop him but, being pregnant at the time, my resistance was quite low! I can't bear the room: it's dark, oppressive and totally out of character with the rest of the house. I suppose we could replace the suite, but what about the tiles? As far as I can see my options are: 1) Buy something to strip the tiles off the walls. 2) Paint over the tiles. 3) Tile over the tiles (but the room is small, so I'd rather not). 4) Sell the house and/or leave my husband. As you can see, I desperately need your help.

Before you leave your husband, first change your bathroom fixtures! For a new suite, try your local architectural salvage company. They should be able to sell you something more in keeping with your cottage. Replacing the suite might leave awful gaps in the tiling, in which case you'll just have to rip them all off. If not, a coat of oil-based paint might be all you need to transform your bathroom into somewhere you'll love. Sugar-soap the tiles first and, when they are painted, use only a gentle liquid cleaner on them.

Q I'm looking for some tiles that would be suitable for a shower that I'm installing. I've looked around and everything seems very similar. I don't want coloured tiles and I don't like borders. Is there anything else you can suggest for a subtle look in a Victorian house?

A There are some fabulous new tiles from Fired Earth that I think are unusual and would be perfect for you. They look like limestone or sandstone but are in fact ceramic, so they do not need the maintenance that stone does. They have a kind of rough edge to them – looking almost slightly chipped, with an appearance of real age and texture. The sandstone has a beautiful soft colouring, but if you want a more neutral effect, then the limestone would be good. Each tile is roughly 6 x 6cm (2¼ x 2¼in). They are easy to lay because they are supplied in 30 x 30cm (12 x 12in) sheets (about 25 tiles per sheet). They cost £71.61 per square metre. Fired Earth has a range of grout to suit the look you want so don't think you just have to have white grout; they do a sandstone-coloured one too. Call them on 01295 812088.

Q Does anyone make unusual tiles that I could use in a bathroom? I'm interested in colour and design and fancy making a real statement.

A Why not use tiles designed by Esther Thorpe? Her tiles are probably as bright as you could get for a bathroom. She also does a dramatic, black bullseye one, as well as other patterns such as spirals, discs, ripples, stripes, boxes, stars, banners and waves. The hand-printed ceramic wall tiles measure 15 x 15cm (6 x 6in), and cost £3.25 each.

✱ **Tessa's tip** There are many ways you can transform a bathroom without spending a fortune. There are lots of fabulous shower curtains around, and fitting them is a simple job. As well as painting wall tiles, you might want to consider painting your floor. Mirrors also help to give added depth to the room. And what about some plants? Ferns thrive in a steamy environment.

walls and ceilings

Q I am replacing cork tiles in a bathroom – the original ones came waxed. The new ones are only available sanded or sealed with a varnish type finish that I don't want. A beeswax polish contains too much solvent and discolours the tiles. The nearest thing I have found is the wax varnish supplied by Windsor & Newton for applying to oil paintings. This makes a perfect finish. Can I get this item in larger quantities or have you any suggestions for the real wax finish as applied in the past?

A The Windsor & Newton wax varnish only comes in one size and that is a tiny 60ml bottle and they won't sell you bigger quantities I'm afraid. It is made from beeswax dissolved in white spirit and is, as you say, designed for oil paintings and not floors. It would wear off much too quickly as it is very soft. Instead, what you need to get is a product from a company called Liberon who sell Floor Sealer, which will seal your cork properly. It will give you a soft satiny waxy sheen rather than the varnish look that you don't want. A litre costs £9.85 and will cover 10-12 sq m (12-14 sq yd). Call them for stockists on 01797 361136.

Q Our bathroom tiles are in good condition except for some discoloration of the grouting in some areas. Is there anything simple we can do ourselves? Re-tiling is out of the question at the moment.

A Many of the tile shops say there are very few good grout cleaning products on the market. One I am told is excellent, though, is available through the Home Free catalogue and is an American product called The Red Devil tile grout cleaner. It costs £5.99 and you can buy a sealer with it for another £6.99, or both for £11.99. Call the Home Free catalogue on 0990 748494.

Q The white grouting in our kitchen and bathroom has turned yellow over the years. We have tried a number of products to restore its brightness but none has really worked. Do you have any recommendations?

A I suggest a new product from Evo-Stik called Colour Fresh. This is not a cleaning agent, but it gives old grouting a skim of new colour. You simply sponge it on and wipe it off, leaving tiles clean and grout re-coloured. Colour Fresh comes in ten shades, including white, and costs £5.49 for a 125ml tube from Focus Do It All. It's certainly easier than regrouting.

Q How can I stop mould forming on the sealant between my sink top and the tiles, which are part of the windowsill in my kitchen? It's so unsightly.

A There are few things worse than mouldy sealant. Pull out all the old sealant and clean the surfaces. Then refill the gaps with flexible mastic, which comes in a tube. Dow Corning does a special anti-fungicidal silicone sealant for kitchens and bathrooms; it costs £5.10 from all good hardware stores. It's easy to apply and is available in clear or white finish.

Q I have a mirror-backed alcove and I would like to cover the sides in small mirror tiles, too. I have had no luck finding these – can you help?

A Mosaic tiles would be ideal. Two good suppliers I know are based in London but will send you what you need by mail order. Nu Line (tel: 020 7727 7748) sell a 25 x 30cm (10 x 12in) sheet of 2.5cm (1in) square mirrored tiles for £4.50 per sheet plus p&p. The Mosaic Workshop (tel: 020 7263 2997) sell a sheet of 425 bevel-edged mirror tiles, each 3cm (1¼in) square, for £20 plus p&p. If you want a catalogue of all their products to inspire you further (and it will), send an A6 sae for Unit B, 443-449 Holloway Road, London N7 6LJ. Be warned – mosaic work is addictive!

Q I'm having a vanity unit made to fit around the bathroom basin, and would like to put a colourful mosaic worktop on it. I'd like to use either conventional bright mosaic tiles or small coloured glass pebbles (the ones usually sold to fill the base of flower vases). Do I need any special kind of grout or adhesive?

A Although lovely in the bottom of vases, coloured glass pebbles have a raised surface and will attract dirt around the sink area. I would avoid these and opt instead for small mosaic tiles. The Mosaic Workshop (tel: 020 7263 2997) have a huge range of small tiles suitable for the job, plus the waterproof grout and glue that you will also need. Mosaic is the easiest craft to master and, I think, one of the most effective and dramatic ways of making an impact. Once you've successfully managed the surround of the vanity unit, why not try the floor as well! We did a bathroom floor on *Home Front* using ordinary ceramic floor tiles that were broken up. Basically, it's the same procedure, but you prepare the floor first. If you don't have a cement floor, then lay a plywood one and draw your rough design on the floor. Then mix up cement, applying a small section at a time and lay your tiles directly on to it. After grouting, leave for an hour, wipe away any excess and polish with a dry cloth.

walls and ceilings

Q I long to try using mosaic tiles to decorate the tops of old bedside cabinets. Do you know any stockists, as I can't get them locally?

A You can get the most fabulous range of mosaic tiles in both vitreous and ceramic finishes. The Romantique Mosaic Centre in Bath offers mail order – their beginner's kit for a mirror surround includes board, tiles, fix, grout and the mirror. After that, your cabinets should be no problem.

Q My daughter-in-law has a large number of odd tiles and wants to do some mosaic in her kitchen. Is there any easy way of cutting up these tiles with, say, a reasonably priced gadget, or is it not worth the bother?

A You mean you didn't see me doing just this on *Home Front*? It really is very easy to do. All you need are some tile nippers that cost about £10 from any good tiling shop. For a beginner they can be a little difficult to handle at first but, once you get going, it's simple. Just remember to use the bottom tooth of the nippers as a lever on the base of the tile rather than trying to bite the tile between the nippers. That way, you have more control over the shapes you make. However, mosaic is about irregularity and there's no such thing as a mistake. It all adds to the fun of doing it.

decorative details

Q My husband, an obsessive type, wants to hang some photos in a dead straight line. How can he do it without lots of trial holes?

A Can he be restrained? If not, and you seriously want to feed his obsession, get him a plumbline, a pencil and a ruler – then lock him in. Just hope your room has an even floor and ceiling. He should mark off on the plumbline the distance between the ceiling and the picture tops, then mark the wall and continue round the room until he achieves the effect – or it drives him mad.

Q We are looking for large colourful pictures at a reasonable price for our large lounge. While in America recently we saw some on sale without glass. Is there anywhere in England where we can purchase something similar?

A Obviously I don't know what you saw while you were there. But for original artwork at reasonable prices, I suggest you look around at local art colleges and evening courses for amateur artists. Go and see them painting and see if there is anything you like and would fit your lounge. People who do courses are usually doing it for the love of painting and will often be very pleased to sell a picture for the price of the materials they have used. If you are wanting prints, then there are lots of poster shops around where you can get all kinds of pictures to suit your taste – from architectural images to abstract. The other thing I think is worth thinking about is using beautiful bits of textile. You can often get fragments – embroidered or otherwise – very cheap. Have them framed without glass and they can look stunning. Or go to a local sale room where you may pick up something you like inexpensively. Second-hand shops are good sources of pictures too. You have to keep looking but you sometimes turn up a gem.

Q Every year on their birthdays I have taken a photo of my two children, now aged eight and ten, sitting in the same place. These photos are very precious to me – it's a source of great delight to see how my babies have grown. Can you suggest ways of displaying them (they are just normal 15 x 10cm/6 x 4in photos) to show them at their best?

A Lots of questions come to mind. For instance, how long will you keep the tradition going? Obviously you will need to be able to add to whatever you decide on. As they are so precious, I would frame them, though they will take up lots of space. First I would decide when to stop the rogues' gallery. At 18, say? Then work out how much space you will need for all those pics. Get a good framing shop to suggest mounts and frames – perhaps two long natural wood frames for the first ten years hung one above the other. Make sure the frames are simple and unlikely to date and get two more made up at the same time for the next ten years. You will not be able to duplicate the frames later. You can always fill them up with other pictures of your children until the yearly one comes round.

Q A friend has had a lifelong wish to wake up and see the world in front of her. I would love to give her a map of the world, something like 120 x 90cm (4 x 3ft) or even larger. Have you any idea where I could get one?

A The biggest map shop in the world is Stanfords, 12-14 Long Acre, London WC2E 9LP (tel: 020 7836 1321), and it will have anything you could want. A 1.5 x 1m Michelin world political map costs £6.95 on paper (for mail order, quote 10217) or £12.95 encapsulated. Postage and packing are extra. Because parcels more than 1m (39in) long have to be sent by courier delivery rather than by Royal Mail, this can add to the cost considerably. The shop stocks a huge range of political, topographical and specialist maps. It even does jigsaw puzzles of the world – maybe this would be a good gift for your friend. She could make it and then frame it. I have seen framed jigsaws and they look very effective.

Q I am looking for a work of art made out of wood to go on a wall. It must be large and stylish. Can you help me out?

A You are most likely to come across something by chance in shops that specialise in Indian and Far Eastern goods. I have seen fabulous carved doors from Africa that make splendid artwork. In London try Liberty's on 020 7734 1234 – they often promote wares from a particular country such as South Africa or Mexico. There are specialist shops such as David Wainwright on 020 7431 5900, while

Camden Market has bargain pieces. Outside London, Dragon's Shed, based in Ascot on 01344 627748, has Chinese wooden screens. Try your local auction houses too.

Q I brought a wall hanging back from Africa and have tried to hang it but it just never seems to look right. I'm sure there must be a better way of doing it. Any ideas?

A I, too, have brought hangings back from abroad and had this problem. You don't say what it is made from. I have some in cotton, wool tapestry, date palm with shells – all have the same problem, which is that they don't look straight when you put them up. Either you accept that they have a traditional look and learn to love their idiosyncrasies, or you can try and control them. I have hung some cotton ones from horizontal poles, with poles at the bottom to weigh them down. Tapestries I have lightly tacked to a wooden batten on the wall; and some really odd-shaped hangings I have stretched, mounted and framed – but this looks fine only if there is enough material around the pattern. Sadly though, whatever you do to them, some things bought on holiday just never look right when you get them home.

Q I saw a beautiful picture of a sunflower in a magazine. I cut it out and would like to fix it on to wood or plastic and protect it with wipeable varnish. Could you tell me how I could secure it and what sort of varnish I could use?

A Why not frame it? Find a junk shop frame that suits the picture. Incidentally, painting the flower with shellac would have made it stiffer and easier to cut out. Decide on a background for the flower and glue it on with artist's spray mount or gum arabic. Then paint over with a matt varnish. Or you could put it directly on your wall. Make an outline of a frame with a felt pen and use a matt varnish over the entire frame area.

Q Where can I buy shellac? You mentioned it a few weeks ago but none of my local art or DIY shops has heard of it. I can't do any of the projects in my decoupage book until I find some. Can you help?

A You can get shellac by mail order from Craig & Rose of Edinburgh (tel: 0131 554 1131). They sell just about every decorative paint finish there is, so you might like to try other techniques as well – how about scrumble glazing, for example?

Q In a recent edition of *Home Front,* leaf skeletons were used as an unusual and attractive alternative to paint or wallpaper. This sounds like the perfect decorating solution for my hall, stairs and landing. Could you please explain how to secure them to the wall. My hall waits eagerly in anticipation!

A To apply these really beautiful leaves to the walls, use Spray Mount from 3M, available at hardware stores and art shops for about £12. To seal them, use a matt acrylic varnish, also available in any hardware or DIY shop.

Q I love Tudor and Elizabethan wood panelling, and would like to create a study in that style. Do any companies reproduce period linenfold panelling, carved doors, etc?

A An amazing company near you specialises in exactly this sort of work. Stuart Interiors (tel: 01460 240349) cover all aspects of period design from medieval to the 18th century. They work mainly for museums and the National Trust, but also do smaller domestic interiors. They will give a free estimate but you can expect to pay in the region of £20,000 for a linenfold panelled study. They can also provide the whole interior for a period room, from textiles and lighting to furniture.

Q We would like to wood panel the lower half of our hall wall but we do not want to spend a fortune. Any idea where we could get wall panelling that looks authentic without costing an arm and a leg?

A Call James Mayor on 0121 643 8349. You don't say what style your house is but James Mayor do three ranges of dado wall panelling that would work well with both contemporary and period homes. They have Shaker, Victorian and Chapel styles. The best thing to do is to send for a catalogue, price £2, which is refundable on the first order. Then you can see which would best suit your setting. They also do an excellent range of wardrobe doors from Georgian, Victorian, Edwardian, Shaker, Classic to Country style. And again the same range in replacement kitchen cabinet doors, which tone brilliantly with older homes.

Q We would like to decorate our living room using reclaimed red bricks. Is there anywhere locally we could buy them?

A Try looking in the Yellow Pages for architectural salvage firms. There is one in Edinburgh called Easy Architectural Salvage (tel: 0131 554 7077). However, the problem with these firms is that you never know what they have in stock. You have to ring to find out, but most of them carry a good selection of basics such as old bricks. You can get bricks from further afield but, of course, carriage will add to the cost. Reckon to pay about £30 for 50 miles. It is also worth contacting Salvo News magazine (tel: 01890 820333), which has all sorts of information about reclaimed materials. Once you've seen a copy, you'll probably get into salvage in a big way! They also produce a Salvo pack for £5.75, which lists the dealers in your region.

Q My hallway is varnished knotty pine and is now looking very dated. Can you please suggest ideas for altering/re-decorating without actually removing the pine clad?

A Simply rub back the varnish to give you enough of a keyed surface to paint. Sandolin have a paint called Harmoni that is water based and quick drying – about an hour between coats. As it's translucent, the natural quality of the wood will still come through from underneath. There are ten standard colours to choose from, and it costs £7.29 for a 500ml tin. Hallways are always busy thoroughfares, so if you want to varnish it for extra protection I'd suggest Sandolin's quick drying clear varnish, £4.79 for 250ml. For stockists call 01480 497637.

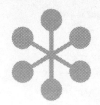

ceiling coverings

Q My husband and I have recently given up smoking. We are now setting about the redecoration of our home and are wondering how best to tackle the ceilings, which are badly nicotine stained. In the past, we have had to resort to using a gloss undercoat before emulsioning.

A Try removing the paper. When the surface is dry, use something called Cover Stain by Zinsser, which is a top quality primer. It takes about an hour to dry and then you can paint over it with any type of top coat you want. Cover Stain is an American product and comes in American sizes so a US gallon (approximately 3.78 litres) costs £25.80 plus VAT, and a US quart (approximately 0.94 litres) costs £8.40 plus VAT. It is available at Travis Perkins, Brewers, and good independent decorator shops. Call Zinsser on 020 8866 9977 for your nearest stockist.

Q The ceilings in our house are covered with vinyl matt emulsion paint, which is peeling and chipping away due to the humidity in our house. Could you please tell us a quick and easy way to remove this paint ready for redecoration?

A My first thought is why is your house so humid? Maybe you should be thinking about sorting that out as well as addressing your repaint job. For the ceilings, rub them down with sandpaper and seal them with Dulux primer sealer (only available in trade shops). It's a solvent-based product so you must leave it for 48 hours to dry. Dulux also do a range of Kitchens and Bathrooms paint which is a moisture-resistant soft sheen emulsion. For other rooms in the house, which are hopefully less humid, try a vinyl silk emulsion, which is easy to wash.

Q Is there any way we can cover up our Artex ceiling? We hate it, but it seems that nothing less than a power tool will remove it.

A I'm no fan of Artex, either. A power tool might do the trick for you, but you'd probably bring down the rest of the ceiling in the process. The best option for your ceiling is to paint it. Ordinary paint will only disguise the problem, but textured paint will partially cover it up. Try Impasto from Paint Magic, £27 for a 5-litre tub. Tel: 01225 469966 for mail order.

Artex can still be a good way to deal with problem surfaces, however, and there are now some modern alternatives to those dreaded peaks and swirls. Try Artex Mediterranean Touch Readymix (£12.99 for 5 litres), Artex powder, £6.99 for 5kg) and the Artex texture brush used for making waves (£7.99). Then colourwash or paint.

Paint Magic also do a textured plaster that contains marble dust, called Marmarino. This gives a subtle crumbling look that is very effective even in small panels. It comes with detailed instructions, but basically you apply thin coats and then tint, wax or colourwash. It costs £45 for 8kg or just £7 for a 1kg (2.2lb) tester tub.

Q I am desperate to get rid of the horrible cork wall and ceiling tiles in my home. I have tried to remove some already but they brought bits of plaster off with them, leaving a pock-marked surface, so I daren't try to pull off any more.

A Try getting the tiles off using a steam stripper. You can hire these for the day – call HSS on 0845 728 2828 for your local branch. The company also has a new catalogue that lists all the equipment it has for hire, including tips on how to use many of the items. It is the sort of catalogue that, once you've seen it, makes you realise how many jobs you can do for yourself at home if you have the right tools.

But back to your cork tiles: first, score them through with a Stanley knife, then go to work with the steam stripper. The steam should get in under the tiles, allowing you to ease them off without making holes in the surface behind. For any areas damaged by previous attempts at removing the tiles, fill the holes with a product such as Polyfilla, then use fine sandpaper to smooth the surface before painting.

Q We have ghastly old polystyrene tiles on our ceiling. Short of using fingernails or a flame-thrower, how on earth do we get them off?

A Your problem isn't getting the tiles off, it's stopping the ceiling coming down when you do it! The tiles may be there for a good reason – for insulation or to stop condensation. As alternatives to ripping them down, consider covering them with lining paper or fit a plasterboard ceiling, nailing through the tiles into the ceiling joists. Also bear in mind that, if you leave a big mess behind, replastering a ceiling could cost £200. If you decide to paint the tiles, don't use an oil-based paint as they will become even more flammable – you won't need that flame-thrower then! If you want to take the tiles off, use a scraper to lever them away from the ceiling. If they were fixed with adhesive, use a heat gun to soften the glue, then remove it with the scraper.

decorative details

Q I live in a very old cottage and would like to use a stencil to decorate between the beams in my bedroom. I want the result to look antique and faded, so should I use watered-down mixed colours, or a wash over it when it is done?

A Why not do both? To start with, I would suggest using a paint from the English Heritage range, because these are softer colours than most. To achieve a muted effect you should dilute the colour with water and use only a little paint on the brush.

When the paint is dry, you can treat it in several different ways to make the effect even more subtle. Antiquing wax – made from beeswax that is coloured brown – will dull down the stencil and give it a patina of age. This costs £6.50 for a 150ml jar from Paint Magic (tel: 01225 469966 for mail order). Or try a colourwash, such as The Stencil Store's Stone Wash White, which costs £14.99 for a litre. If you are a beginner, it is a good idea to use these techniques because they help to make the result look more convincing.

Call The Stencil Store on 01923 285577 for their mail-order catalogue, which costs £1.50. This contains a wide range of stencils, but if you can't find the one you want, they can access the Stencil Library for just about anything you can imagine.

Q I have a large, plain plasterboard ceiling that is skimmed and painted. It's 3.6m (12ft) from the floor, rectangular, and measures 10 x 7.3m (34 by 24ft). How can I make it more ornate?

A You haven't made it clear what kind of property you have or how industrious or artistic you want to be, but here are a few suggestions. You could paint it decoratively – though you'd need to hire scaffolding in order to reach. It might also be best to hire someone to paint the ceiling for you. In the north, Sebastian Wakefield (tel: 01756 760809) specialises in mural and trompe l'oeil work. Ceiling paintings can look fantastic. I saw one recently with lavish cherubs and rich jewel colours. It changed an ordinary bedroom into an exotic lair.

Or you could wallpaper the ceiling. There are some wonderful wallpapers around, but you have a pretty large area so think carefully about the design and cost. If cost doesn't matter, how about some gold leaf work or gold paint? Then, of course, you could commission some dramatic or floral plasterwork for the edge or as a central motif or you could use a simple colourwash and some stencilling. The Stencil Store on 01923 285577 has a new range of stencils available. Good luck!

Q Help, one of my twins is missing. Let me explain: the sitting room of my Victorian house still has its original ceiling rose, but its twin has long since gone from the adjoining room. Can we get an exact copy made by taking a mould of the remaining one?

A The chances are there is an interior decor shop near you, selling copies of your missing ceiling rose. Most Victorian houses were built from standard pattern books and a rose from a Victorian terrace should present no problem.

Q We are renovating a Victorian terraced house and have some original cornicing in the dining room that we would like to recreate in other rooms. How can we do this and would it be very expensive?

A A company called Troika Architectural Mouldings (tel: 0114 275 3222), does custom-made cornicing at about £30 a metre. If you can cut into your cornice or get at an end, trace its outline on to a piece of card and send it to them. They will then quote you a price for making up new cornicing in the same style.

Depending on how big your rooms are, matching your old style might be rather expensive. But don't worry, Troika also sells 'off the peg' cornicing in a range of eight standard Victorian styles, at about £9 per metre. It might be a better idea to replace all your cornicing with this. Troika has a brochure and will send out samples.

Q I have a DIY disaster. I live in a cottage with old beams in the sitting room. The beams are painted black and are very oppressive. I started to sand the beams but it's taking an age. A friend suggested sandblasting but I can't find a company that will do it. Please help save my sanity.

A Let me put you out of your misery immediately. You can transform your beams with woodwash, which is available in a range of colours. In no time you'll have banished the black and introduced something much less gloomy – even white or pink. First you need to establish what sort of paint your beams have been covered in. If the paint is oil based, then you need to apply an acrylic converter to act as a primer. If the paint is water based, then simply sand back enough to give a key for the woodwash. Contact Paint Magic on 01225 469966 for a colour chart of all their woodwash shades – it costs £7.50 and is available by mail order.

Q The wooden beams at the top of my conservatory are full of a sticky resin or glue that drips on to the carpet. I've rubbed them down with emery paper but it always comes back. It is worse in the summer when it is really hot. Can you advise me what to do?

A It is quite unusual for timbers to drip like this inside, though I have seen it when railway sleepers are used in gardens, especially when the weather gets hot. One solution would be to have your woodwork sandblasted and then sealed, using a surface sealant rather than one that penetrates the wood. I wouldn't varnish them – that might look wrong. Before you start, though, it may be worth getting someone in to have a look at these timbers, as they sound rather odd. It may be a DIY job by the previous owners, using untreated wood. If not, you could try to find out which company built the conservatory and ask them for advice.

Q I would like to divide my through-lounge and I'm quite keen on using old railway sleepers as beams. Do you know where I could buy some?

A Old railway sleepers can often be bought pretty cheaply. We paid £100 for one we used in a *Home Front* house project. It took six men to fit it but it looked fantastic when it was in. It was bought from an architectural salvage yard: it pays to look around locally in such places. Yellow pages will help you.

* floors

The flooring boom

means most of us will have probably been on our hands and knees in the last few years fitting some kind of new floor. What we put on our floor makes a huge impression on the room. I have just taken up some carpet in my sitting room and replaced it with dark wood flooring. Suddenly I have a sophisticated living room! You can choose to use wood, laminates, Marmoleum (what we used to know as linoleum), rubber, stone, beautiful Oriental rugs, tiles, natural grass woven matting or even paper flooring. I worked on a leather floor once, but at £250 a metre, that is only for the rich and famous. What you decide, determines the look.

Make sure you think about the traffic of the room and the dirt factor. With small children, I do not recommend natural flooring – Playdough gets stuck in it and Ribena stains! Go for easy-to-wipe-clean surfaces of laminates, wood or rubber. However, in a loft with only adults skipping through it, natural flooring looks great. Warmth is obviously an issue too. There is no doubt that wooden floors are colder than a carpet so if you live in a draughty home and need to preserve the warmth, think carpet.

 wood

Q I have a Georgian house with lovely floorboards. I would like to strip them and have them on show, but there are quite large gaps between several of them. How best can they be filled?

A What I've done in my own house is to cut thin slivers of wood and bang them down into the gaps. I did have rather large gaps and I wanted to do it the traditional way. Once the floor has been varnished, the wood fill blends in very well.

Q Can you advise us on wooden flooring for our new flat? We need to cover two bedrooms, the lounge/kitchen area, small hallway and bathroom. What should we use and should it be the same throughout?

A There are various sources of wood flooring you could consider. Old wooden flooring is more expensive than new, and different woods vary hugely in price. Some architectural salvage companies specialise in these woods, so find a local one in the Yellow Pages. Dark woods are popular at the moment and tend to be expensive. If you are covering your entire flat and you want to make it look bigger, I would go for the same flooring throughout because it will give uniformity to the space and enlarge it visually – also, there will be less wastage when laying it.

There are some very good laminate floors around now, too, which are much less expensive than wood, so have a look in some of the big superstores. A word of warning, though: I keep seeing flyers quoting cheap clearances of wooden flooring – half price sales and so on. Avoid these and go to a reputable shop. A large department store would be a good place to start your research.

Q I'm having to put down a new floor in an old house, but I don't know what to go for. Have you any advice on where to start?

A It really depends on the kind of look you want to achieve and what use the room is going to have in the end. Reclaimed boards are far more expensive than new ones because they have had to be removed from houses and there is a lot of waste involved in fitting them. Reclaimed oak boards, for example, can cost as much as £100 per square metre, which is going to leave you with a hefty bill to pay after laying costs are included – old boards are not tongue-and-groove jointed so they require an experienced carpenter to lay them. New boards come cheaper. There is a wide range of woods to choose from, depending on the colour you want. Also, think about what you are going to put on the floor. If you do not intend to put down rugs, you may want to splash out on reclaimed boards as these will blend in with the age of the house. However, if you plan to have rugs, new boards may suffice. Whatever you do, it won't be cheap but it will change the look of your room entirely. You don't say why you need a new floor – if it is because the present boards are rotten, then you need to find out what has caused this. Many people simply accept that old houses have some damp and live with it. But it may be that you need to put in a damp-proof course or have the joists treated for wet or dry rot before laying a new floor. Get advice, go to reclamation yards, talk to timber merchants and work out your budget.

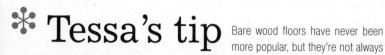

✳ **Tessa's tip** Bare wood floors have never been more popular, but they're not always easy to keep in tip-top condition. From Scandinavia comes a new concept in wood care. Trip Trap Hardwood Oil seals and protects all wood surfaces, giving a surface that doesn't mark and is easy to wash. Because it is an oil, not a varnish, the wood can breathe, and will never need sanding again. Hardwood Oil is ideal for high-traffic areas such as kitchens. For areas that get less use, seal with Trip Trap liquid soap. For pine and other light woods there is Trap Trap Lye, a mild bleach that produces a limed effect, and is ideal for pine as it stops it yellowing. Use the lye first, then seal with Trip Trap oil. For more information call Eva Johnson on 01638 731362, or Foxell and James on 020 7405 0152.

Q We are about to have a laminated floor fitted and, although we are told constantly that they are extremely hard-wearing, we are concerned that moving our furniture may cause scratches. We are trying to find some felt pads that can be stuck to the bottom of the furniture to reduce the possibility of scratching. Any ideas?

A Most hardware and haberdashery counters only sell very thin felt pads designed to stop ornaments from slipping. Ikea do sell felt furniture pads – it's obviously a problem they are familiar with in Sweden with the amount of wooden floors there. But I'm afraid I can't give you a price or any details because I can never get hold of Ikea on the phone! But they won't be expensive and will definitely do the trick. Taskers DIY on 0151 525 4844 have 6mm-thick self-adhesive felt which can be cut to fit. A pack costs £2.99 plus p&p.

Q We are just about to lay an oak floor in our sitting room. What is the best way to seal it? We want to keep the natural look of the wood but don't want lots of maintenance.

A Fired Earth is mainly known for its tiles, but the company has recently introduced a hardwood floor range, and to care for these it has developed a product called hot wax oil. This is a clear, oil-based liquid sealer that protects the wood without spoiling its appearance, leaving just a low sheen. Use two coats for a durable finish. How long this will last without further attention depends on the traffic in the room, but in a sitting room it should have at least 5 years' maintenance-free life, more if busy areas are covered with rugs. Hot wax oil costs £16.99 for enough to cover 9 sq m (10 sq yd), or £47.99 for 30 sq m (35 sq yd). Called Fired Earth on 01295 812088 for local stockists.

Q We want to restore the wooden floor in our Victorian house. Should we buy new planks and stain them to match the originals or try to track down more Victorian boards?

A Always go for old boards – they're easy to find in salvage yards and look so much better than new ones. You will never get a new board to match the old, however hard you try. In my house we moved all the old boards in good condition into two rooms and then bought random widths of reclaimed cedar to make entirely new floors where we had run out of the original boards.

Q I'd like to have bare floorboards in a bedroom I'm redecorating, but the old carpet had a foam backing and left black foam sticking to the boards. I intend hiring a sanding machine. Can you give me an idea of how much this will cost and whether the foam will be a problem?

A Try to get the foam off before using the sander as it might clog the machine and you'll spend a fortune on sandpaper as it will wear through very quickly. Buy some heavy-duty sandpaper and work on lifting the foam by hand first. You should be able to hire a sander for no more than £30 a day including VAT, and the job shouldn't take you more than a day as long as you remove the foam first.

Before laying laminate flooring, think ahead and plan any cabling that you want. By laying speaker cable in set areas you can hide unsightly cables and give a clean look to your room.

Q I want to have a 'proper' old-fashioned parquet floor in my hall, but the only flooring I can find is modern long wooden strips. Where can I find the original, smaller blocks of wood as in days of yore?

A The parquet flooring that DIY superstores sell is a totally different product to original parquet. You'll probably find what you want at your local reclaimed wood floor specialist – there are lots of reclamation yards around these days. LassCo Flooring in London is a huge reclaimed flooring specialist with prices starting from £20 a square metre. Call them on 020 7237 4488.

✳ Tessa's tip

Wooden floors are always popular – but one wood you have probably never thought of using is bamboo. We Brits have yet to catch on to it, but bamboo is brilliant for bathrooms, because it is 100 per cent moisture repellent. It is also extremely strong – so hard, in fact, that it has to be softened by steaming and soaking before it can be flattened and cut into strips.

Bamboo is easy to lay, supplied in long sections that are grooved on one edge so that they slot together. You simply nail or glue them over a wooden sub-floor, or directly on to concrete, provided that all cracks and holes are filled first.

You can order bamboo flooring directly from a company called Charltons (tel: 01761 436229). At £64.50 (including VAT) per square metre, bamboo is not cheap, but for a small bathroom it may offer a solution to those problems of water leaking through wooden floor-boards.

Q This is a desperate cry for help. After much persuasion I got my husband to sand a parquet floor in our hall. Many layers of dust later, we got down to the bare parquet floor. My husband doesn't want to revarnish it. I've visited many DIY stores, which advise that I use beeswax or linseed oil. Please help.

A Well it really depends what sort of finish you want. Why does your husband not want to revarnish, I wonder? Varnish is really the simplest and least maintenance in the long run. So if he is tired out after sanding, tell him that, with a little more effort, he can save himself work in the future! Use a spirit or water-based primer and then a good quality lacquer/varnish – that way you will have five to ten years of wear without further work (although the time it lasts obviously depends on how much use the hallway gets). There is a large range of matt or high-gloss varnishes from which to choose. If your husband is opposed to varnish, then use oil on the floor. This will give the wood an untreated flat, natural look, but will need several coats to get a good finish. You will then need to maintain it every six months for at least four years to keep it looking good. It will also need regular dusting. Am I putting you off? Alternatively, you can apply a primer and then wax with what you have been told – something such as Briwax – but, frankly, that is very high maintenance. Personally, I would go for varnish. Having oiled my own floor – never again!!! Call Lassco Flooring on 020 7739 0448 for details of products.

wood

55

✱ **Tessa's tip** Think very carefully before you respond to fliers or handbills pushed through your letterbox telling you about cheap household repair companies, specialist window replacement teams in your area and bargain carpet sales.

Recently, I sent off for a brochure about flooring. A letter then arrived in the post, saying that the company had been unable to contact me by phone but had a representative in the area who would come round on Sunday morning – at 10.30am – to discuss my needs. I phoned the company to tell them that I don't appreciate such high pressure selling, only to be abused by the company representative and have the phone slammed down on me. My advice is to look at some of the house magazines around and find some trade directories before deciding on improvements in your home. I guarantee it will pay you not to respond to fliers: these companies are mostly cowboys and are best avoided.

Q Our bungalow was built in 1937, and fitted with parquet floors throughout. Unfortunately these were rotten in places when we bought the house, and all had to be removed. After they were lifted, a sealant was put down, but now we find the floors are damp again. Is there another product we can use to seal them properly? We have heard there is some sort of latex that might do the job. Can you tell us where we can buy this, and how to apply it?

A It sounds as though you have quite a problem on your hands, and I would suggest getting a flooring expert in to have a look at it. You must have spent quite a lot on this floor, and I wouldn't like you to throw good money after bad. Does your bungalow have a damp-proof course? If not, that might be the source of your problem. The latex you suggest is good for helping with damp floors but it will not cure the problem. It is simply a rubberised material that you put over a screed before laying another flooring product on top of it. You can buy it from a builder's merchant such as Travis Perkins and it costs about £24 plus VAT for a 25kg bag, but I wouldn't suggest laying it yourself. You need to ensure you get a flat surface, and that is a professional job.

Q My daughter has a house that has quite a lot of parquet flooring. She has had some building work done and the floor has suffered in the aftermath of the alterations. How can she restore it?

A Obviously, try washing it first and see just what you are dealing with. If the builders have left stains and scratches on the floor, it is possible to sand it. Parquet is usually laid in patterns, so you have to sand the floor in two directions, the second time at right angles to the first. You should then sand down again with a very fine sander, again in both directions. Having just sanded a floor, I would try a thorough cleaning before resorting to sanding. It makes a terrible mess.

Q Please help with ideas for a cheap and practical floor covering. I have four cats and their fur gets everywhere. I like the look of wood or marmoleum flooring but £10 per metre is the maximum I can pay. I have cork in my hall, which is warm and easy to clean but looks outdated. I am not a great DIY person. Please suggest some alternatives for my budget.

A You don't give the measurements for your hall – is it long and thin or small and wide? I have used second-hand Persian runners in halls, which you can pick up cheaply at auction sales. They are usually multicoloured, don't show the dirt and will brighten up a long dark hallway. If they're your style, you could put one down over the cork floor and there'd be no DIY involved at all! Otherwise, you could replace the cork tiles and then paint the new ones with wood stain in bold geometric patterns. Varnish afterwards with matt acrylic varnish to preserve your handiwork. You don't have to be a great artist to do this and it can look very effective. Alternatively, if you live near an architectural salvage yard, you may well be able to find some reclaimed wooden boards that suit your budget. These yards often clear out old factories and offices and there are great deals to be had. Have them laid professionally to achieve the best possible finish.

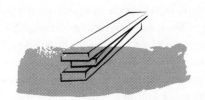

 tiles

Q I bought my house a year ago and lifted cork tiles off the kitchen floor to find a beautiful terrazzo floor underneath. My problem is that I cannot get it to scrub up clean. I have tried everything from bleach and chemical floor cleaners to paint thinners but I cannot get the glue off. I am very disappointed, because I feel I will have to tile over the floor which would be a real shame.

A There is one product that I can assure you will work, but it is pretty nasty to use and the company that sell it ask you to talk to them before going ahead with it. They do sell it to the DIY market but it is very strong and has to be used carefully. It is called Stain-Away and is made by Casdron Enterprises Ltd (tel: 01962 732126). In your area, a company called Evode Industries distributes it (tel: 00353 1840 1461). It is four times stronger than Nitromors and will melt your Wellington boots if not used carefully. It can even make you pass out if you inhale too much of it. Casdron work with a company called Stone Care Knight (on the same number) who will do the job for you if you are nervous. If you do decide to do it yourself, protect yourself with a mask and gloves, and keep windows and doors open while doing it. You will need to mask off skirting boards as the product will strip all paint off and will anodise stainless steel if it gets near it. Also you will need to dispose of the residue carefully by putting it in a drum and taking to the council dump. Altogether a job for experts, I would say, but it will bring your floor back to its original state. After that all you need do is seal it. Casdron do Stainstop, which will protect it and is undetectable. Do please phone them before you start any work on the floor.

Q I am desperate to find the traditional formula polish to clean and shine my hall floor tiles. I know it contains beeswax, but what are the other ingredients and their quantities?

A First of all, let me say that you don't have to use this old-fashioned way to clean your tiles. There are products on the market that will do the job just as well. But, if you do want to get traditional, first clean your floor with a floor scrubber, hired from any hire service shop for around £30. To polish the tiles use a mixture of boiled linseed oil and heated beeswax – about equal quantities. Simply rub it on with a soft clean cloth and polish until they look wonderful. Alternatively you can get a range of products from Lithofin that will clean, seal and wax your tiles. You do need to check what your hall tiles are made of as there are hundreds of products on the market to suit different tiles and the particular finish you want.

Q We covered our quarry tiles with linoleum tiles and then put cork tiles on top. Is there a relatively simple way to strip back to the original floor?

A I'm afraid there's no quick, easy solution. You should be able to prise off individual tiles with a wide stripping knife. It's manageable, but they'll probably come off in bits and some glue will be left behind. You can use Nitromors paint stripper to clean glue off the quarry tiles, then white spirit for a final clean. You'll then need to seal the tiles – brush on linseed oil and white spirit in a 5 to 1 solution. When dry, buff up with a light wax polish. Alternatively, HG Systems produce a range of specialist floor cleaning and sealing treatments which may do the job. Call 01206 795200 for advice or stockists.

Q After reading in your column about polish for slate floors, I wondered if you know of anything for quarry tiles?

A You can polish quarry tiles with a regular stone polish. First, decide on the look you want. You could try a matt, clear wax, antique wax or low-gloss finish. If the floor is grubby, you will need to clean off existing wax or polish with turpentine. A company called LTP (tel: 01823 666213) has cleaners, sealer and polishes for all kinds of floors.

Q We have four large, slate steps leading up to our front door. However many times I scrub them, they always look dull and in need of a jolly good clean. Is there anything I can do to improve their appearance and bring them more to life?

A The trouble with slate is that it always looks good when it's wet, but as soon as it dries it looks dull. The solution is to seal it. Try a product from Liberon called Floor Protector: this is a clear liquid that makes porous materials water resistant and works equally well indoors or out. All you have to do is clean your slate by scrubbing with water – but not detergent – then brush on two or three coats of Floor Protector when it's dry. Floor Protector gives a satin finish, and you can also use it on terracotta, marble, quarry tiles and stone. One litre costs £13.55. Call Liberon on 01797 367555 for your local stockist.

Q We have Welsh slate-tiles on our conservatory floor that look bright when wet but lose this beautiful sheen when dry. Is there a product we could use to achieve a permanent shine?

A First remove any dirt and then apply Fired Earth's Stoneshield Sealer (£13.95), ring 01295 812088 for mail-order details). However, most slate floors have already been sealed and you should not do it again. Instead, use Stone Finish (£11.95) which you mop on. It will need to be reapplied once a year. For a high sheen use Johnson's Traffic Wax Paste, £25.20. Ring Freefone 01784 484100 for your nearest stockist.

✳ **Tessa's tip** An exciting new product has caught my eye – aluminium floor tiles. I have seen aluminium used in factories and hotels, and always thought it was a durable, waterproof, not too slippery flooring. Now the manufacturer is launching it for home use, with a range of 30-cm (12-in) square tiles available in packs of nine. As with ceramic tiles, you simply glue them on to a level floor surface. They are easier to lay than ceramic tiles as they can be cut with a domestic jigsaw and, once in place, are simple to keep clean. Each square yard pack costs £49.99.

You can also buy stainless steel tiles. If you are interested in these, call Luxomation on 020 8568 6373. The company makes sizes from 20mm (¾in) (suitable for mosaics) up to 200mm (8in). The most popular size for wall tiles is 100mm (4in), and these are available in satin or mirror finish, £1.99 and £2.17 each respectively. Luxomation also does steel electrical sockets and light switches of the type used in industrial kitchens.

Q I have a large piece of slate in my fireplace that has been marked by a plant pot. I tried to clean it with Jif without reading the instructions first – they actually say it should not be used on slate. All it has done is make the mark worse. Is there anything I can use to restore the slate to its original condition?

A Slate is slightly porous so it will absorb cleaners. You need to try and get all the Jif off first, so scrub it back with washing-up liquid. Seal the slate with olive oil and then rub that back, too, so it is not sticky and likely to attract dust. It's as simple as that. There are specialist companies that make slate sealant, which could help hide the mark if the olive oil doesn't do the job well enough. Casdron on 01962 732 126 makes Lithofin slate sealant, which costs about £15 a litre and gives a glossy finish, and KF Stainstop at about £31 a litre for a natural look. The Welsh Slate Company on 020 7354 0306 sells its own sealant for £12.95 plus £4 p&p, for 250ml.

Q Our kitchen used to have lovely white and cream floor tiles with white grout. Three cats and a boxer dog later, the tile grout looks filthy. I tried bleach on a toothbrush and tile grout whitener but to no avail. As a last resort I added a thick layer of brown grout over the white, but after a few mops the white began to show through. Will I have to re-tile?

A If you hadn't put the brown grout down, I would have suggested an excellent cleaning product, made by a company called HG. The best thing now is to hack out the old grout with a grout rake, then re-grout with ivory or light grey. You could try the two-part epoxy grout that is used in hospitals and industrial kitchens. This is very hygienic but extremely complicated to use.

HG makes a wide range of grouting products that are generally available from independent hardware shops rather than DIY superstores. For your local stockist, call the MICA hardware chain (tel: 0161 339 2011), or the Home Hardware chain (tel: 01271 326222 for nearest store).

Q When we took up an old fitted carpet in our Victorian house we uncovered a lovely tiled floor. The tiles had been varnished, so I used Nitromors to remove this unwanted coating. Now I want to treat them with something to protect them and bring out the lovely colours. I have heard that a mixture of linseed oil, beeswax and turpentine is the traditional way to seal tiles. But how should I mix and apply this solution?

A You can certainly seal them using that mixture, but it is hard work and there are now preparations on the market that are easier to use. If you choose to seal the tiles with linseed oil, the first coat should be diluted with equal parts of turpentine or white spirit. Then you'll need to apply at least five or six coats – and for very porous terracotta tiles sometimes as many as 12 coats – of neat linseed oil. Use a paintbrush to apply it, and remove any surplus from the tile surface with a dry cloth. A few hours after the last application of linseed oil, polish the tiles with clear beeswax, or with a tinted one for a darker look. Ideally, two or three further coats of beeswax should be applied in quick succession with follow-up coats once a week over the next month to build up a hard-wearing finish. If you decide to opt for the less arduous, modern method of protecting tiles, LTP and Hagesan produce a wide variety of acrylic sealants for terracotta tiles. You will find both firms' ranges on sale in tile shops.

Q I have recently laid some rather nice terracotta floor tiles in my kitchen and used sandstone-coloured grout. When I polished the tiles, the grout absorbed the polish and now the floor looks dirty. Did I do something wrong? The sequence of work was to seal the tiles with two coats of linseed oil, then grout and finally polish. I buffed the tiles by hand.

A You did the right thing in sealing the tiles with linseed oil. What you should have done after you had put on the grout was to coat the whole surface with another layer of linseed oil. That would have darkened the grout slightly, but kept it clean when you finally polished the tiles. No grout cleaner is going to work now because they are either an acid to remove grout off the face of a tile or a bleach to clean up dirty looking grout. The only thing I can think of is to give the floor another coat of polish and hope that this darkens and evens out the patchy, dirty look. Failing that, you may have to remove the grout and start again.

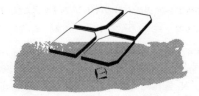

carpets

Q I have a good carpet that is some years old but in perfect condition, once pale blue but now silvery grey. How can I dye it in situ? There are a few small stains but a dark colour would cover them. Could I tackle it myself?

A As far as I'm aware there is no foolproof method to dye a carpet successfully. Most dyes need to be dissolved in water to activate them and must then be washed out. I think it would be better to employ a company to come in and steam clean your carpet. If the stains still offend, move the furniture round. Failing all else, buy a new carpet.

Q I live in an old cottage and want a new 45cm (18in) wide stair runner, but can't find one. Please help.

A Three ideas for you. The Alternative Flooring Company has just introduced two runners in the standard sizes of 60 x 236cm (2ft x 7ft 9in) and 68 x 320cm (2ft 3in x 10ft 6in). The company will also make up any size you want. Phone Freephone 0500 00 7057 or call the company on 01264 335111. Prices start at £30. Alternatively, you could try calling Roger Oates Design on 01531 632718 who do a 60cm (24in) and a 68cm (27in) runner – their 68cm (27in) one can be cut down to fit your needs. You would probably need to choose one of their designs with no border, so it is easy to cut to size. The extra sewing and binding would cost an extra £10.25 per metre. Prices start at £62 a metre. Finally, ask your local antiques shop to keep a look out.

Q Although not worn out, my stair carpet is showing signs of wear on the edge of the treads. Is there anything I could put on them that would save them from showing more wear and not look unsightly?

A You could use stair nosing that is normally used in offices and meets the treads and the risers of the stairs. You can get it in lots of different materials – plastics, aluminium, and also in different colours so there may be one that's suitable for your stairs, but it's quite unusual to use it domestically. Call Volanti on 020 8947 6561 for more information. You could think about moving the carpet a little to shift the wear to a different part.

Q We've recently moved into a new house where the carpets were provided by the builder. However, I'm now rearranging my furniture and find that I've got ugly indentations in the carpet where the sofa, chair and table legs have been and which I cannot get rid of. Can you help?

A If it's a good quality carpet, the indentations should disappear by themselves about a month. It may be that the builder used cheap carpet, which will show the marks more. You can try attacking the problem with a butter knife – one with no sharp edge – to try and lift the pile a little. Vacuuming over a period of time will loosen the pile, too. If the dents don't come out in a month or so, I think you can assume they're there to stay and you may want to rearrange your furniture again or buy a rug to cover the offending spots. Alternatively, have you tried placing a damp cloth over the mark and ironing it with a hot iron? Another trick is to place an ice cube on the indentation and let it thaw. Leave the carpet to dry overnight and the pile will lift.

Q We are keen to find natural floorings for our new flat, but would rather not have tiles, as these are a bit cold in winter. Can you help?

A It sounds unlikely, but the answer might be paper. A company called Crucial Trading offer Papamat, a reversible mat made out of paper with a cotton binding. It comes in red, green, blue or black, and can be vacuumed or washed by hand. It is also amazingly durable. Call Crucial Trading on 01562 825200 for details.

Another possibility is The Alternative Flooring Company, who sell 100 per cent coir matting in a wide range of colours. Call free on 0500 007057 for stockists. For natural upholstery and curtain fabrics, try the Natural Fabric Co on 01488 684002.

Q We want hard-wearing fashionable flooring and wondered whether seagrass, coir or sisal would be suitable for every area, bathroom and stairs included? Who stocks it?

A Coir is the hardest-wearing of all these natural floorings and it's cheaper than most. But it does react to moisture and joins can split open. Also, these floor coverings are not great if you have children – try getting Plasticine and mud out from between the weave. As they can be rough underfoot, stain quite badly and sometimes wear on staircases, they are best for trendy couples who don't stay at home that much! I would never use any moisture-absorbent flooring in a bathroom – it just gets damp and smelly. Natural floorings do look good but carpet can often be a cheaper option in the long run. Crucial Trading (tel: 020 7221 9000) has a huge range of natural floorings.

Q I went on holiday to a cottage in Wales that had a central vacuuming system that worked by suction from underneath the carpets. How could I go about installing such a system when I renovate the house I hope to move into?

A These systems are becoming standard fare in self-build homes. However, you can install a system into an existing home quite easily, although it will cost you slightly more. For a new home, the average spend is about £500 excluding VAT and, with fitting costs, works out to about £700. Basically they work by installing a cylinder in the garage, utility room or under the stairs. The cylinder collects dust and dirt via an inlet on each hallway into which you attach the hose part of the vacuum. The hose is approximately 9m (30ft) long, so you can work out how many inlets you would need. Call Paragon on 01224 735536 for a brochure.

✳ # Tessa's tip
I have bought two vacuum cleaners in my life and inherited one, and I've never thought much about their different qualities. They all more or less clean the place, which is what you expect. When you buy a vacuum the salespeople tell you all sorts of fancy things about the different models but you never get to try them out until you decide on one and get it home. It was only when I tried a friend's Dyson that I realised there is a huge difference in how cleaners perform. The Dyson model pictured, the DC05, weighs only 4.7kg and is easy to use on stairs, something I've been struggling with for years. Also, for someone who is always forgetting to buy spare dust bags, what a joy – the Dyson is bag-free. And if you suffer from allergies, it picks up everything from tiny pollen to pet hairs easily. This one costs £240 but there are cheaper models available. Oh, and they look pretty good, too.

Q While I was away on holiday, the person looking after my house let her dog wee on the carpet. I cannot get the stain out with the usual cleaners. Can you help?

A I have no idea how you get dog wee out of a carpet. What I do know is that it can make a difference if it is a male or female dog. The urine can be more acid in a female and actually burns the colour out of the carpet. It also loosens the colour and causes colour run. One of my mother's dogs weed on her velvet curtains and I can still see the blotchy stain quite clearly in my mind. If it is a valuable old rug, you could try phoning Behar Profex on 020 7226 0144 as they can work magic on rugs and bring back colour from the dead. The rug would still need to have a pile on it to allow them to draw the colour back from the base of the rug, so if it is a flat weave kelim, you will have no chance. However if your carpet was a fitted one, the only thing to try is lots of cold water to dilute it, mop it up and then put loads of salt on top and bottom. But this only works when the wee is still wet. So for you, I think the answer is a large rug to cover the problem.

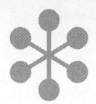

rugs

Q My white sheepskin rug is very old and I'd like to replace it. I've enquired all over Cornwall, from Plymouth to Penzance, and come up rugless. Can you help?

A I recommend Morlands (tel: 01458 835042); they do mail order, and p&p for a rug is around £4.70. A single skin rug in natural colour is about 90cm (3ft) long and costs £36.99. The double, where two skins are matched and sewn together, costs £89.99. Coloured skins are also available in a wide range of colours including black, bright green, chocolate, mulberry and navy at £39.99 for a single. They also have a snow leopard-effect – a natural skin with brown tips – also for £39.99. If you want a colour guide they'll send you examples of the various shades. They also supply short-haired rugs that are sheared short and are good for babies and the elderly – single costs £39.99. And for long car journeys or sore patches of skin or joints, they do a square that you rest on to relieve the pressure – cost £14.99. Clean the rugs by combing with a large-toothed comb and then beat on a line. If you need to wash it, choose the wool programme and use a very mild detergent, then a softener. Dry naturally. Never dry a rug near heat or the skin will harden.

Q Some years ago, I washed a white sheepskin rug but ended up with a dirty yellow one, although, underneath, the fibres were still white. Is it possible to restore the outer fibres, please?

A Probably not, is the short answer. This advise will be too late, sadly, but the safest option may have been professional dry cleaning. For future reference, you should protect a rug from dirt to start with – Scotchguard and Meltonian do a protective spray for sheepskin. If it does start to get grubby, the tricks is to clean it before it gets really dirty. Use a liquid soap and froth it up with tepid water; then use only the foam on the rug. Don't let the leather under the wool get wet as it dries out and goes hard. When it is dry, beat it with a broom to restore the pile.

Q I want to make a rag rug but the local craft shops don't seem to know what I am talking about. Where can I get hold of the backing material, tools and, perhaps, some advice?

A What kind of craft shops have you been visiting? People have been rag rugging for centuries. I once filmed a house for *Home Front* that was entirely carpeted with rag rugs and it looked amazing. The company to contact is Fred Aldous (tel: 0161 236 2477). Its mail-order catalogue contains everything you will need, including a guide to making rag rugs. It sells two types of hessian for the backing material. The more open-weave one is easier to work with, costs £1.79 a metre and is 1m (40 in) wide. The finer weave one costs £2.88 a metre, is 91cm (36 in) wide and comes in various colours. The tool you will need is a rag rugger, £6.99, which looks like a large pair of scissors with tweezers on the end. You poke the point through the hessian, pick up some material and loop it back through the cloth. The company also does a starter kit that includes some hessian backcloth, a rag rugger, rag rug gauge and instructions, for £9.25.

Q I wish to replace my lovely Indian Namdha rugs as they are very, very old. They're made of felt and are hand embroidered. Can you suggest somewhere in the Newcastle-Darlington or Leeds-Harrogate areas where I could buy new ones?

A Oxfam sell them. The rugs are not listed in the current Oxfam catalogue, so call the Oxfam helpline on 01865 313 6000 for details of shops in your area (the nearest is probably in Hexham). The Oxfam Namdha rugs come in two sizes – 60 x 90cm (2 x 3ft) and 90 x 120cm (3 x 4ft) - and cost £10-£25. Patterns depend on what's available but they are all embroidered by women in India. There are also some exciting contemporary Indian rugs around – they are more expensive than Namdhas but last just as long. For example, there is a range by Guru, which start at £350 for one 180 x 120cm (6 x 4ft), in 12 designs and six colourways. For a catalogue and direct mail order, call them on 020 8960 6655.

Q We are the proud owners of a Turkish rug that is about 11 years old. Sadly it is showing signs of wear at the ends – even though we have tried not to walk on it. The tasselled bits at either end have begun to break off. I wondered about cutting them off, turning the tightly woven strip next to them under and then sewing or sticking it. Would this work? Or is there a specialist company that could sort it out for us?

A Well, you are not so wide of the mark. Professional carpet restorers will sometimes remove the tassels and turn the end of a rug to give an even edge, if some tassels have completely gone. Alternatively, they use something called an invisible stopping stitch between each warp of the rug to stop it from fraying further. Once the tassels have started to go, you cannot ignore it or it will spread into the main part of the rug. If you look at most old carpets, it is the ends that go first. The vacuum cleaner is often to blame. Try the stopping stitch yourself if you are handy with a needle – as you get better they may even become invisible! If you want some professional advice and an estimate of how much it would cost to repair, call David Black Oriental Carpets on 020 7727 2566. They can provide an estimate from a photograph of the rug. Or try Yellow Pages for a local carpet dealer to ask for advice.

Q I am being driven slowly mad by 'creeping rugs'. I have a lot of floor rugs on top of the carpet and just cannot find anything to hold them in place. I have wasted money on products guaranteed to work but so far none of them has. Please can you help?

A You don't say what products you have already tried, but here are a few suggestions. John Lewis sells sheets of a sponge-backed material called Rug Hold, price £8.50 a square metre. Place between rug and carpet, a patch of this should stop slippage. Mail-order firm Scotts of Stow do a cut-to-fit, anti-slip mesh, about 1.47m x 81cm (58 x 32in), price £7.95. It needs no glue to fix it. They also offer cat-claw rug grips. These are 5cm- (2in-) square pads, each with rows of tiny metal hooks that hold your rug in place. Price £7.95 for four. Scotts of Stow are on 0990 449111.

Q I have a runner on top of a jute carpet. I found that neither 'cats' paws' nor rubber mesh could keep it in place. Double-sided tape held it for a long time but, alas, has come away. Any ideas for keeping the runner in place?

A Roger Oates Design (tel: 01531 632718), a company I mentioned recently as making narrow runners, also supplies two types of anti-slip underlay. One is an anti-slip polypropylene mesh that sticks to floorboards and would work well on your jute carpet. It comes in 70cm (28in) widths and costs £4.60 a metre plus p&p. There is also SRF underlay, which is spongier, but more suitable for bare floorboards than jute carpet. It costs £8 a metre plus p&p.

Q I recently purchased a reindeer-skin rug in Norway. Unfortunately it is moulting rather a lot and I wondered if there is anything with which it could be treated. I would be grateful for any tips you might have.

A When I read your letter, I was reminded of some advice I was given by a neighbour and I see no reason why it wouldn't work for your rug, too. I bought a very hairy and moulting mohair scarf that left bits of fluff all over my coat. I didn't know what to do until my neighbour recommended that I wrap it tightly and put it in the freezer for two weeks. Amazingly, it worked, so, if your freezer is big enough, why don't you give it a go?

Q I would like to clean my Chinese rug, which is 150 x 90cm (5 x 3ft) in pink/cream basic colours. I cannot afford to have it done professionally but after 11 years' service it needs help!

A If it is valuable, then professional cleaning would be safest but, as you want to have a go, do the basics first. Hang the rug on your washing line and give it a good bashing – I use a wooden broom. You'll get off all the surface dust and dirt and you may find it's enough to lift the pile and liven up your rug. If it needs more attention, use a squeeze of a gentle wool detergent in a pint of water – just enough to make frothy water. Then, with a soft brush, gently rub the bubbles into the carpet. Wait until it dries and vacuum off. Try a small area first for colour-fastness. Remember that good carpets grow in character as they age and are often the better for it. A bit like us, really!

✳ Tessa's tip

Lots of people are buying old rugs to put down on wooden floors without realising that such floor coverings need to be cared for correctly. It is fine to vacuum them, but when you do, be sure to use only the suction part of the vacuum cleaner – not the brush. The suction action flicks up the pile of the rug and stops dirt penetrating further into the rug. Once you have done this, add two drops of fabric conditioner such as Comfort to a bowl of lukewarm water, dampen a cloth with it and very gently wipe over the rug, going with the pile. This closes the wool and brings dirt to the surface. Be careful with kelims as the colours in some are prone to running. If you need your rugs cleaned professionally, try Behar Profex. It has been cleaning beautiful rugs for decades and is expert at it – many firms merely use bleach products to take out stains, which also lift the colour. Cleaning a small rug starts from £50 and repairs cost from £120. Call Behar Profex on 020 7226 0144 for details.

Q My sister has removed the carpet from her bathroom and was hoping to lay sheet vinyl. However, the floorboards are in poor condition and not level and vinyl would show the joints. She doesn't want to sand the boards because of the dust, nor re-carpet nor paint the floorboards. Help!

A One of the simplest ideas for a bathroom is to use canvas floorcloth and you can paint your own very cheaply. You need canvas, PVA glue, acrylic primer, water-based paint and water-based acrylic eggshell varnish. Buy canvas slightly larger than you need, because it shrinks. Pin it flat on a floor or table, paint with the PVA glue and let it dry. Put on the acrylic primer and, when dry, fold back the edges and glue down. Then paint or stencil your design on the canvas. Finally, when dry, treat with at least three coats of acrylic eggshell varnish. Fix to floor with double-sided carpet tape.

✳ Tessa's tip

Helen Yardley makes some of the most beautiful rugs I know. They are modern, stylish, and once you have seen one, it is easy to spot her look. She has just produced a new range of pure-wool and hand-tufted rugs and runners using cut and loop pile for extra texture in many of the designs. There is a huge range in other sizes and colours, including reds, oranges, hot pinks, moody purples and creamy neutrals. The best way to buy a rug is to call Helen Yardley direct on 020 7403 7114 and discuss your needs. You can be sure that you are buying a future classic that will look great on your floor or wall. Prices start at £975.

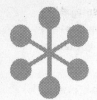

flexible flooring

Q Some time ago you answered a question about cleaning vinyl floors. My kitchen floor get heavy traffic from three dogs and, despite regular cleaning with products such as Flash and Kleer, it never seems to come up with any shine. Can you recommend any alternative?

A Try using a Marley Floor Cleaner and then polishing with two coats of Marley Floor Gloss.

Q I am in the process of redecorating my bathroom after having a new bathroom suite fitted. I am looking for suitable flooring that is childproof. I am interested in rubber tiles and have heard of a supplier called Dalsouple. Could you please give me some more information about rubber tiles and where I can get them?

A You are quite right – there is a company called Dalsouple that does a massive selection of rubber tiles in all kinds of sizes. They have 60 colours and 30 different textures to choose from, so there should be something to suit your new bathroom colour scheme. As with any tiled floor, you need to make sure the floor is level before you start laying tiles, so if you have a timber sub-floor you will need to put down a plywood base for the rubber to go on. As it's a bathroom and you have small children, I would advise going for tiles with a textured surface because this will be less slippery than smooth-surfaced ones when wet. Rubber is a great product for bathrooms – it is easy to clean and looks great. It costs about £41 a square metre and unless you are handy with flooring, you will need to get someone to fit it for you. Call Dalsouple on 01984 667551 to find your nearest retail outlet. They will also advise you on the correct adhesive to use. It is made in France so expect to wait between four to six weeks for delivery.

Q A year ago we put down some black and white vinyl tiles on what seemed like reasonably even floorboards in the hall. Since then, however, the tiles have cracked badly and now we have gaping holes between the boards. What can we do?

A Vinyl tiles should work well in a hall – it sounds as if you didn't sort your floor out beforehand. Floors must be flat, smooth and dry before you start work. Floorboards generally need to be covered with a sub-base, such as a layer of hardboard, or they start to show through. To get the effect you want, I'm afraid you'll have to go back to the beginning and do this now.

Q I've recently moved into a new house and the kitchen floor has horrible worn vinyl tiles. I like the look of linoleum, but how practical is it in a kitchen, and is it very expensive?

A I'm a great fan of linoleum. It's hard-wearing, easy to clean and looks beautiful. It comes in lots of colours and is warm on bare feet – ideal for the kitchen! You can design your own pattern and have it cut by your supplier for a truly original look. Or there are ready-made decorative borders available. It's more expensive than other soft floorcoverings and has to be fitted by an expert, but I think it's well worth it. Forbo-Nairn (tel: 01592 643777) is the only British manufacturer of Marmoleum, a natural lino, ideal for allergy sufferers. Contact the company for local suppliers and fitters.

Q I have a lino-tiled floor that has lost its colour and finish because of age and water. Can you suggest how to restore it? I would like a gloss surface that is non-slip. Some of the tiles, which are 23cm (9in) square, are beyond repair. Do you know where I can find replacements?

A Any gloss surface is likely to be a bit slippery, I'm afraid. But Forbo-Nairn, which makes Marmoleum (as lino is called these days) does a dresser to polish up tiles. It is a liquid polish and although not sold as a non-slip finish, is not too skiddy underfoot. John Lewis in Glasgow sell it for £5. You would probably need a couple of coats to get a good shine. As for restoring the colour lost because of age and water, you could try stripping off the old polish with a cleanser, which Forbo-Nairn can also supply. This is simply applied with a mop. It costs around £3.50, again from John Lewis. Forbo-Nairn doesn't sell tiles of the size you want, but you could buy its 33cm (13in) or 50cm (20in) sizes, and get a floor specialist to cut them down for you. For local stockists, call Forbo-Nairn on 01592 643777.

Q I want to redo my kitchen floor, ideally with a completely smooth surface. I have vinyl at the moment but it suffers from digs and cuts. Is there anything else?

A Well, there are lots of different surfaces you could use on your floor. It depends on the look you want and how much you want to spend. For the simplest finish in a kitchen, and for warmth, I would recommend wood, as it is kind to the foot, easy to clean and looks beautiful. There are hundreds of different colours and finishes available. Or you could go for Forbo-Nairn's Marmoleum (similar to lino) which is made of natural materials. It's also warm to the touch and comes in masses of colours. If you are worried about marking it, think about using tiles. If you happen to damage an area, it is relatively cheap to lift a tile and replace it. Quarry tiles are popular but getting difficult to find, and they are expensive. You also need a good strong finish on them to prevent marking. I would steer clear of tiles as they are cold to the touch. If you are putting down underfloor heating, tiles are not a problem and neither is stone. With the sophisticated sealants and waterproof grouts around now, limestone and sandstone are easy to use and look great. For stone floor enquiries call Stone Age on 020 7385 7954.

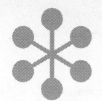

decorative
details

Q My husband has cleaned and restored an old pine staircase. We want to show it off by putting a strip of carpet down the centre, using some lovely brass stair rods that we have found, but we can't find clips for the rods anywhere. Can you help?

A If your brass stair rods are antique, you will have trouble finding suitable clips at carpet retailers, because most modern stair rods are 12mm (½in) diameter while older ones are 3mm (⅛in) diameter. But a firm called Stairrods (UK) (tel: 01207 591176), will manufacture clips to the size you need. They can also make rods in any material you want, including chrome, brass, bronze and wood.

Q We are in the process of building a lean-to and want to know if it's possible to paint the concrete floor. If it is, could you advise on the best product to use?

A The people you need to speak to are Sealo Crete (tel: 01706 352255), who will advise on stockists in your area. They do two types of concrete paint: a polyurethane one, suitable for exteriors, and an epoxy one that will suit your needs. The polyurethane paint comes in red, grey and green, costs around £40 for 5 litres and takes two to three hours to dry. The epoxy paint comes in red, blue, green, medium grey, light grey and buff, is harder wearing but loses its colour in sunlight, so is unsuitable for exteriors. It takes 24 hours to dry and costs around £60 for 4 litres. To apply concrete paint, first use a brick cleaner called Sealo Clean (£2.50 a litre). It acid-etches the surface to remove any grime. Simply dilute it, brush on and then rinse away. Be aware that any painted exterior surface will tend to get slippery. You can buy an aggregate that you paint on between coats to help prevent this problem. Available in 5kg bags, for around £10.

Q The flooring in my new house is wood and I'm keen to do something simple and inexpensive with it. The local authority has given me permission to paint the floor: could you advise me on which paint to use?

A Painted floors can look fabulous and are easy to do. Use vinyl matt emulsion and, if you're feeling adventurous, why not design a simple pattern, too? If you go for a pattern, make sure you use masking tape to keep the edges of your design sharp. Always clean the floor of any dust before you begin. Use an acrylic primer first (this dries very quickly). When you've painted your floor, varnish it well. The number of coats of varnish depends on the wear the floor will get.

Q I have a cork floor in my dining room that has been varnished – it looked lovely with my pine furniture. However, I have now furnished the room with old oak furniture and would like to darken the floor and/or paint it. I have no idea if I can remove the old varnish without damaging the cork, or if I can paint or stain over it.

A The standard method of stripping varnish is with a machine sander. You can imagine what would happen to a cork floor. The best way to tackle it is by hand. Lightly sand or use a varnish stripper to give a surface for the new varnish to stick to. If the varnish is worn in places you may need to first use clear varnish over the worn areas. Leave to dry before applying a darker stain over the whole floor. If you wanted to paint the floor, use gloss paint after you've sanded, but I think you'd get a better finish with the varnish.

Q My bungalow is tiled with thermoplastic tiles on concrete. The tiles are in sound condition and I wondered if I could paint them. There seems to be a large number of products on the market to help you paint floorboards, work units, etc – could I use one of these?

A A paint called Vinyl Flair from International will do the trick. You must make sure you have cleaned and dried the floor well before you start. If the floor has been polished, all residue must be removed before painting. Use a synthetic brush to paint it on and do a test patch first to check that it adheres to the tiles – it ought to be fine. Simply paint on and allow four hours to dry before repainting. You can walk on it in about eight hours. Clean with a damp cloth or a mild detergent. Colours are oyster, peppercorn, Shaker blue and green, buttermilk and terracotta. It costs £11.99 for a litre, and is available in most DIY superstores. Call 01962 717001/2 for stockists or look at www.plascon.co.uk.

Q **The previous owner of our house painted the original Victorian porch and path tiles with what appears to be cardinal red. It is now very worn and shabby. We have tried everything to remove the paint but with no success. Can you help?**

A Try a paint stripper. It won't harm the tiles as Victorians used hard-wearing encaustic tiles made from natural clay. They shine up beautifully using boiled linseed oil and beeswax. Apply two coats with a soft cloth – hard work but the results are brilliant. If tiles are damaged, modern equivalents are available, or try salvage yards. Mail-order tiles are available from Original Features on 020 8348 5155.

Q **I have a smallish bathroom floor that is in need of some help. It has very boring off-white vinyl flooring and I want to go for something a bit more exciting. Any ideas?**

A Well, it depends on your budget and the sort of finish you want. You could try your hand at laying a mosaic floor – a lot less difficult than you think; then there's linoleum, which is very trendy these days. People are also using rubber floor tiles, although you need to be careful as they can get slippery in bathrooms. You could paint and seal cork tiles or you could try a company called Harvey Maria on 020 8516 7788, that will make up any design you want on a cork tile with a PVC laminate top. They also do their own great designs with beautiful cork tiles that you can buy in a pack of nine, enough for 91 sq cm (1 sq yd). They are water-resistant, and easy to clean, so would be great for your bathroom.

Q I have an oak floor in my hall. Apart from painting it, is there any way that I could lighten its colour? I have tried to sand it, but that made no impression at all.

A If I had an oak floor I would leave it alone, because wood is very trendy at the moment. But if you want to lighten it, look for a product by Paint Magic will do the trick without too much work. It is called white colour wax, and works in a similar way to liming wax but without all the effort. The colour wax must be applied to bare wood, but since you have sanded your floor already, the preparation is done. White colour wax costs £6.50 for 120ml. Call Paint Magic on 01225 469966 for mail order.

An alternative technique would be to use a wood wash. Simply dilute the paint to the consistency and colour you want and paint it on. Then varnish with a matt, semi-matt or gloss varnish to protect the floor. For a one-step treatment, there are white or yellow tints that you can mix with acrylic varnish, and these would also lighten your floor.

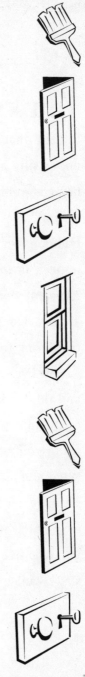

✳ doors and
windows

You know what they say – you

can tell what kind of person you are from your front door. It is not as silly as it sounds. Your first impression of someone's home is waiting at the front door. Is it cared for? Does it need a paint? Is it modern? What about the door furniture – is it traditional or contemporary? Does it have a Beware of the Dog notice? Is there a number or a name? What colour is it? Apparently red is a hugely popular colour for doors, but come across a door painted mauve and you'll probably find a sensitive type living there. So what does red say about us?

Now I've scared you into considering redoing your door, stop and think about your windows too. There is an awful lot to contemplate there. What frames should you have? Can you restore old windows? What type of glass should you put in? What style of fittings? How do you clean them and remove scratches? I hope there's something in this section to help everyone who wants to improve their frontage. Even those of you who live at the seaside whose brass door knockers never stay clean!

painting

Q I live in an Edwardian cottage which has a functional but ugly PVC front door. Can you paint exterior PVC doors and, if so what should I use?

A Why not change the door completely? Despite all its virtues, PVC can look out of place, particularly in a period cottage. Go to a salvage yard with your measurements – you may find something more in keeping with your cottage. If you really want to keep the door, paint it using ICI's Weathershield, which is specifically designed for discoloured PVC. However, it only comes in brilliant white. ICI tested darker colours but these absorb sunlight and make the surface warp. I would head for the salvage yard.

Q Our house, built around 1912, has the original front door with coloured glass inserts. The door has been painted very badly in the past and now has many layers of paint, which need removing. Is it safe to have the door dipped and stripped or is there a risk of the glass falling out in the process? If it is not safe, which method of paint removal would you recommend?

A I'm afraid that there is a risk of the glass falling out if you dip the door. To avoid the problem, find a good dipper and make sure they submerge the door beading side down – the beading around the glass will hold it in place when the paint and putty come off.

Alternatively, you could strip the door yourself. With modern products this needn't be a tiresome job, though you will need to be careful as an old door like this will probably have been painted with lead paint. Left alone this is perfectly safe, but you shouldn't sand it, because the dust is hazardous. Instead, I recommend a product called Kling Strip. This is a poultice that you spread on the door, and leave overnight. Then you simply remove the poultice in the morning and it brings the old paint with it. Kling Strip costs £17.45 including p&p for a 5-litre tub, or £59.75 for 25 litres. Call Strippers on 01787 371524 for mail order.

If, for any reason, your stained glass does come to grief, there are some excellent reproduction glass companies that can replace it for you. Philip Bradbury on 020 7226 2919 is one you could try.

Q I have a nicely shaped, half-paned glazed front door, that needs a makeover. Any ideas?

A Smartening up your front door is easy. There is a product that Dulux does called Instant Sander that you simply paint on and leave to dry. Once dry, you wipe it and it gives you a key on which to start painting. It will not strip all the paint off the door. Instant Sander is available in Homebase and the better independent DIY retailers. Once you have done this, the choice is yours as to the look you want. If you would like the woodgrain to show through, then Dulux does a paint called Brushwood that will give you a natural wood effect over your painted surface. If you want something longer lasting, then I suggest you go for a satinwood or high-gloss finish. Again, if you have used the Instant Sander, you will be able to paint these directly over the prepared surface.

Q How can I clean the aluminium frames on my sliding door and, once I've done that, what can I paint them with, if anything?

A Clean the aluminium with soapy water, then dry it well. To paint it, I recommend Dulux's Weathershield range. If the aluminium has a smooth finish, Dulux manufactures a mordant solution that you paint on first to give a key – essential to ensure subsequent coats are evenly applied – to the metal, though you won't need to do this if the frame is already rough to the touch. Then apply a coat of quick-dry metal primer before painting with a top coat of Weathershield gloss or satin. The gloss takes about 16 hours to dry and the satin about six. Call Dulux on 01753 534225 for more information about the Weathershield range and its uses.

Q I have several veneered interior doors in need of revarnishing. They have been polished with a silicone spray polish, which makes a bad surface for the varnish. I sanded one of them down to the wood and then scrubbed the surface with fine steel wool and white spirit, but the varnish still ended up looking like water on a greasy surface. I know that you can use cellulose spray paint on top of silicone, but how can you get rid of the silicone to make varnishing possible?

A Where you went wrong was to use white spirit. You should have used wire wool with methylated spirits. Try again with that, and if it isn't strong enough, use a wash of soda crystals dissolved in water. If traces of varnish remain, you could try a product called Libnet Furniture Cleaner – it contains solvents that will break down the silicone and allow you to revarnish your doors. It costs £3.79 from all good hardware stores or you can buy it by mail order from Foxell and James on 020 7405 0152 plus p&p. Libnet is also good for removing the silicone wax finishes of some cheaper polishes and it will not harm the veneer.

Q The entrance hall of our bungalow is a bit dark, due mainly to the seven doors that lead off it. The doors are made of brown wood veneer, and I would like to paint them white or some other light colour. Do they have to be prepared in any way beforehand?

A Make sure the doors are clean and dry, then apply a melamine/tile primer. Once this has dried, apply two coats of acrylic eggshell paint. You will need to put some varnish over this. Acrylic varnishes take less time to dry than oil-based ones, and are far less smelly. They come in eggshell, matt and gloss finishes, so take your pick. International (tel: 01962 711177) and Paint Magic (tel: 01225 469966) are two companies that do the full range of paints you will need.

Q How can I stop the knots from showing through on some pine doors we have. I have given them several coats of paint but the knots still come back through. They look such a mess.

A I'm afraid you will have to get back to the wood and start again. What you should have done was to seal the wood with a special knotting solution before you painted it. International do one, which you can buy at all good hardware stores. If you are intending to overcoat in a natural varnish, there is a special clear knotting solution you can use. Otherwise it comes in natural resin yellow/amber in 125ml tins. Alternatively, you can try an excellent product called primer sealer, which also seals off knots in wood. It costs £11.75 for a US quart (1.3 litres/2 pints). Call Zinsser on 020 8866 9977 for stockists.

Q We live in a 1970s bungalow which was 'abused' by its previous owners. We have spent long hours restoring the building and sorting the basics. The floors in the dining room, bedrooms and hall are parquet, a kind of dark oak colour. The doors, however, are a horrible 'hollow' type and have been painted in gloss. Here on the Isle of Man, salvaged wooden doors are very expensive – to replace eight doors would cost us £1,250! As money is tight, have you any ideas what would make them look better?

A I can see the problem, living where you do and also having a modern house, so even good quality salvaged doors might not suit. You could remove the gloss paint, attach some cheap and easy to fix beading, then repaint the doors in a more subtle eggshell finish. Changing the handles can often dramatically improve things. Or perhaps you could remove, say, your sitting-room door and replace it with a heavy velvet curtain?

Q The windows and front door of our new home are UPVC, but the windows are white and the door is wood-effect brown. Can I paint the door to match the windows?

A Yes, if you use Dulux Exterior UPVC paint. Fortunately for you, it only comes in white. It costs about £16 per litre plus VAT, and most DIY stores sell it. You don't need an undercoat but you must clean the door first. The paint is pretty durable and should last four to five years. For more information call the Dulux advice line on 01753 550555.

Q The south-facing window and doors in my house are in terrible condition, particularly the sills. The windows have been treated with a mahogany stain, and I was wondering what I could use to get rid of it before I repaint. It needs something more powerful than sanding. Any ideas?

A If it won't come off with sanding, then try a product called HomeStrip. One coat should be enough to strip most finishes. All you have to do is apply it with a paintbrush, leave it for the appropriate length of time – this varies from 15 minutes to an hour, depending on the finish you are stripping – then remove it with a paint-scraper or, for ornate carving and the like, stainless steel scouring balls. Then wash down the surface with water and lightly sand it when dry. HomeStrip's suppliers claim it can take off five coats of paint in one application, and does not dry out as you work, so large areas can be stripped at one go. It clings to vertical surfaces and will not discolour timber. Unlike many paintstrippers, HomeStrip is water-based and solvent-free, so should not cause side effects such as headaches and skin irritations. But if you are stripping old paintwork, be sure to check for lead in the paint first, as removing lead paint is hazardous and requires special precautions. Kits for checking lead content are available in most big superstores. For HomeStrip call Ray Munn on 0845 601 0803. Cost is £11.95 per litre plus p&p.

doors and windows

Q My daughter has just moved into a new home and, though it is fine in every other respect, the windows have all been replaced with plastic ones that have brown frames. Is there a product that we can use to paint them white?

A Dulux do a paint called Weathershield UPVC that only comes in brilliant white. All you have to do is clean the surface of the frames with a plastic scouring pad, then apply the paint using a brush. For larger surfaces, such as a door, a roller or spray gun would work well, too. The paint should be touch-dry in two to four hours, but allow for longer in damp conditions. Don't thin the paint, as it has been designed for use at full consistency. Weathershield contains a fungicide to discourage mould and should last five to six years depending on conditions. You are unlikely to find it in the big DIY stores, so go to Travis Perkins or a similar builder's merchant.

Q Is there any product for removing mastic from UPVC window frames with ease? No one seems to stock such a thing, although I think I have seen it used on television programmes.

A If the mastic is silicone-based then any silicone remover will do, and will be safe to use on UPVC. Call Dow Corning on 01676 528000 for more details. If the mastic is oil based, acrylic or polyurethane, then I'm afraid the only answer is elbow grease and a bog standard scraper.

Q We have just moved into a new home, previously occupied by heavy smokers. Can you tell me how I can remove all the silicone sealant from the inside of UPVC windows? I have tried everything to clean it but it is still dark brown.

A There's a sealant remover you can buy for £3.50, which will loosen the sealant and make it easy to remove. You squeeze it on like toothpaste. New sealant is very easy to use – you can buy a special gun to help you apply it.

Q The outdoor wooden window sills of my house blister and crack from being exposed to the elements, and I have a constant battle to keep them in good weatherproof and decorative order. I have tried most of the fillers in the DIY stores without any lasting success. Is there anything you could recommend?

A Your woodwork does sound in a bad state, so I would advise sanding them right back and starting again. Wood is particularly vulnerable to our British weather, and breaks down quite easily in moisture and sunlight. The Dulux Weathershield range includes a preservative primer that will seal bare or new wood before you paint it. The primer helps to stick the wood together, and it kills algae and fungi, helping to prevent rot and mould. Then use undercoat from the same range. This is flexible enough to move with the wood and so helps stop cracking and flaking. Leave for two to four hours before repainting. Then apply Weathershield exterior high gloss paint. This is designed to let the wood breath and it also has fungicides in it to help stop mould growth. The pigments in the paint are resistant to the ultraviolet rays of the sun. It takes about four hours to dry and Dulux say it should last for up to six years. Available from Jewson and Travis Perkins.

Q I need some advice on preparing the structure of my wooden conservatory for painting. It has been treated with Sadolin for a natural mahogany finish and my intention is to undercoat and paint the woodwork with ordinary interior paint to lighten the room.

A I'm afraid you have a lot of work in store. As the mahogany stain is so dark you will have to strip it back first with a paint remover like Nitromors. You will then need to scrape and sand it back further to get the stain out of the grain of the wood before you embark on your undercoating and painting. An alternative is to take the wood back to its untreated state and then use a lighter stain than the deep one you have now.

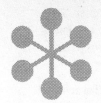

replacements

Q I have recently moved into a 1930s house that has a lot of original stained glass, including a large, circular panel in the front door. This is very delicate and obviously not burglar-proof, so I wondered whether it could be 'double glazed' by having clear glass fitted on either side? Some of the other windows are a worry too, as they have started bulging in the middle. Can you help?

A Yes, you can get security glass fitted on your front door. I had the same problem as you – when I moved in to my present house, it had the most beautiful stained glass in the door, but you could have put your finger through it very easily. On the outside I fitted toughened glass, which comes in 6mm or 4mm (¼in or ⅙in) thicknesses. This is very strong, and only needs to be fitted on one side. It won't detract from the appearance of the stained glass either, because from the inside you will still have the more fragile original showing.

Regarding the second part of your question, bulging happens when the horizontal metal ties that give the window strength become corroded and come adrift. Unfortunately, this means that the window should be taken out and repaired, and temporary glazing installed while this is being done. Do go to someone who can do the whole job, as it will cost you far more to get separate people to do the temporary glazing and the stained glass repair. Look in Yellow Pages under stained glass suppliers for someone qualified to do the job.

Q My Edwardian front door has stained-glass panels down the sides, but the panel above is missing. Where would I find a replacement?

A Specialist glass shop, Philip Bradbury (tel: 020 7226 2919), should be able to match your panel. Then you'll want to start using glass all over your home. You could even design your own Edwardian-style glass door or how about fitting glass panels in cupboards? Yellow Pages will list other glass suppliers.

 Q **The original front door of our late-Victorian house is slowly crumbling away. It is made from heavy wood with panelling and we want to replace it with something very similar. Where can we buy either a new door in the same style or an original from the same period?**

A I would always try to find an original door first. Heaps of salvage companies throughout the country reclaim such things and don't charge you a fortune. Check your measurements before starting the search. If you can't find the perfect fit, get something slightly bigger and plane it down when you hang it.

 Q **I am looking for an interior door, new or reclaimed, size 201 x 81cm (79¼ x 32in), for my lounge. Most DIY stores stock only standard sizes and I don't know where else to try.**

A Try Premdor Crosby (tel: 01793 708200). They have an enormous range of doors in stock, one of which may be suitable for your needs. If they can't help, don't worry, because they also make to measure. You can choose between six different veneers, inlaid, panelled, with or without glass. For a made-to-measure door, allow six to seven weeks for delivery. If they have a door the size you want in stock, it should be with you within a week.

Q **We have a thirties detached house with metal-frame windows in small panes. I know the trend is to retain authentic features, but the wooden pieces between the metal are starting to rot and the metal gets very dirty and blackened at the bottom with condensation. They are also not double glazed. What should we do? I like the look of white PVC windows but would they fit the character of the house?**

A Plastic windows always look out of place in a period home. I would take out the windows, rub down the metal frames and repaint them. Then have new timber frames made for the surrounds. To reduce condensation, try secondary double glazing.

doors and windows

Q I have recently sanded some window frames and accidentally scratched the glass. Can you suggest a way to remove the small scratches, or do I have to replace the glass?

A If the scratches are not too deep, go to a good jewellery shop and ask for jeweller's rouge and a salvyt cloth (these are used to polish jewellery). The rouge will cost about £1.50 and the cloth £2. Put some rouge on the cloth and rub gently on to the glass. It may reduce the small scratches to an acceptable size. If not, I think your only option is to replace the glass but this needn't be an expensive job. If you can't find the rouge, phone Jewel Tools Supply Co. on 020 7242 8528.

Q I have some plain glass that I would like to decorate, preferably with a stained glass look. Would I be able to wash the glass on completion?

A You don't say what you want to paint. If it is a window already in situ, then I suggest you use coloured film. You can buy a Decra Art Pack that contains ten assorted coloured sheets for £11, including p&p, from North Western Lead (tel: 0161 368 4491). The company also does templates for door designs in diamond, square or rectangular shapes, and self-adhesive lead coil to make up into panels. If it is a flat glass surface, the same firm does glass stains in red, green, blue and yellow at £3.30 for 15ml. When using a stain, make sure to use a good quality artist's brush and keep the surface flat until it is completely dry or the colour will blob. Alternatively, there is something called Glass Etch. You can get a very effective etched glass look on mirrors, windows and glass doors. Simply cover the area you don't want frosted with a stencil of your choice and spray the Etch over the rest of the glass. It dries in minutes. Humbrol sells Glass Etch at £3.99 for 150ml and it is sold in Sainsbury's Homebase stores, Hobby Craft and Great Mills stores.

Q We live in a Victorian house that has lovely sash windows with some unusually shaped panes. The only problem is that they are draughty and we don't know how to go about sealing the gaps. Can you double glaze sash windows, or do we just have to live with this cold?

A There's a company called The Sash Window Workshop (tel: 01344 868668), who specialise in restoring sash windows and can help you out with your draughty windows. They are the only company I know who can double-glaze a sash window without ruining its appearance. They use heat-reflective glass to improve the insulation of the window and to reduce condensation, and they laminate it to help with noise and security. The company say their double-glazing system is about two-thirds of the cost of brand new double-glazed sashes, and they undertake work all over the country. If a sash window is beyond repair, they can replace it altogether.

Q **Some of the sash cords in the windows of my early 18th-century house have perished. If possible, I would like to replace the cords with spiral balance lifts. Can this be done, and do you know anyone who can help me with it?**

A Instead of the cord and weights of traditional sash windows, two spring mechanisms control the opening and closing of spiral balance lift windows. Each spring is covered by a metal tube, visible on either side of the window frame. My first thought is that adapting your windows may prove more troublesome than simply replacing the cords. Also, because your home is so old, conservation may be an issue. I suggest you call English Heritage on 020 7973 3000. They can point you in the direction of your local conservation officer who can advise you. They also do a range of free booklets about renovating old windows. Call 01793 414910 and ask for the booklets called *Framing Opinions*. The Society for the Protection of Ancient Buildings has also produced a free booklet in association with English Heritage specifically about sash windows, and you can get this on 020 7377 1644. Also, St Blaise is an excellent restoration firm in your area that specialises in fine joinery using traditional materials. It can be contacted on 01935 83662.

fittings

Q Our front door suffers from seasonal mood swings! In summer it's too loose and during winter months it jams fast. Is there an obvious solution without replacing it?

A In wet weather doors often swell – rub candle wax on the frame. If this fails, plane it down gently, but wait until the wet weather has stopped to check how far you should pane back as it may improve when dry. A build-up of paint can cause a door to stick – again rub it down. With a loose door you really need to make new fixings entirely as the old ones could be worn.

Q Please help me find a new letter box to fit my front door. Because the existing one is an awkward size, I am having great problems finding a replacement. The fixing centres are 24cm (9½in) apart and the plate depth is 9cm (3½in).

A JD Beardmore (tel: 020 7670 1000) stock a selection of letterplates in brass, black wrought iron, imitation bronze and chrome. They can

---

✳ **Tessa's tip** Locks may not be the most exciting aspect of home improvement but they are a vital bit of equipment. My tip is to get a 'snib' lock fitted to your front door. Before they go to bed many people double-lock the front door and put the key in a safe place well away from it. But what if you need to get out of the house in a hurry because of fire? Seconds spent searching for keys and unlocking the door could make all the difference. That's where a snib lock comes in. The 'snib' is a small button on the body of the lock that enables you to double-lock the door from inside without using a key, and unlock it again the same way. This is an especially good idea if you have children, as they are notorious for hiding keys.

A top-of-the-range snib lock is particularly good if you have glass panelled doors. It costs about £70 from architectural ironmongers, superstores including B&Q and Homebase, and specialist locksmiths. It should carry the BS kitemark, which most insurance companies now insist on, and not be difficult for a do-it-yourself enthusiast to fit. Ask for cylinder rim locks when deciding on which one to go for – there are at least 20 variations available from Yale alone.

obtain other sizes on request, from small to the larger sizes that you require. They do mail-order worldwide, and issue a catalogue so you can see the different styles of door furniture they offer. To give you an idea of price, letterplates start from £25 plus p&p. They also stock a range of postal knockers – these have a door knocker integrated into the letterplate.

Q Can you tell me where I can obtain stainless steel door furniture. We are near to the sea and brass is hopeless to keep in good condition. Also, would it be possible to paint over the brass furniture we have on the front door?

A Specialist architectural ironmongery shops can get hold of stainless steel but they tend to keep only a limited range as it is expensive and normally used only for industrial purposes. However, Nicholls & Clarke on 020 7247 5432 do have a range of stainless steel letterplates, handles, hinges, etc. It is possible to paint stoving lacquer over brass but this must be baked on – not something you could do easily. I would go for the new stainless steel fittings. You know the saying: first impressions start with your front door.

Q I have recently had a large fitted wardrobe and cabinets installed in my bedroom. They need about 30 knobs or handles, and I would like something more interesting than those available I many of the DIY superstores. Do you know where I can obtain these reasonably cheaply? So far I have discovered only Clayton Munroe, which charges £25 each.

A You are right: while Clayton Munroe does have some fabulous handles, they would work out a bit pricey for your project. Anyone looking for a smaller number of handles should give them a call, though, on 01803 762626. Don't reject the superstores – they often do stock interesting items if you are prepared to look. You didn't describe your cupboards, but I'm sure that B&Q's range of WOW handles would have something to suit. To give you an idea of the range, there's a stainless steel dimpled knob at £3.80, which is ideal for revamping cupboards and doors; there's a small 'vee' handle in stainless steel (£4) and in black (£3), which is more minimal in look; and a four-leafed-clover doorknob for £9.90 in silver effect, and £14.50 in cast iron. Alternatively, try Top Knobs on 01626 363388, who have a wide range from which to choose.

Q A couple of years ago I saw some very beautiful but very expensive door handles – one in twisted pewter was particularly wonderful. Recently I have installed some new bedroom doors but they're still handle-less because I can't find any lovely handles. Can you help?

doors and windows

A It shouldn't be too much of a problem getting unusual doorknobs. If you're looking for twisted pewter, such as the one you mention, then try Clayton Munroe (tel: 01803 762626) who do a wide selection of twisted metal handles and other door furniture. There is also a stunning range of handles, cabinet pulls and robe hooks from a company called Glover and Smith (tel: 01256 773012). Their double ammonite handle can be used as a push/pull. It is made of pewter, costs £25.30 and comes in a range of finishes from natural to antique to bronze finish. The 'Sapling' style, also strong enough to be used as a push/pull, costs £14.50.

Q 20 years ago I bought some lovely coloured glass door knobs. The store I bought them from no longer stocks them. Do you know where I might get some more?

A Try Liam Carey in Cornwall. The colour range includes cobalt blue, bright blue, peridot green, amber, teal, amethyst and clear. The door knobs come in three shapes – smooth, ribbed and daisy – and cost from £39 a pair. Single cupboard handles are £12.50 each and come in four shapes. All handles can be frosted for an extra £1.50-£2.50 each. For more information call Merlin Glass on 01579 342399. Allow 28 days for delivery.

Q I have recently had a new kitchen fitted but I'm disappointed with the cupboard handles. I have looked around various DIY shops but can find nothing out of the ordinary. I think some pewter-coloured handles would look good. Can you help?

A Many people try to keep costs down by using basic trimmings, but one of the best tips around is that if you are buying a standard kitchen or ordinary pieces of furniture, changing the handles can give their appearance a real lift. A company called Clayton Munroe sounds as though it might have the answer to your needs. It has a huge range of metal-turned handles, and cupboard pulls in a number of metal finishes. For further details or a free catalogue, call 01803 762 626.

Q Could you possibly help me to find some glass door knobs? I have searched everywhere but so far have found only small drawer knobs rather than full size door knobs.

A A company called Aaronson Noon does the most amazing range of glass knobs for doors and cupboards, as well as coat hooks, finials and tiebacks. There are 47 different shapes and styles, each of which can be made up into any of their range of products. The company also does vases and one-off commissions, such as fountains, tiles and furniture – they have even made a glass four-poster bed! All Aaronson Noon products are handmade, and delivery takes about four weeks. The firm's brochure carries full details of all the colours and shapes on offer. To obtain a copy of the brochure, call 020 7610 3344. You can also find cheaper glass door knobs in the latest Nice Irma's catalogue – they come in blue, green, turquoise or clear glass and cost £16 each. Call 020 8343 9766 for a copy of the latest Nice Irma catalogue.

Q Do you know any companies that sell interesting door furniture? I am looking for something that looks old and is in keeping with my house, which is an old barn conversion. I cannot find anything I like in our local shops and don't know where else to look.

A There's a very interesting company called Dartington Steel Design and they have a range of door furniture that would look great on your barn. It is their Rustix range, which is based on traditional designs from the 17th and 18th centuries. Each piece is hand forged and prices vary from about £11 to £55. They can also supply made-to-order electrical switches and sockets to go with the range. Call them on 01803 868671.

✳ **Tessa's tip** A bit of a gimmick for you – but I thought it could be helpful, too. Mobile phones are personalised now, so why should the humble front-door key be left out? I'm always searching for the right one on my bunch, so one of these snazzy designer keys could be the answer. What's more everyone in the family can have their own distinctive pattern, so no more arguments about who has lost theirs!

The keys are made by Fashion Fun Kee and there are 24 different patterns to choose from, price £4.95 each; call 0800 169 3161 to find your nearest outlet. There are 400 of them around the country so there should be one near you. Simply take your door key along, choose your pattern and have your key cut. The key cutting company, Minit, say they have tested one of the designer keys 50,000 times and found it very durable.

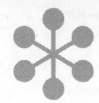

decorative details

Q I have recently redecorated my bathroom and would be grateful for your thoughts on a quick and easy way to modify some 1970s' style cupboard doors without having to take each one off its hinges to be painted. The doors are made of chipboard with a mahogany veneer and covered in polyurethane varnish.

A I recently saw a brilliant idea for just such a problem. A young girl had similar doors in her bedroom and her mother wouldn't let her paint them. So she bought some cheap muslin and dyed it three colours – one for each door. Then it was stretched across the front and tacked at the back of the door. It was so simple and looked fantastic. You should obviously choose colours to go with your new decoration. This cheap, easy and effective idea is also great if you're renting and can't change the decor too radically.

Q Our house is plagued with flies in summer as we live near an orchard and the apples attract them. I can't leave the back door closed all summer. Have you any suggestions?

A Try a company called Breezeway who manufacture a range of American-style insect screens for windows and both internal and external doors. They are made of a grey mesh and are pretty much undetectable once in position. They let the light and air through but keep all insects out. They are like the screen doors you see in American movies and open in the opposite direction to the existing door. They also make roller blinds for doors and windows and sliding screen frames for sliding patio doors. All the products are supplied in kit form. Price depends on size. The instruction leaflet tells you how to measure the space and gives detailed prices for hinged screen doors, roller screens, lift-out screens and hinged window kits. Allow 21 days for delivery. Call them on 01234 781000.

Q I'm trying to find a flyscreen door like the ones they have in America and Australia. How would I hang it and how would the postman get mail through?

A I would abandon the idea of a fixed flyscreen door and try an inventive and practical flystopping screen from CIC Screens. These screens are made of aluminium chains and come in 13 colours. They provide a physical barrier that is heavy enough not to billow around in the wind, while the links shimmer in the light to deter insects and birds. Ready-made screens are available in wonderful stock designs, sized 91 x 198cm (36 x 78in), but any size or pattern can be made to order. Prices start at £100. Call CIC Screens for more details on 020 8560 3337.

Q Please can you help me locate a supplier of beaded curtains? I like my French doors open during the summer but unfortunately my grandchildren, who visit almost every day, become upset at the sight of anything that flies – bee, wasp, fly or gnat. I thought that beaded curtains would be the answer, but I've looked everywhere, without luck.

A Brats (tel: 020 7351 7674 for mail-order service) have fabulous beaded curtains that will keep your grandchildren amused for hours. They even do a 'disco' silver ball version for £48 if you really want to go wild. Or you can go for glass-effect Perspex in purple, green or blue for £29.99, or a rather more skimpy curtain with beaded flowers.

✳ # Tessa's tip
If you want to make your door really stand out, buy it a decent hook. Crummy hooks are all very well when you don't see them, but often they sit on the door unadorned by a coat or hat. The door hook is usually one of the first things you see in a hall when you walk in and a good looking one can make a big difference to your hall. Coexistence is a shop that specializes in furniture and fittings for architects and interior designers fitting out new homes so you would expect them to have pretty state of the art stuff. Most of their range comes from Italy and they do sell amazing door hooks. They are pretty expensive at £45 each but worth a look at their website if you are thinking of splashing out. www.coexistence.co.uk or call them on 020 7354 8817.

Q You recently mentioned a special paint that you can use on glass, but my local department store does not stock it. Can you help?

A Your local store sounds as if it needs a lesson in service. Call the London Graphic Centre (tel: 020 7240 0095) who sell a water-based gloss paint called Decor Glass and a solvent-based one called Glass Art by mail order. Both retail at £3.39 plus p&p. They come in a range of 15 colours as well as white, black and clear. Remember that these paints are suitable only for decorative work and are not intended for covering large areas. Now is a good time to decorate glass bottles or the undersides of glass plates as original Christmas presents.

Q We want to colour a glass panel. Professional glaziers have quoted £70 for a pane measuring 104 x 24cm (41 x 9½in), which we thought was excessive.

A For a panel using a variety of colours, their quote doesn't sound excessive to me. However, if you want to go for a cheaper option you could do it yourself. James Hetley (tel: 020 7790 2333) can supply cold paints that are suitable for glass. They also sell contour paste, which can be used to make an artificial lead line. It costs £3.69 a jar – you would probably need two jars for your panel. A word of warning: I have tried to paint glass and there is a knack to it. For a start, you need a steady hand. For a relatively large surface area like yours, I would advise doing a pattern. That way, any mistakes will be less obvious. If you are really keen, you could go to a class and learn how to do it first. You can use the college's kiln to fire your work and you will have learned a new skill. Contact your local further education department. You could also consider buying a pane of glass that is already coloured. James Hetley has a large selection of etched, antiqued and plain coloured panes.

Q What suggestions do you have for covering a bathroom window without having to resort to curtains?

A I have opted for etched glass in my bathroom. The lower half of the bottom pane is etched, which provides a privacy screen but still allows all the light in. A good quality glass merchant should be able to do the job for you. If you want to try your hand at frosting glass yourself, choose a design that will cover the window sufficiently to offer privacy. Clean the window, then attach a stencil of the design to it with masking tape. Paint the frosting on the window and allow to dry between each application to prevent smudging. Frosting can be bought in DIY stores and paint shops.

Q I have recently moved house and my bathroom window is round; about 60cm (23in) in diameter. It is set in the wall to a depth of 20cm (8in). Any ideas on how to dress it so that we can still see that it's a round window from the inside?

A My inclination would be to leave it completely free of dressing because it sounds like an interesting feature in a bathroom. Find a design you like, photocopy it and take it to a glass merchant specialising in etching. Get him to cut the glass to size, etch the design on and fit it for you! Why not use fish – they always look beautiful etched into glass, or go for a nautical look with a pattern of knotted ropes. Alternatively, etch a small circle in the middle of the window and leave the rest plain – this will give you privacy but allows lots of light in.

❊ **Tessa's tip** The BBC Good Homes show in Birmingham is always packed with the latest DIY ideas. Among these, a company called Armfield Glass is doing amazingly innovative work. It predicts that we'll be using far more glass over the next 20 years, for everything from doors to ceilings, worktops, and even entire homes. People tend to be scared of glass, thinking it will break easily, but the toughened variety is quite suitable for floors. Armfield have even done glass rafters in a conservatory with a glass roof. There are all kinds of decorative effects you can get, too. As well as sandblasting and etching, you can incorporate items within a laminated finish – so, for instance, you could commission a door with a silk panel embedded in it. But if you commission something, remember that once it's made, that's it. You can't slice a bit off a glass door if it doesn't fit! Call Armfield on 01268 793067.

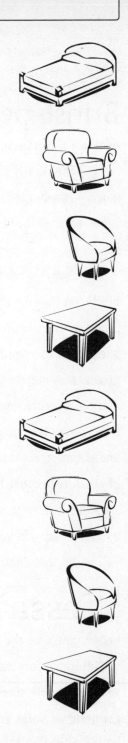

* furniture

British people are funny about furniture. Most of us don't buy much of the stuff. A lot of it has been hanging around the family for a long time, even if we don't like it that much – it belonged to old uncle someone and it has sentimental value. I am all for history but I think if you don't like something, sell it and buy something that you do like.

You always write and ask about restoring old pieces – particularly tables and chairs that have seen better days. With the products that are around now it is so easy to really bring a piece back from the dead. All you need is a bit of time and elbow grease. It is hugely satisfying to get off the horrible old lacquer that years before someone put on a perfectly respectable table and then re-wax it to give it a different look. Over the years I've given lots of tips on restoring cane and rush chairs, which gives me lots of pleasure because I like to see good old chairs used. Then there are sofas. Where to start with sofas? They have been focused on by every shop and you simply have to look and try to decide what you want. Remember they look smaller in the shop than when you get them home – as I know only too well! Think what you want to use it for. And remember, your needs might change before you have the money to buy another sofa.

Children's furniture has also been developed in the last few years as people spend so much on their little darlings. You can get designer sofas and chairs for them – but do they appreciate it? I'm all for children having interesting furniture as long as it can be hidden under, jumped on and sat on to read a book.

 beds

Q I want to jazz up my bedroom and have been looking for a headboard with a difference. So far I've seen only wooden ones and the more traditional material-covered type. Any suggestions?

A I saw a fantastic idea recently at the Country Living Fair in London. A woman called Felicity Irons (tel: 01234 771980) uses rush to create all kinds of things for the home, including double and single bed headboards. She can also work to a specific commission.

Q Can you help me find a headboard for my 12-year-old son's room? He hasn't the space for a bedside table, so I would like a light fitting incorporated into it.

A Department store headboards in wood will cost anything up to £250 and won't have a light fitting. Why not try designing your own and then get fretwork specialists Jali to make it for you? They can make up almost any shape you want. Their headboards are made from MDF and are supplied raw or primed ready to paint. Simply call them on 01227 831710 and state the width and height you want along with a rough description of your design and Jali will quote you a price. As an indication of cost, their standard bedhead is £120 for a single and £185 for a double – both plus VAT.

Q I've always wanted a four-poster bed but they're so expensive. Where can I get one for under £1000? I don't like those iron ones.

A You are right – four-poster beds are horrendously expensive. Obviously you have to pay more for one than a normal bed as you are getting something which has far more work than the standard bed. The iron ones you don't like are the cheapest as it is fairly simple to add poles and drape fabric across them. You can even make one yourself with poles. We did one on *Home Front* for under £100 but it was made of copper tubing. Personally I think if you want a four poster you are after a grand statement and making one of cheap metal doesn't really work. You could try commissioning a carpenter to build you something. At a recent show in Paris I saw a wonderful four poster using thick squared off wood poles. The wood had been blasted to give it a whiteness and it looked gorgeous but wood again is expensive. If you can source some cheap wood and find a good carpenter I would go down that route. Alternatively, seek out second-hand ones in auction sales or advertise for £10 in The Architectural Salvage Index on 01483 203221. Someone might just want to get rid of one! Remember that when people sell four posters the price they quote is for the bed only, you then have to add the cost of the mattress. Avoid shops as you will never get one for £1000.

Q **We have converted our loft into a bedroom, but now we can't get the base of our double bed through the hatch. Our friends think this is wildly funny.**

A I met a woman who lived in a water tower and she had her sofa built in the sitting room at the top as she couldn't get it up the stairs. If that is not practical, you could always opt for a futon or a pine bed, as most come in handy plank lengths that you can assemble when you're up there. I have been to a flexible furniture show where the designers obviously had you in mind! You could have bought a desk, chair, bed clothes rack and bedside table all designed to fit through your loft hatch. Call the Crafts Council on 020 7278 7700 for details.

Q **Can you please send me details of companies who stock wallbeds. I have tried local stockists but with no luck. A television programme recently featured a flat with one installed.**

A I think you saw it on *Home Front*. We were doing up a studio flat with a wallbed and they are now becoming more and more popular. The company you should ring is Wallbeds on 020 7434 2066. It sells single and double beds that are suitable for regular night use. They use interior sprung mattresses and standard bedding and can be folded away, fully made up, into fitted cupboards or alcoves. A 15cm (6in) deep mattress and bed frame costs £425 for a 90cm (3ft) bed, £549 for a 120cm (4ft) and £549 for a double, including VAT and free delivery to anywhere on the mainland. They can also be made to measure.

Q I am looking for bunk beds that can be installed at right angles, rather than in the usual arrangement of one directly above the other. I have seen these for sale in Canada but not in this country. Can you help?

A I wanted something like this for my children's room – but I had no joy either. My suggestion would be to get a local carpenter to make them up for you. Surprisingly, this needn't cost very much more than bought beds (if you could get them!). Alternatively you could try Ikea. They do something called a loft bed, in white metal, which comes with a ladder and costs £199. You could then place another bed at right angles underneath it. Unless you particularly wanted small beds for children, this could prove a good option as it leaves your bedding arrangements flexible for the future.

Q My child is ready to go into a bed but her room is small and a full-size single bed won't fit. I also want to buy some furniture. Any ideas?

A I've been working on a child's bedroom where the smallness of the room was its charm. With imagination you can create a really enticing room. Children's furniture is widely available. The Bofink chair, for example, costs £8, while the Mammut range costs from £8 for a stool to £180 for a wardrobe, all from Ikea. When you are decorating a child's room, think low. Create decorative paintwork at their height so they can see it. Also, try putting up some hooks at child height – you may even get them to hang up their clothes!

Q We have two small children and not much space. Do you have any suggestions for suitable beds? The more fun the better – it might make bedtime more attractive?

A I have two small children too, so I know just what you mean. There are now lots of bunk beds available such as a range from Dico called Tricolore, which is made of tubular steel and costs £279.95. But the children should be over five years old. Contact Dico on 0161 665 1417 for stockists. Ikea's range includes slides and other fun attachments. Alternatively, if you know an imaginative carpenter, why not design your own? Make some rough drawings and get a quote – it might not be much more expensive than a bought one.

beds

103

Q Several years ago we bought a foldaway bed for our daughter's bedroom to allow her to have a larger play area. My niece would now like to buy one for her young son. Could you please let me know if these beds are still made and where to get hold of them if they are?

A Try a company called the London Wall Bed Company on 020 8742 8200. Depending on your DIY skills and your budget, they should have something to suit you. They do a flat pack, steel frame pivoting mechanism bed base which will fold away into a cupboard of your own. It costs from £395 but that is just for the frame – a standard mattress will fit on it or they do one for £177. If you are not so handy, they also do a fold-down bed for £1,075 which has doors attached to the underside of the bed that disappear when the bed is down. There is a horizontal version for a narrow room or a vertical one for a bigger space. All the add-on furniture is also available. Ask for their Leonardo range.

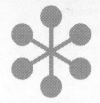

painting and restoring

Q Are all stereo speakers black, or is it possible to buy them in white or cream? My partner has recently moved in with me and wants to mount his speakers on the sitting-room wall. However, I find them visually quite oppressive, even if I enjoy the sound they produce! I could paint the cases white, but the front mesh would still be black. Can you help?

A As your partner has only recently moved in, I wouldn't touch his speakers ... yet! Wait till the relationship is well established, then gently suggest that you'd like to re-cover them. Remove the fronts before you paint the cases, then use an acrylic primer as a key, followed by whatever paint you fancy. If the fronts are fabric, you can simply re-cover them in any material of your choice, provided that it is lightweight and has a wide mesh to allow the sound through. Plastic fronts can be sprayed with car paint. Alternatively, The Cornflake Shop (tel: 020 7631 0472) sells excellent speakers by B&W for £250 a pair in a range of colours, including white.

Q I would like to crackle glaze a melamine wardrobe and two melamine bedside tables to blend in with a more modern decor. Do I need to prepare the rather shiny surface any differently from natural wood, and if so, what do I use as a base coat?

A First you should sand down the melamine to give it a slightly rough surface as a base for the paint. Then apply two coats of an acrylic converter – Paint Magic do one for £7.50 for 500ml plus p&p, available by mail order on 01225 469966, or ask them for a local stockist. To achieve a crackle glaze you need to decide on the two colours you want to see in the finished look, the dominant top coat and the base coat. Then apply a basic matt emulsion as an undercoat. When it is dry, paint on the base coat of crackle glaze – again Paint Magic do one for £10.50 for 500ml, or The Stencil Store do one for £8.99

for 300ml (tel: 01923 285577). Remember in which direction you painted the crackle glaze – either top to bottom or left to right – as the top coat must be applied in the opposite direction, otherwise the crackle glaze won't work. Try using a woodwash paint for the top coat (Paint Magic, £12.50 for 500ml). Finally seal with an acrylic varnish, either eggshell or gloss. Remember, crackle glazing takes practice, so try your hand at something small first rather than starting out with your entire bedroom furniture!

Q My daughter's bedroom contains fitted furniture in honey pine (varnished over). I would like to give it a more up-to-date look buy lightening the wood and giving it an old 'white wash' look. How can I achieve this?

A The first thing you need to do is to remove the old varnish with varnish stripper and some wire wool. I imagine what you mean by an old white wash look is a rough knocked-back paintwork effect. You can achieve this easily using simple matt emulsion. It would be better to use a darker colour for the base coat and 'old white' for the second, as the first coat will eventually appear through the top coat. Paint your first colour over the furniture. When it's dry, use a candle to rub wax over the paintwork and then apply the white matt emulsion.

Q I am 14 years old and I'm interested in interior design. My bedroom is in the attic and has plenty of light through three windows but the walls are painted white, which I think is boring. Also I have drawers with plastic panelling on the front and these look repulsive. Could you give me any ideas for the wooden furniture and the walls?

A For starters, I hope you saw the Junior Decorator competition we held on *Home Front*. Everyone was under 16 and their ideas were fantastic. The three finalists each had a small bedroom with a window and some furniture to decorate, and they did great things. One painted the floor red, with silhouettes on the walls, and customised the furniture with ordinary paint, using aluminium for the tops. Another sprayed theatrical busts gold and made plinths from wood. The winner created a tropical beach scene by dyeing the carpet blue for the sea and yellow for sand, painting a mural on the walls and cutting out palm trees from MDF. Inspired? If not, choose something you love in your room and take a colour scheme from it, or think of a theme you like and start there. I imagine you have limited funds, so keep it simple but bold. Use two contrasting bright colours. Check you have parental approval before you rip the plastic panelling from your drawers. And don't worry about it all going wrong – where better to make a mistake as a budding interior designer than in your own bedroom? That's how you learn. Send me a photo of before and after – I'd love to see what you do!

Q **I have a white melamine bedroom unit that I would like to either paint a different colour or stencil to brighten it up. Do I need to use a sealer before painting it? And what type of paint should I use?**

A International do a melamine primer that is available through B&Q stores. It's ideal for painting bedroom units, kitchen cupboards and wardrobes. You can also use it on other laminated surfaces and even glass. Don't use it on kitchen surfaces or small stencil areas, though, as it is likely to chip off: it's designed to cover large areas. To prepare your surface, it must first be clean and dry. Sand it down lightly to give a grip for the paint, then apply one or two coats of the primer. Once it is dry, you can paint with emulsion, gloss or eggshell. Use a synthetic brush, as natural bristles absorb water from the paint and leave heavier brushmarks.

Q **I have found scratch marks on some furniture and wonder if there are any touch-up pens available for wood. If so, do they come in different colours for different woods?**

A Yes, there are. Try Liberon Waxes (tel: 01797 367555 for stockists), they sell them direct at £3.99 each. There is also a three-part touch-up pen that has three different colours – pine, mahogany or oak – for £4.29. They are all water resistant.

Q **On a recent television programme I saw a product called Easy French Polish being used on a coffee table that had been stripped of its painted surface. I have tried to obtain this product from various DIY stores, but without success. Could you help, please?**

A I think the product you mean is Rapid French Polish, which you can get in some B&Q stores in the north of England. Alternatively, you can buy it by mail order from Foxall and James (tel: 020 7405 0152), price £6.83 plus p&p for 500ml. Foxall and James sells a range of other products that may be of interest. If your French polished table is simply in need of a boost, try the firm's French Polish Reviver, price £5.73 plus p&p for 500ml. If you have decided to strip back your table, you will need to apply a wood sealer base-coat before you use the polish. This costs £4.47 plus p&p for 500ml. Allow the base coat sealer

painting & restoring

107

to dry for at least two hours before applying the polish. Use a rag – something like an old pillowcase is perfect – to apply polish, and leave it to dry for 12 hours before recoating.

Q I have a small oval table that is highly polished. Someone put something on it leaving a circular milky stain. How can I remove it?

A For water-marks on highly polished surfaces, try Hard Finish Reviver made by Liberon. This revives French polishes and varnished surfaces by removing a very thin layer of the finish. It should work well for most polished wood surfaces, though a mirror finish may be left slightly dulled. For scratched wood, Liberon do a wax filling stick that looks a bit like a Yorkie bar! It comes in 24 different colours to match almost any wood, and you simply rub into the scratch, then cover with Hard Finish Reviver. Hard Finish Reviver costs £3.96 plus VAT, and the filling sticks are £2.09 plus VAT, both available by mail order on 020 7405 0152.

Q We have a very old Lloyd Loom children's chair in need of repair and restoration. The weave is broken and at some time the whole chair was repainted. Are there any reputable restorers, please?

A I would suggest you throw it out – radical, but it sounds to me as though it is beyond repair. The weave of the old chairs is different from the weave used now, so a repair wouldn't be possible. If it were just the paintwork that needed attention, you could do it yourself: simply scrub the chair with a stiff brush and sugar soap, then take it outside and hose it with a strong jet of water to remove as much old paint as possible. When you repaint, use a car spray paint, but remember to wear a face mask and spray outside – when it isn't windy.

Q I'm looking to buy a small church pew to fit into my bay window. Some years ago one of the 'house' programmes on television featured a company that specialised in this type of reclamation. Do you have an address for this or any other company that could help?

A The best way to track down a reclamation yard is through The Salvo Pack (£5.75). This has a list of dealers in your county, plus details of architectural auctions. Also subscribe to *Salvo News* magazine (£50 for 25 issues). For details call 01890 820333.

Q I have tried in vain to find decorative mouldings to use on furniture. Most DIY outlets have straight lengths of moulding but I'm looking for curves, bows, etc. Is there anyone who sells these by mail order?

A Shortwood Carvings do a huge selection of fancy plastic carvings, from cherubs to bows, friezes to panel designs, and you can attach these to your furniture or fireplace with panel pins or PVA glue. Lengths can be joined using acetone and bent around corners by gently warming the plastic. Paint them with emulsion or spray paint for a good finish.

Q Our house has been on the market for two and a half years, and we have had six different valuations, all around £180,000. It is in a desirable location, has four bedrooms, 46m (150ft) garden, conservatory, gas central heating – everything we thought people would like. But it just won't sell. What are we doing wrong?

A One of the classic tips is to make your house seem as spacious as you can, so if you have a lot of clutter around, remove it. It may also be worth giving the rooms a quick lick of neutral white, because potential buyers may find it hard to visualise their own style on top of someone else's. Make sure the front door is painted and that the entrance is clear and fresh. The old chestnut about enticing smells such as fresh coffee is worth remembering, too. Talk frankly to your estate agent about why they think it isn't selling: they might come clean and tell you something you aren't aware of. Ultimately, though, you can always sell a house if the price is right, so you may have to accept that your valuations were a little over-optimistic.

❋ **Tessa's tip** Everyone knows that moving house is one of the major stresses of life, so you need to think it through like a military operation. It's worth paying your carriers to pack and unpack for you, unless you have very few possessions. Good movers are used to delicate items and know how to pack well – you are far more likely to break things if you do it yourself. Check heights and widths of doors in advance to make sure things will go in, and give your movers a rough plan of where things are to go – it will save you time and money on the day. Get a contact number for the previous owners because there may be things you need to ask. Leave your old home clean and tidy – there is nothing more depressing than arriving at a new place and finding a terrible mess. And don't pack your kettle. Take it with you for that all-important first cup of tea!

Q I would like instructions on how to make a room screen. I was very taken with one I saw in a recent magazine feature about a couple who live in a converted chapel. What had it been covered in and how could I make something like that?

A Screens are easier to make than they look and can transform a room, not to mention hide a lot of clutter. The couple featured in this magazine had simply found an old screen and decorated it with strips of wallpaper patterned with faux book shelves to create a trompe l'oeil effect. To make a screen from scratch, buy 12mm (½in) plywood and mark a design – remember the top can be quite a decorative shape. Cut it out with a jigsaw. Paint, wallpaper, stencil or decoupage whatever you want on to it. Use acrylic varnish to seal your design. Then screw on some hinges. If you just feel like doing the decorating, you could ask the timber yard to cut the shape out for you. Then get to work.

✱ Tessa's tip One thing I learned when shopping for furniture for my house in London is that it is so much cheaper to shop out of London. You can often find real bargains in strange out of the way places where maybe the trend for sixties furniture hasn't caught on yet! But I never knew how easy it was to get these things back home. Someone asked me the other day about transporting bathroom fittings across the country. Try ringing some courier firms from the Yellow Pages. I found one called Crewkerne Carriers on 01935 477003 who were local to where I bought a table and they transported it to London for around £50. The same thing in London would have cost three times as much.

Companies like this will also do house removals all over the country. They don't have to be local to where you live. If your pick up coincides with another drop off, you could get bargains that you may not get locally. A table and four chairs going from Manchester to Dorset would cost you around £85 plus VAT. You may have to wait a week or so for delivery to get these sort of prices but couriers also do special drops for a higher fee.

✳ soft furnishings

I'm always amazed at how expensive fabric is. Making new curtains can be more costly than wallpapering a whole room, so you need to think carefully about what you buy and where you get it from. There are all kinds of unusual suppliers of fabric – think theatre, art shops and display manufacturers and you find interesting cloth to suit your budget. Try to see if you can find local areas where there are Indian, African or Middle Eastern fabrics being sold as you will get great value products.

Blankets, throws and cushions have become thrust into the limelight with our homes becoming so important to us. Everyone can afford to buy a cushion to transform a space. It's much cheaper than changing the curtains. So cushions are being sold by everyone and have everything on them – from feathers, to glass to buttons – and are made of all sorts of fabric. Old weaving firms are redesigning their product and selling exclusive contemporary blankets for those in the know. Who would have thought that the old blanket would be high fashion?

Blinds have also come into their own. Traditional blind firms are seizing the moment and reinterpreting their ranges for modern loft living. It is no longer the day of the Venetian blind for every other style of blind is now available.

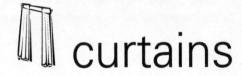 curtains

Q I'm looking for a supplier of heavy-duty, best-quality silk damask cloth for curtaining and upholstery. I know it's very expensive, but my present bedroom curtains and covers need replacing as the silk is rotting in the sunlight.

A Try Silk Shades Interiors, mail-order silk specialists whose prices are extremely competitive. The company sells a heavy-duty damask Dupion silk at £22.50 per metre for 112cm (46in) width in ivory, cream, old gold, antique gold, ruby and jade. It also does plain Dupion silk in a host of colours for £10.95 per metre for 120cm (48in) width, as well as tartan silks, striped Dupions, satin brocade, embroidered Dupion silks and York taffeta silk. Call them on 0115 988 1846 and send £5 for a large Dupion swatch-pack of colours. Silk Shades will also send out up to five swatches if you are looking for silk to match your carpet, wallpaper or upholstery. Just send in a relevant sample. Their special offer silk sale list is also available for £1.50. Postage and packing for small orders is £4.50 and £6.50 for larger ones.

❋ Tessa's tip

Look out for Allied Carpets' new soft furnishings range, launched soon, which features lots of lovely delicate fabrics. Curtains have a layered look, combining ready-made panels of hand-woven silk underneath with organza panels on top. Panels measure 110 x 220cm (43 x 86in), prices are £44.99 for silk and £59.99 for organza. There is also a very pretty silk tassel panel, and one in embroidered shell silk, plus matching throws and cushions.

Aside from the ready-made section, Allied have a new custom-made gallery where you can choose from hundreds of new fabrics and have curtains made up for you. Call 0800 192192 for local branch details.

Q My everyday-use crockery is Portmeirion, in the Botanic Garden design, and as most of the shelves in my kitchen are open, I thought I would like to have matching curtains. I have been advised that they have discontinued the fabric. Do you know of any place that would be likely to have stock still available?

A I suggest you phone the factory that made the fabric. They have a factory shop where all the unsold fabric returns to. I have checked and they do not have any at the moment but if you give them your name and phone number they will call you when it arrives. They were hopeful that you would get some. You can call the shop on 01782 744721.

Q I am completely hopeless with a needle and cotton. Is there any way of making curtains without having to sew?

A You can easily make curtains and blinds without sewing. Fold the hems on all rough edges of fabric. Put Wundaweb (from department stores and haberdashers) along the inside edge of the fold. Press with a hot iron through a damp cloth to seal the hem. To hang the curtains or blinds, use an eyelet puncher to make holes in the fabric, then thread string or wire through them. Or buy curtain clips that slide over the curtain rod and clip on the top of your fabric. For instant effect, drape material over a curtain pole and use a decorative hook to hold the curtain to one side.

Q Do you know a company that will dye cotton velvet curtains? I have tried high-street dry cleaners but none can help. My curtains are about ten years old but still in good condition, except for fading at the edges. As they are quite large, it would be very expensive to replace them at today's prices.

A It is extremely difficult to find local cleaners who will take on a job like this but Harry Berger Cleaners and Dyers (tel: 0161 485 7733) have been operating for 40 years and get mail-order packages from all over the UK. Send an sae enclosing £2 for the mail-order brochure, which includes a colour chart and explains how to measure

✳ Tessa's tip

Before you take down unwanted curtains, take a photo of them. A picture on a noticeboard in a shop window often brings results. And don't forget that if you want to sell old good quality curtains, there's a company called The Curtain Exchange.

curtains

soft furnishings

your curtains and pack them for posting. Up to 23kg (50lb) in weight will cost about £12.50 to send and the dyeing will cost around £15 per square metre, plus return postage. Cotton velvet is perfect for dyeing – it takes colour well – and dyeing could save up to half of the cost of new curtains. They can also be dyed lighter because the colour is stripped out of the velvet in the dyeing process, then added again.

Q Is there a curtain-lining fabric that reflects sunlight? I want something that will protect the curtain from fading, and help keep the room cool.

A Try blackout lining from John Lewis. This is available in 137cm (54in) widths, in white or cream, and has been chemically treated to reflect heat and light. It's especially good for children's bedrooms in the summer – it really does keep them in bed for longer! Call John Lewis on 020 7629 7711 for mail order.

Q My house has extremely large picture windows, most of which face south or west. As a result, the curtains fade very quickly. I need to replace some of them and I wondered if you could advise me which type of fabric would be most fade resistant.

A All fabrics will fade if exposed to sun, but the colour that is known to fade fastest is blue, so avoid blue if you can. However, there are linings that can be used to stop your curtains fading.

Q On each side of my front door I have small windows, both measuring 53cm (21in) wide and 114cm (45in) tall. I need them to let light into the hall but I also need net curtains on them for privacy. Every time the front door is opened the curtains flap in the breeze and get caught in the door as it closes. Is it possible to buy nets that have a rod top and bottom to keep them in place?

A The best thing I have found for such a problem is something called Jago net rods. They come in brass or waxed steel and are either self-supporting – across a window frame – or can be screwed into the frame. John Lewis stores have a wide selection. They start at around £20 for a small one, and for your job you obviously need one top and bottom to hold the nets steady. You simply hem the net top and bottom and slip the rod through it.

curtains

115

Q Can you please tell us where we can get some brass eyelets about 5cm (2in) or larger in diameter, plus the tool for inserting them into canvas. My daughter wants to make some curtains to cover the alcoves in her bedroom but wants to thread poles through the eyelets instead of wires.

A You need to try a yachting supplier for something like this, as department stores only usually stock eyelets up to 11mm (½in). I have found some at a shop called Harry Beals (tel: 020 7836 9034) of 4.5cm (1¾in) external diameter if that is wide enough for you. You will need to buy a punch and die at £41.37 and a cutter for £17.57. The brass rings cost £19.27 for 100. These are beginning to sound like an expensive set of curtains! You can get eyelet kits and the eyelet tool, hemming tape and twenty 11mm (½in) rings for £8.25 at good department stores, so you might want to reconsider wire rather than a pole! However, don't ignore yachting suppliers – they do often have extremely interesting attachments, coloured ropes and fixtures that make highly unusual decorative features.

blinds

Q My daughter and her boyfriend have recently bought a house and sunk most of their money into it. In the kitchen they have installed a roller blind to match the wall frieze. But when the blind is down the room appears even brighter as the blind has a white background and reflects the light. Is there a way they can darken the effect without having to buy a new blind?

A The best thing to do is to get the blind laminated with a dim-out or black-out backing. Most materials, apart from voiles, can be laminated. Tidmarsh & Sons (tel: 01707 886226 for mail order) can laminate most fabrics. They could, for example, laminate a Thomas the Tank Engine duvet cover and make it into a black-out blind for a nursery.

Q I have some roller blinds made from the same sort of material as shower curtains. Is it possible to dry-clean them?

A First, it is not possible to remove a roller blind from its casing. It is stuck in with heavy glue, so all you can do is to clean it in situ. If it is dusty, just use the upholstery attachment of your vacuum cleaner, but if it is marked and grubby, use a clean, damp cloth and gently wipe off what you can. Don't scrub at it, as most roller blinds have a textured and stiffened finish that you will destroy if you rub too hard.

Alternatively, take the blind apart and buy new fabric, but that is the most expensive part. A local art shop might be able to recommend a suitable acrylic craft spray. It's difficult to suggest something without knowing what the fabric is like, but if you're willing to risk it, there's a product called Buntlack Spray that is made in about 30 colours and costs £11 a can. It's used on theatre backdrops and might well prove suitable. Call The Artshop on 020 7734 5781 for details.

Q Can you please tell me how to clean Venetian blinds? I can remove and wash the smaller ones but I daren't remove the kitchen blinds, which are 243 x 180cm (8 x 6ft) long. I would get into a most awful tangle. Also, being in a kitchen, they get a sticky dust film that needs a good rub. I feel like throwing them out.

A With Venetian blinds, first use a feather duster. If you regularly do this, you shouldn't get too much build-up on them, but if they are sticky, all you can do is use a cloth with detergent. As Venetian blinds are aluminium, the detergent will not hurt them, but again, do not scrub. Other types, such as Roman and reefed blinds, can safely be removed and dry cleaned.

Q The bay window in our bedroom overlooks the street: can you suggest something to give us a little more privacy?

A Well, where can I start? After rejecting curtains, which I assume you have, you could consider some blinds such as those made by Alison White, which have a clean, contemporary look. While giving you privacy, they also have small square, round or L-shaped cut-outs in them, that allow more light through. They are made of Swedish cotton and come in 12 colours. They are ideal if you keep the blinds drawn during the day. This cut-out style also looks great from the street.

Q I want to make a Roman blind from voile to give maximum light but also privacy. I've looked in DIY shops for a kit but to no avail. Do you have any idea where I could find one?

A John Lewis offers two sizes of Roman blind kit, and your nearest store is probably the one at Cheadle in Cheshire. You can telephone them on 0161 491 4914 to order a kit. There's a free delivery if you are within 30 miles, and a few pounds' charge for p&p if you're further out. The two sizes of kit are 120cm (4ft) (£25) and 180cm (6ft) (£33). The kits can be cut to size with a small hacksaw and come with everything you need except the fabric.

Q My daughter, who has moved into a small house in a renovated Victorian school, has a beautiful arched bedroom window with a ledge beneath it that's about 60cm (2ft) in depth. Do you have any ideas for curtains, blinds or shutters that would suit an arched shape in a modern setting?

A Tidmarsh (tel: 01707 886226) do a range of shaped blinds for openings such as arches or triangular roof panels. Certain shapes will require stiffening rods to hold the fabric in position. The firm won't be able to visit your daughter for a single window, but if you send them the drawing you sent me, along with the window measurements, they will advise you about what is possible.

Q I want to put up blinds in my sitting room. I have seen rather ordinary ones, but do you know of anything more unusual?

A A great new catalogue from Eclectics (tel: 01843 852888) should have something you will like. All the blinds in it work well in a contemporary setting. The blinds come in 12 colours, and there are ten different shades of Perspex bars, which sit at the bottom, to suit your room. The maximum width in this range is 200cm (78in). If you want wider blinds, Eclectics offer Kyoto sliding panels that go up to 465cm (15ft) wide and come in five different materials. Each panel is 65cm (25in) wide. All blinds are supplied with brackets for easy fixing. The catalogue explains how to measure your windows, but be sure to get it right, as every blind is made to measure.

Q Have you any suggestions for covering the lower half of an exposed window? I have seen some really smart pull-up blinds that would do the job, but I am renting my flat and don't want to spend too much money on it. Is there anything with a contemporary look that I could use to solve this problem?

A Etching the lower half of the window is very effective but, as you are renting, you probably won't want to do this. Instead, why not try something incredibly easy like fitting a push-fit rod and curtain half way down your window. You simply extend the rod to fit and then twist it to lock it into place. The rod is easy to remove when you move. Use whatever fabric you like to create a contemporary look.

Q My Victorian terraced house has a sitting room that is right on the street. I feel very exposed in the room unless the curtains are drawn, and so I hardly ever use it except at night. Have you any suggestions about how I can make the room more private during the day?

A I must say that arrangement sounds pretty gloomy and hardly to be recommended. Everyone needs as much natural light as they can get, especially in the winter months. I suggest trying something such as the pull-up blinds, which are fitted to the base of the window and operated by a pulley system fitted either to the side or to the centre of the blind and are simply pulled up the height you require. So if you want some privacy during the day, you can raise the blind and it will still allow light to come in from the top section of the window. Also, if you have a feature such as coloured glass panels in the upper section of your

blinds

119

windows, these blinds allow it to be seen. Tidmarsh & Son make such blinds and can be contacted on 01707 886226. The company offers a free measuring service for customers inside the M25 but if you live further away, they will send you a brochure. Then take measurements of the window and the company will quote you an approximate price. The blinds can be made up in any fabric you choose, as long as it is suitable for the lamination process. Remember that the thicker the fabric you choose, the larger the roll of blind at the base of the window.

Q **I am changing the colour scheme in my living room, and there are some vertical blinds in a soft grey that I'd like to spray-paint gold. Does that sound possible?**

A If your blinds are the plastic Venetian type, they will be very difficult to repaint – I don't know of any gold paint that would be suitable. But if they are wooden blinds, Plasti-Kote (tel: 01223 836400) does a gold paint that would work, providing you lightly sand and prime the wood first.

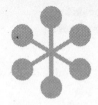

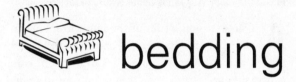

bedding

Q Can you help me find a supplier of 'flock', which is a modern equivalent of the cotton filling used for pillows. I want to make up a firm, non-collapsible pillow.

A I suggest Dainty Supplies (tel: 0191 416 7886), which supplies all sorts of craft and haberdashery materials. Wadding costs about £1.15 per metre for 50g (2oz) weight, and £2.25 per metre for 175g (6oz) weight. Or try Jersey Vogue Fabrics on 020 8952 7751, which can send you a sample by post.

Q I would like to renew some of the plastic fasteners on my duvet cover, but I would rather avoid having to sew them on. Is there a tool to carry out the job?

A As far as I know there isn't a tool that helps with this job, but if you don't fancy sewing, why not use iron-on Velcro? You buy this by the metre from the haberdashery section of department stores.

Q I have a bag of duck feathers from worn-out pillow cases that I would like to re-use. Do I need to clean the feathers and, if so, how?

A They may not need cleaning at all. Feathers from damp old pillow cases often need nothing more than a good airing. If you do decide to clean them, make sure the bag they are in is securely sewn so that the feathers will not come out. Handwash them in hot, soapy water and rinse well. You can spin the bag in the washing machine to take the excess water out. Then dry it on a washing line on a hot, sunny day, shaking it occasionally.

Q I'm looking for some stylish, contemporary blankets for my new double bed. I have seen lots of brightly coloured ones but I'm after something more subtle to suit the room. Any ideas about where to look?

A I suggest you write for the latest brochure from a mill in Wales called Melin Tregwynt. It has a beautiful new range of blankets, throws and cot blankets in masses of different colours. The mill has a concession at Selfridges so if you are ever in London you can see the range, or a mail-order catalogue is available. I love the large circle-felted blankets that come in grey, bean brown and ecru, and are 100 per cent pure wool. A double blanket, 210 x 240cm (7 x 8ft), costs £235; a single, 170 x 240cm (5½ x 8ft), is £188. Matching cushion squares and floor cushions are available, too. Melin Tregwynt also produces a beautiful, simple soft Aran wool woven bedspread, 160 x 240cm (5 x 8ft), that costs £150. The mill's new range has all kinds of muted colours and surface textures from light lambswool and angora blends to heavy felted blankets, any of which would look great on your new bed.

Q Can you tell me where I can find a combination duvet? The type I'm looking for has two layers, a thin one and a thick one, that you can fasten together or use separately, according to the season.

A John Lewis does two types of combination duvet: a polyester one from Snuggledown at £44 for a double, £55 for a king-size; and a goosedown from Natural Feeling, at £119 and £155. Both have two layers, of 4.5 and 9 togs, and used separately or together they certainly give you flexibility. The only disadvantage is that when you combine them they tend to get crumpled up inside the cover.

The prices above are summer sale discounts, and that is definitely the time to buy bedding – you can get some real bargains on warm winter duvets when it is sweltering outside. Call John Lewis on 020 7629 7711 for your local store, and they can arrange delivery.

Q Can you help me find some of the fake fur used to make cosy throws and bed covers? No local shops stock it and I would like to have a go at making a luxury throw.

A I don't know what your local market stalls are like, but I have often seen fake fur on ours. If you are having trouble getting hold of it, call some of the larger department stores: they will definitely have stocks. I have called John Lewis in London for you and they have some luxury brown fake fur at £65 a metre. Their other range is more reasonable at £29.50 a metre. They can send it out to you, £3 p&tp. Call them on 020 7629 7711.

soft furnishings

Q I have a real eiderdown that's not used now. If possible I would like to make it into a duvet. Is there a firm that would do this for me?

A There's a firm called PA Tex Ltd (tel: 01386 442794) who can help you. They convert eiderdowns into duvets and also re-cover old eiderdowns. The best way to start is to call them for a price list and sample fabrics. A rough guide for converting an eiderdown to a duvet is £30 for a single and £35 for a double. Re-covering an eiderdown costs about £100 for a single and £120 for a double, plus the cost of your fabric. If you are supplying your own fabric make sure it's not too heavy. If they need to top-up your eiderdown, the cost depends upon what the filling is – down feathers are expensive, about £3 per 25g (1oz). Please note that they only offer this service for down and feather eiderdowns. It shouldn't cost much more than £8 to send the eiderdown by parcel post.

Q I'm looking for some pretty bedlinen for my teenage daughter. She is very keen on checks but I can't find anything suitable locally. Do you know of any manufacturers who sell bedlinen like this?

A Mail-order company Peacock Blue does a sweet range of gingham bedlinen that's really fresh and pretty. I particularly like their Venice blue colourway but they also have rose pink, sage green and freesia yellow, so there's plenty of choice. The range includes duvet covers in single, double, king and superking sizes, at £39, £55, £65 and £75 respectively. Matching fitted sheets are £22, £28, £28.50, £32 and £38.50. Standard pillowcases cost £10.50 each, square ones are £13, and baby ones are £8.

Mail order is a convenient way to buy heavy bedlinen, so it's worth having a look at the rest of the Peacock Blue range, including feather and man-made duvets, mattress covers, towels, robes, bath mats, bedspreads and traditional merino wool blankets with a satin edge. There is also a free fabric swatch service so you can check the colour match with your decor. Call Peacock Blue on 020 7384 3400 for a catalogue.

Q I have recently decorated my 10-year-old son's bedroom on an army theme, with sponged walls and camouflage netting across the ceiling. It looks fantastic and he loves it. To finish off the room, I want to make him a duvet cover from camouflage material. I've looked everywhere for some but with no luck. Do you know where I can get it from?

A What a great mum you sound! There's a wonderful shop in the middle of Soho, London, called Borovick which sells just about every type of fabric you could think of. They do two colours of camouflage – blue or green – it's 150cm (60in) wide and costs £10.25 a metre. Phone them on 020 7437 2180 and they will quote you a p&tp cost.

Q We have a rather nice double duvet that has started to leak feathers. We have tried to find a re-covering service, but had no success. Do you know of any company that can help?

A Phone the Eiderdown Studio on 01395 271147. It re-covers duvets and eiderdowns: single duvets cost £37.30; doubles are £46.75; kingsize are £54.45; all plus £5 p&tp. You can have them covered in ecru or white 100 per cent cotton and the feathers are put into channels. A brand new eiderdown using your own fabric costs £82.30 for a single, and re-covering an old eiderdown costs £73 for a single, again using your own fabric, plus p&tp. The company also re-covers pillows.

Q I have some perfectly good merino wool blankets but the satin edging is starting to look tatty. What do you suggest?

A Phone Early's of Witney on 01993 703131. They sell replacement taffeta or silk edging for blankets. The narrow width is 30p a metre and the wider one 60p a metre plus p&tp.

Q I have bought a 120cm (4ft)-wide bed but cannot find the bedding to fit it, even in a trawl of the major department stores. Please help.

A Call Keys on 01255 432518 for their catalogue of special-size bedlinen. They even cater for round beds. Materials are poly/cotton, 50 per cent percale/cotton mix and 100 per cent cotton. The mixes come in a wide range of colours and prints but the 100 per cent cotton is available only in white or natural. Keys can provide fitted and flat sheets, pillowcases, valances, duvet covers, fitted mattress covers, extra-long and extra-wide quilts and bedspreads. Call them for a quote and colour swatches.

Q I would really like to tie-dye some bed linen but don't know where to start. Can you help?

A First, you need to tie-dye by hand and not in a washing machine. Dylon (tel: 020 8663 4296) does two types of dye that are suitable for bed linen. The first is called Dylon Hand – available in 21 colours – which comes in a box with fixative, will dye 225g (8oz) of dry fabric and costs £2.75. The second is a cold-water dye for £1.55, plus 49p for the cold-water fixative. Available in 26 colours, this type of dye will also colour 225g (8oz) of dry fabric. Tie-dying is simple. Just block off the areas that you don't want the colour to reach with rubber bands or string. If you want to use more than one colour then start with the lightest colour first, rinse thoroughly, then apply the darker shades.

bedding

125

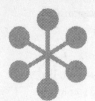

decorative details

Q My son changed the colour schemes in his lounge, thinking he could leave the suite as it was. He now realises that this won't work and, having checked out the cost of having professional covers made, I came up with the option of having the existing covers dyed. I do not feel like attempting it myself because of the size of the covers.

A If the covers weigh more than 1.5kg (4lb) (dry weight), you are right not to attempt them yourself as the dye would not take evenly in the washing machine. But for those people with smaller covers, Dylon machine wash works well. You must use the correct amount of dye for the weight and make sure that each load is exactly the same weight or again you will get patchy results. Also remember: if your covers are faded or worn, these areas may well show up as different shades. If you want to get the covers dyed professionally, try a company called Chalfont Cleaners.

✳ Tessa's tip

Bute is a company on the Isle of Bute in Scotland that has a fabulous range of woven upholstery fabrics suitable for everything from industrial spaces to the domestic market. Bute specialises in tough-performance fabrics and its range of colours and designs suits an enormous range of settings. With its sophisticated looms it can also custom-weave fabric to your own design. You can buy their fabrics direct from the company on Freefone 0800 212064.

Q I have a 1930s suite that belonged to my parents and I want to make it more comfortable and up to date by replacing the throw cushions that go with it. Where can I buy new cushions? I intend to make the covers myself.

A Why not make the cushions too? Feather filled cushions are more comfortable than polyester ones and are not that difficult to make. But you do have to plump them up after sitting on them. Get soft, small feathers. John Lewis in London (tel: 020 7629 7711) sells curled chicken feathers at £3.50 per kg (2lb 4oz). Or you can use the feathers from old pillows: just machine wash and tumble dry the pillow – the feathers fluff up well. You'll need to double seam the cushion and rub soap along the seams to stop the feathers escaping. If you don't want to do them yourself, give your measurements to any good department store and they will make them up for you.

Q I am looking for some exciting new cushions. I have just been visiting a friend who had a beautiful range of accessories in her sitting room, and I want to brighten up my sofa. Any suggestions where I can obtain these locally?

A I don't know what the shops are like near you, but why don't you try mail order? Nice Irma's have a fantastic range of new cushion covers in their spring catalogue, and I'm sure you would love the colours. Call Nice Irma's for a catalogue on 020 8343 7610. Postage and packing for cushions is free for orders of £35 or over; under that it's a fixed rate of £3.95 whatever the order. They also do a range of curtains, poles, photo frames, doorknobs, lampshades and storage items, all in fresh, bright colours.

✳ **Tessa's tip** There are so many new fabrics about in all kinds of amazing textures that it's an exciting time to start using them in your home. I've just recovered my sofa in bright pink and what a different it makes to the room. Whatever your budget, you can do something – even a cushion makes its own statement in the right fabric. The latest range of sculpted, structured materials from Monkwell are just great. There are lots of sheer fabrics in fab colours, such as platinum, steel, aluminium, bronze, copper, amethyst, malachite and quartz, which are suitable for upholstery, accessories and curtains. Call 01202 752944 for stockists.

Q Could you please let me know where I can buy some jazzy buttons to add the finishing touch to linen cushion covers? I would like something to liven them up. The only place I know that sells a decent range of buttons is John Lewis but they had nothing suitable. Please help!

A Call Celestial Buttons in north London on 020 7226 4766. They do a fantastic selection of buttons suitable for clothing, and for interior design purposes such as trimmings for curtains, cushions and other decorative uses. Simply send them a cutting of the fabric or yarn and some idea of what you would like. They will send you a selection of sample buttons by return of post. They will include a size card, too, as they say many of their clients are unsure how big a button should be on a cushion or a garment. They are quite used to running this service and are on first-name terms with many of their customers.

Q I have inherited some very beautiful linen tableware, which I have no use for. Do you know of a firm that might be interested in taking it off my hands?

A Try an antique shop that specialises in linen. A very good one is Lunn Antiques who do beautiful antique linen and lace (tel: 020 7736 4638). Call them and describe exactly what you have and they will be able to tell you whether it is the sort of thing they are looking for and quote a price. They will refund postage when you send it to them if they are buying. Alternatively, there may be a local antique shop that would be interested. Call a few and get some idea of prices. Don't sell to the first one – you may have something valuable.

✳ # Tessa's tip

One of my favourite fabric companies has always been Ian Mankin. It offers a great range of utility fabrics such as calicos, butchers' stripes and tickings, gingham, cotton net and Indian ribbed cottons in stripes, checks and plains, all of which are suitable for upholstery and curtaining. Their new translucent cotton net is particularly delightful, and costs only £3.50 per metre. My favourite is the Madras Check range, which comes in indigo, sky blue, pistachio, yellow, pink, peony, navy and black. It measures 137cm (54in) wide and costs £9 per metre. To get a catalogue, send £3-worth of postage stamps to 109 Regents Park Road, London NW1 8UR, or phone 020 7722 0997.

---

soft furnishings

Q Can you help? I am looking for fringes with bobbles for standard-lamp shades. I want long ones – 10cm (4in) or longer. I have tried department stores and specialist shops but they sell only short fringes. Any ideas?

A Decorative Textiles of Cheltenham (tel: 01242 574546), is a small, long-established family business that sells both silk and beaded fringes suitable for your lampshades. It also stocks replicas of old fringes and antiques. If you can't visit in person (which I recommend), send a sample of what you are trying to match and they will send back to you as close a match as they can find. It is one of those shops that you wished existed everywhere because of the staff's helpfulness. It is open from 10am to 5pm, every day except Sunday.

Q I would very much like to find some pretty bedroom accessories made from fabric. Do you have any ideas?

A Hot off the press is a 16-page catalogue from DWCD interior accessories, a company that has made its name selling all kinds of beautiful scented lavender and rosebud bags. These are perfect bedroom accessories and make great gifts, with prices starting at about £7.50. The bags are made in pretty fabrics like organzas, Irish linens and Liberty florals. The new range of hanging items includes a fabulous handbag-shaped feather-trimmed lavender bag in aqua or pistachio to scent your wardrobe. It has to be the ultimate in luxury for £15. There are also lavender bolsters for the bed, and hanging lavender hearts. Aside from the lavender, there are 75cm (30in) square floor cushions in a gorgeous French fabric striped in shades of brown and green that are shot through with burnt orange and lime (£75) and 60cm (24in) square sofa cushions in the same fabric for £35. Call 020 8964 2002.

129

❋ **Tessa's tip** I get a lot of letters asking how to repair items brought back from holidays – everything from bits of sculpture to ornamental pots. My tip this week is to think about bringing back textiles. If you are travelling to somewhere unusual, it is well worth looking out for interesting examples of embroidery, weaving or dyed cloth. Scour local markets and shops for such things: they make good – and unbreakable – souvenirs. If your holidays are long since gone, you could contact Joss Graham Oriental Textiles (tel: 020 7730 4370), which has a wide range of fabrics from £50. The company can send a digital photo of any rug to your computer. Better still, go to London and rummage through its vast range of fabric.

Q I have some cushions made from antique fabric and would love to have some more. Do you know if there is anyone I can commission to replicate the material?

A There is a fascinating company that I have just discovered - well my mother did really. She saw some beautiful fabric hanging in someone's house and tracked down the makers. Together we went to find them in the middle of the Somerset countryside. It is a company run by father and daughter. The man used to be a farmer and then went to Florence to learn how to weave and has an amazing collection of looms in the barns of his old farm. He can recreate fabrics and carpets from patterns from the 15th to the 20th century, so if you want to match an old fabric or design something yourself, they are the people. Their range includes silk damasks, fabrics for wedding dresses, crewel work, hand knotted and flat woven carpets and cotton plain weaves and checks. It is best to call and discuss your needs, then they can advise you on cost and what they can do for you. But they also do small end pieces, which are brilliant for sumptuous cushions and upholstering chairs. Definitely worth calling Renaissance Weavers on 01398 361543.

✳ **kitchens**

Kitchens and what we put in them must account for the biggest spend in redoing our homes. It is incredibly expensive to refit kitchens and most of you are always asking for handy hints to reduce the load. We all move into places that aren't exactly our style and most of us, unless we are very lucky, have to put up with the fixtures. But the home decorating boom has pushed to the limits the kind of things we can change without spending a fortune. The types of material available for the domestic market range from rubber, glass, Formica, all kinds of beautiful woods and laminates to aluminium and stainless steel, zinc, tiles in every size and shape – there is so much out there, the choice is what is difficult now.

The paint you can use for colouring Melamine must be one of the biggest sellers – it is so easy to paint over drab units without spending masses. And even professional decorators are getting daring in the materials they will try. The television makeover programmes have forced them forward – they no longer turn up their noses when you ask for a zinc splashback and tell you it can't be done. We have seen these things being done and want them.

One of the areas that I think is so exciting is in the retail world. It wasn't very long ago – in fact, only seven years – when I was buying a new fridge and I wanted a stainless steel one. All the shops shook their heads and said no. Now stainless steel is commonplace – you can have your fridge how you want it. It can look like a fifties' one in a choice of colours. White goods are no longer white. The consumer has won over the slowest of trades. Even now your washing machine can look trendy if you want it to.

There is so much choice that it is hard to know what look to go for and to get something that works and lasts. I have been furious with manufacturers over things like toasters that are designed to last only for a year or so. Apparently if you buy a new dishwasher it will only last you five years. If you have one that was made ten years ago, hang on to it as it is worth repairing, unlike one you buy now. That is the downside of wealth of choice – we are all too keen to throw away and buy again. I still think that once you have bought items for your kitchen you should be able to sit back and enjoy it and not have to spend more Saturdays looking around again, so I try to help people repair and maintain their products.

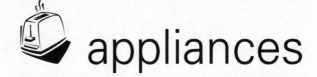
appliances

Q I have a new glass ceramic hob that unfortunately has a scratch on it. Although it is small, it is quite deep. Any suggestions as to how I can buff this out, or is there a company that can do it for me?

A Shallow scratches can be removed from glass hobs with a product called Hobrite, which has a little bit of pumice in to act as an abrasive. But it sounds as though you have gone through the thin laminated surface, and that, sadly, is irreparable. I think you are in for a new hob if you can't face looking at the scratch. Personally though, I'd regard it as an occupational hazard of cooking and not worry about it. Ceramic hobs are very practical in some ways, but they do scratch. The best tip is to keep them very clean and lift, rather than drag, your pans.

Q I have bought a second-hand cooker – a Creda Trimline Four. I have only one wire cooking shelf measuring 37cm (14½in) wide by 35.5cm (14in) long. I need another shelf to cook on. Can you help with an address for Creda so I can purchase a wire shelf?

A Hotpoint looks after Creda now so you need to get in touch with their parts department. The number is 08709 077077. You'll need details of the cooker to hand, the measurements of the item and a credit card to pay with. Alternatively, you could try your local department store, who may be able to order it for you.

Q I have looked everywhere for a knob for my Atag built-in gas oven, model OGR220, without success. Not even the manufacturers can help. Although old, my oven is in good working order and it seems sad if the alternative is to buy a new oven for the sake of a little knob. Can you help?

A I have contacted Atag, the oven's manufacturers and, as you say, they do not carry the parts any more. Your oven is about 20 years old and the policy of all the electrical companies is to try and keep spare parts for at least 10 years for any such repair. After that, it is a question of contacting your local domestic electricity shop and seeing if they have something that would fit the shaft or spindle that the knob sat on. I agree with you that you should be able to repair it, so if this line of enquiry proves unsuccessful, what about trying a local DIY handyperson? They may well be able to make a replacement knob for you. It will not match the original but it will save you the cost of a new oven. Twenty years' life for a cooker is pretty good going but I'm sure you will be able to keep it working even longer.

Q **My husband and I live out in the country where there is no supply of natural gas. Our electrical cooker is rather elderly and, as we now have a microwave/convection cooker, we would like to purchase four rings and a grill for use with bottled gas. Is this possible? If so, can you suggest names of suppliers? We have looked locally but have found only tops without a grill and these are ugly and difficult to clean. We have seen tops in Spain that are attractive and easily cleaned. Can we purchase something similar here?**

A I think you are going to find it extremely hard to find a grill without a cooker to use with liquid petroleum gas (LPG), as it is known. The only place you may find something that might work is in a camping shop but it probably wouldn't look quite right in a kitchen. The other alternative is to go for a single oven with a grill inside. Stove do one that can be converted to LPG. German manufacturers such as AEG, Bosch and Neff do four-burner gas hobs with jets that can easily be changed for use with LPG. Call Hot and Cold on 020 8960 1300. They deliver nationwide and their prices are very competitive.

appliances

135

✳ Tessa's tip With space at a premium in many kitchens, more and more people are going for a single oven with a grill incorporated into it. If you are buying such an oven, be sure to take a look at pyrolytic ovens. Most manufacturers, including Bosch, Belling, Neff, Miele, Hotpoint and Neff, now make them. What's their advantage? With a standard single oven, fat from the oven often splashes on to the grill. This causes the oven to smoke next time you turn it on. Pyrolytic ovens, though, are self-cleaning, which prevents this from happening – although you do still need to clean the shelves and trays separately. So if you lead a busy life, take a look at easy-clean ovens. They cost a bit more – from about £500 – but avoid all the fumes and smoke.

Q It's always been my dream to own an Aga but there just isn't room for one in my small kitchen. Is there anything else you can suggest that would give the same warmth and look but isn't so large?

A Aga have just come up with an oven that may suit you. The Aga Companion has a vitreous enamel, cast-iron exterior in the same style as the original Aga and is available in the same range of colours. But instead of a constant hot oven, it is a conventional cooker with two steel electric ovens. The top one has a grill, and the bottom one is fan-assisted. The hob can be either gas or electric. The ovens are self-cleaning and heat up in about 12 minutes. You wouldn't get the continuous warmth an original Aga gives, but you do get the look and a very flexible oven into the bargain.

Q Is there a way of making the towel rail on an Aga less slippery? The drying-up cloths regularly fall off mine and, if I'm not there, the dogs lie on them.

A Aga does make a tea towel with a long loop which can be tied to the rail to stop this happening. It's in black and white checked 100 per cent cotton towelling, available from all Aga stockists, price £5.99. Call 0345 125207. There is also an anti-slip material that you can put round the rail, from Falcon Products on 01706 224790. The fabric is useful for all sorts of purposes – to stop chopping boards and mixers from slipping; as a grip to open jars; to keep telephones, computer keyboards, sewing machines and fax machines in position. The fabric is 30cm (12in) wide, comes in green, burgundy, black, air force blue, cream and white, and costs £2.30 a metre.

136

 Tessa's tip The Aga has always had a special place in our affections. It's not cheap, but there has never been a shortage of customers for its old-fashioned, chunky charm. Sometimes, though, it's more of a sentimental than practical choice, and modern homes don't really need the 24-hour heat it provides. But now you can have all the prestige of the Aga name on an up-to-the-minute design. The new Aga Masterchef is a dual-function cooker with three electric ovens (two large fan ovens plus a slow cooker), a five-burner gas hotplate and an electric ceramic grill. It's available in racing green, claret, dark blue and cream and fits into a space of 100cm (40in). Sadly, though, its price is a thoroughly traditional £2,950, including VAT.

Q I'm having great difficult finding Aga pans in my area. Can I buy them mail order and how much would that cost?

A Apparently, Aga pans are hard to find outside big towns, despite the fact that Agas are still more popular in the country. You can buy pans mail order – phone 0345 125207 and this will automatically connect you to your nearest stockist. They can send you out a free catalogue and then you can choose what you want. All year round Aga do very good offers if you are starting your collection of pans. As one Aga pan can cost £50, it is worth thinking of buying a few on offer! If you buy one, p&tp is £4.95, but an order of £100 or more, p&tp is free. Colours are available in their cast iron range are racing green, claret, dark blue or gloss black or matt black.

Q I read your reply on how to smarten up an old white fridge by using car spray paint. I love the idea, but is there a simpler way of making it more attractive? Just now, all I have on it are photos, which look messy and grimy.

A I've come across a great idea that is much less messy than painting the fridge and is especially practical if you are house-renting and can't really change its original white. It's a huge magnetic poster that will cover the entire fridge door. It comes in two sizes, will trim to fit and is easy to attach, wipe clean and take off. There are five designs, including brightly coloured food, classic paintings by Carl Larsson, and even a Christmas scene. Contact Fridge Art on 01293 820861.

Q My fridge and freezer have become very tatty on the outside. Is there a suitable paint that I can use to smarten up their appearance?

A Try a car spray paint. Halfords, the car accessory store, has a wide range of colours. A 200ml tin costs £3.99 and you shouldn't need more than a couple of cans. Wash down with sugar soap and mask off all areas you want paint-free. If you can, take off all handles and accessories. Make sure you spray the fridge in ventilated conditions and wear a mask. I know someone who painted a big American fridge bright red. It looks great but it was quite a job. Alternatively, you could splash out on one of the latest Ariston creations, from £649 at John Lewis.

Q I have just bought a new fridge freezer that seems to need something to break up its stark whiteness. Can you suggest a way to decorate it so it's more pleasant to look at?

A Plasti-Kote does a super enamel spray paint that's easy to use, ideal for fridges, and dries in minutes. It's available in 35 colours,

appliances

137

so there's bound to be one to suit your colour scheme, and costs £4.99 for a 400ml can from most DIY stores. Alternatively, there's lots you can do to decorate a plain white fridge. The Craft Depot (tel: 01458 274727) sells large sheets of different-coloured stick-on foam that you can turn into fridge magnets (it sells the magnets too), and The Great Little Trading Company (tel: 0990 673009) sells magnetised photo frames especially designed for fridges. They come in sets of two, 15 x 10cm (6 x 4in) at £6.99, and 7.5 x 10cm (3 x 4in) at £4.99.

Q We have acquired a fifties GEC refrigerator. It is in good working order but the door seal has perished. Can you suggest a supplier to replace it, or could something else be adapted to fit?

A Well, it was a long shot, but I phoned GEC spares just to see if they had an old seal lurking in the store room. Unfortunately, they didn't. They do keep spares for their refrigerators (now Hotpoint) but only for about ten years from the date of manufacture.

Unfortunately, the whole sealing mechanism has changed since the fifties. Then, the door was secured by a handle, but modern seals have built-in magnets, so it is highly unlikely you will be able to get a replacement for yours.

I sympathise with you, as it seems such a small thing to prevent you enjoying what is now an extremely trendy item to own. Replica fifties fridges are available, but these are at least £900, so that may be no consolation. Sorry to be the bearer of bad news. However, if anyone reading this can help with the perished seal, contact me and I'll put you in touch.

✳ Tessa's tip

In response to the enquiry from a reader wanting to repair a fifties fridge which had a broken door seal, lots of readers suggested draught excluder as a seal, in single or double widths. Someone else suggested silicone sealant, which sets to a rubbery texture without shrinking and can be built up in layers. He says that before each layer is added, you should wait until a skin forms. Another suggestion was a vintage car supplier called Paul Beck, who can be contacted on 01692 650455: he has all kinds of bits and pieces that may work. Or how about suggested using the door seal from a chest deep freeze as these tend to have larger seals than the normal fridge doors? Use RTV sealant, which comes in lots of colours and is available from DIY stores, to bond the seal. Alternatively, a classic car supplier Coachtrimming Centre (tel: 020 8659 4135), could supply a car-door draught excluder.

Q Would you advise me on a paint I should use to remove rust from my dishwasher? A patch of it has appeared below the door.

A You really need to get off as much rust as you can before painting the area. Plasti-Kote (tel: 01223 836400) has an anti-rust primer for £6.49 that you should apply before painting. The company does a 'rust-not' paint, which will prevent further rusting, but will not get rid of any existing rust. It comes in a limited range of colours – black, gloss and stain white, brown, bright red, dark green and royal blue – and costs £6.49 for 400ml.

Q Can you help me find a small automatic washing machine? The space I have available for one is only 58cm (23in) wide, and local shops have nothing suitable.

A Candy makes a washing machine called the Aqua No 8, a 50cm (20in)-wide automatic front loader that should be ideal for your kitchen. Unfortunately, smaller doesn't mean cheaper – it costs the same as a standard model, £399. Ask a local department store to order one for you, but be aware that it may take up to eight weeks for delivery.

Q You gave advice recently on small washing machines. In similar vein, I have been trying for some time to purchase a free-standing, eye-level grill gas stove with a depth of less than the standard 600mm (24in). Any ideas?

A A London company called Hot and Cold (tel: 020 8960 1200) has what you are looking for. Made by Stoves, it is 550mm (21½in) wide, 430mm (17in) deep, is free standing, has a double oven and an eye-level grill, with a gas hob. It costs £722.50 plus carriage. For readers outside London, Hot and Cold can deliver anywhere in Britain. Sending a cooker to the north of Scotland, for instance, costs less than £40, so ring for a quote.

appliances

139

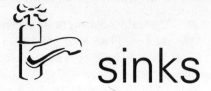 sinks

Q I'm about to refurbish my kitchen and would like to fit a round stainless steel sink. I'd also like a round stainless steel draining board, but this is proving very difficult to find. Could you suggest any catalogues we could send for or any stores that stock these items?

A You could try Ikea for a sink, but I suspect that to get the look you're after you will probably have to have one specially made. The firm you need to speak to for both the sink and the draining board is GEC Anderson on 01442 826999, but remember they only do only flat surfaces, not ridged ones. To keep flat draining boards looking pristine you have to wipe them down regularly. Measure up and GEC will quote you a price over the phone. They can do everything from sinks, baths, bowls and even loos in any shape or size. Delivery time is five to six weeks.

Q Five minutes after cleaning the stainless steel sink in my kitchen, it looks a perfect mess. How do I keep it sparkling?

A Bar Keeper's Friend is an environmentally friendly powder, available in most supermarkets and branches of Boots and John Lewis at around £1.70 for 200g (7oz). You can also buy it via Kleeneze Homecare for £2.99 – call them on 0117 975 0350 for your local agent. Apparently, the powder was first made 100 years ago in the Wild West, but it is just as effective today. It's a non-abrasive cleaner that works on stainless steel, bone china, copper, chrome, marble and plastic, as well as white and coloured composition sinks. It is also recommended by Wedgwood for removing stains in fine porcelain.

Q I have just spilt some bleach all over my beautiful stainless-steel sink and, no matter how hard I rub with cleaners such as Jif, I can't shift it. I'm desperate, it looks awful, any ideas?

A Don't worry – there is something that can help! A product that I guarantee will shift the stain is called Shiny Sinks. It's a very good product for cleaning stainless steel sinks and keeping limescale at bay. Used regularly on sinks, the product will keep them shiny and beautiful. For your problem, you will have to use some elbow grease as well, but it will work. Give yourself a few stints at it; then wash it off and dry the surface. You can buy Shiny Sinks at any supermarket for just a few pounds.

Q Would you have any details of suppliers of imperial-measurement kitchen sinks (enamel or stainless steel) preferably in the Surrey area?

A I'm not quite sure why you are worried about this. Even though everything is now sold in metric sizes, any plumber can work out the dimensions. Just go into any good kitchen supplier in your area and ask for their help.

Q I have a traditional Belfast porcelain sink. I'm trying to locate a firm to supply a white enamel draining board to go with it. Any ideas as to where I should look?

A As far as I know, you can't get hold of these now. (I always hesitate when I say things like this because I know I'll get a postbag full of letters saying that you can.) People who buy a Belfast sink tend to get a free-standing wooden draining section to go with it. Any of the good kitchen shops will be able to help you design something along these lines, or you could get a local carpenter to build something to fit your space. If you want to keep trying for an enamel one, check out your local reclamation yards (see Yellow Pages).

sinks

141

Q Having seen some taps in a service station cloakroom that operated by 'remote control' (the water starts when you put your hands under the tap), I thought I'd like to have something similar installed at home because they'd be very easy to use. Where can I find such a thing?

A There are a number of companies that make this type of tap and they do seem a good idea but it will probably be expensive to change your fittings. Some are programmed to stay on while your hands are there, others are programmed for a set amount of time. Armitage Shanks (tel: 01543 490253) is one company to talk to. Other companies to try are Dart Valley Services (tel: 01803 529021) and A & J Gummers (tel: 0121 706 2241).

Q We have an old kitchen sink that frequently blocks. A plunger always fixes it but only for a while. What do professional plumbers do to unblock sink pipes?

A The only way to stop a sink blocking once and for all is not to put things down it! A plumber will remove the u-bends and clear out trapped waste with high pressure jets – at vast expense – and your sink will still clog up again. A plunger is fine, but get a really huge one! I used caustic soda in my shower for years when all I needed was a big plunger. Also buy a plug-hole shield to stop debris going down.

units and worksurfaces

Q My kitchen has good units but the overall colour scheme is brown and cream, which looks dated. We hope to move house in the next year, but we don't want to spend very much on updating the kitchen. The units are cream and the work surfaces are dark brown. The wall tiles and floor covering are also cream and brown. The walls are also magnolia. We had thought of replacing just the worktops but that might damage the tiles.

A If you're trying to increase the value of your home, don't bother tinkering with the kitchen. Anyone buying the house will probably rip it all out and start again, so you'll never recoup your money. Or is it just that you can't stand the kitchen a minute longer? If you still want to have a go, you could paint the units and the tiles. If the units are melamine, wash with sugar soap, then lightly scour with a rough pad and paint with acrylic primer. When dry, paint with matt emulsion and acrylic varnish to protect the paintwork. As for the tiles, you should clean them, paint on a tile primer and then paint with oil-based paint. When cleaning the tiles, use a gentle non-abrasive cleaner. The worktops would cost more to replace. As the units and tiles are neutral shades, I'm tempted to say leave it, as neutral sells.

Q What do you recommend I use to revarnish a pine kitchen that will be hard wearing, yet will not turn orange with age.

A First you need to remove the old varnish. Use a stripper to get back to the bare wood. Liberon does a methylene chloride-free one, or there are plenty of others on the market. Once you've got back to the wood, instead of using a protective polyurethane coat – probably what was on it originally, which does tend to yellow with age – try some finishing oil instead. Liberon do a 250ml tin for £3.39 and this will cover 2 to 3 sq m (2$\frac{1}{3}$ to 3$\frac{1}{2}$ sq yd). Call on 01797 367555 for stockists in your area. You will need four coats of the oil, which seeps into the wood and seals it when it dries. Simply apply with a brush or cloth and leave for five to ten minutes between coats. After each coat, rub back lightly with wire wool and dust off any stray dust before re-coating. Depending on the wear and tear you give it, it shouldn't need another coat for a year or two. Then just rub down lightly with wire wool to prepare the surface, and apply a top-up coat.

Q **I have painted our wood-effect kitchen units with blue emulsion paint. To prevent chipping, I wanted to give them a protective coating and have tried many types of varnish from water-based, quick-dry ones, which leave a very streaky finish, to solvent-based ones, which produce a slight browning effect. Do you know of a suitable clear varnish/coating that I can use?**

A I'm a bit worried that you have not prepared your surfaces properly. Wood-effect kitchen units usually have a plasticised coating that emulsion paint will not stick to properly. The correct procedure for painting them is to clean the surface thoroughly, then use a melamine primer, which is suitable for use on any plasticised surface. Apply two coats of this and then two coats of satin finish paint as a top coat. If you use a satin top coat you will not need to use a varnish. Emulsion paint is not designed to go over non-porous surfaces and will chip off even if you coat it with varnish. What you will have to do is to strip back the emulsion paint you have already put on (this shouldn't be too difficult to do). Then follow the above instructions for a long-lasting finish that won't chip. International do a melamine primer that is available in most DIY superstores and good independent stores. Call International on 01962 711177 to find your nearest stockist.

Q **The Formica worktops in my kitchen are badly scratched. Is it possible to tile over Formica and if so, which tiles and cement should I use?**

A There is no adhesive specifically recommended for sticking worktop tiles to Formica, so try to remove the Formica if you can. If it proves too difficult to get off, sand down the surface in order to provide a key before you apply the tiles. You will need to put a wood beading trim around the front of the worktop. Then use a strong, epoxy-based flexible floor adhesive – Fired Earth (tel: 01295 812088) supply one called Vitraflex. They also have three types of tile suitable for worktops: Stone Lustre, Fossil and Tuscany. It's vital that you check carefully with a tile shop before starting this project. If you don't buy a suitable tile, you will end up with cracks and marks the first time you put a hot pan down on them.

Q When I moved house I inherited a three-year-old solid oak kitchen. I loathe the worktop and would like to replace it with a granite one, but I cannot seem to find any suppliers of these worktops in the Berkshire area. Can you help?

A The biggest selection of granite you're likely to find that is not too far away is probably at Pisani, on the Great West Road in Brentford, Middlesex (tel: 020 8568 5001). They stock more than 30 different granites to choose from. People in other parts of the country who have the same problem finding a supplier of granite or marble should contact the National Federation of Terrazzo, Marble and Mosaic Specialists (tel: 08456 090050), and they will be able to put you in touch with a supplier in your area.

units & worksurfaces

145

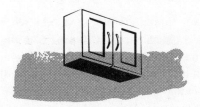

replacements

Q I am desperate to find replacement wires for my marble cheese cutter. I have tried all my local kitchen shops and no one seems to be able to help me. Any ideas?

A There's a fabulous independent kitchen shop in Taunton, called The Cook's Shop, which is crammed with wonderful things. They regularly win prizes for their stock – and they have cheese wires at 25p each! Send an sae and 25p in stamps or a postal order to The Cook's Shop, Riverside Place, Taunton, Somerset TA1 1AG and they will send you one. Call them on 01823 271071.

Q You once wrote about a company that can help people find out-of-date china. I have inherited some old bone china that I don't want to keep. Does the firm also buy items to replenish its stocks?

A The firm you are thinking of is called TableWhere. They most definitely do buy old china. Call 020 8361 6111 and tell them the maker, the pattern name, how many items you have and what they are. TableWhere will offer you a price and organise collection if you accept the bid. The china must be in good condition and not crazed, though it is fine if it looks used, as people want replacement items to blend in with their own sets.

TableWhere is a fantastic shop that specialises in discontinued china, from 200 manufacturers, dating from 1900 to the present day (although they specialise in post-war items). If you are missing a piece from a dinner service, first try to find out who made it, along with the pattern and name and number. If you don't know the pattern, send a photograph to the shop and they will try to identify it. It's a staggering service when you think that Wedgwood alone produced 250,000 patterns, sometimes with five or six colourways within each pattern. Call TableWhere on 020 8361 6111 (or fax on 020 8361 4143) for details of their worldwide mail-order service.

Q Somebody once told me of a company that could make blue glass linings for silver salt cellars or mustard pots. My mustard pot is lacking one and I wondered if you knew where I could buy a new lining, and whether I need to send the cracked one for size?

A There is a company that can do this for you. Call Facets on 020 8520 3392. There is no need to send the broken one: Facets can provide the blue glass liner if you send them just the silver outside section. The glass is specially ground to suit each item. If the company can supply your mustard pot lining from stock, it will cost you £10. If it has to have one specially blown to fit, it will cost £18. The company also does sugar-basket glass: the stock size costs £25; if one is specially blown, the cost then depends upon the size. If your liner is chipped, the company can mend it or recut it. Facets can also rebristle old brushes, which many of you write to me asking about. Ring the company on Monday and Tuesday, 1-5pm. When you send your mustard pot to them, send it registered post: this is a special service that insures the article you are sending. Recorded delivery is not enough.

Q Is there anywhere I can get replacement lids for my saucepans? The knobs on mine have all broken, but the pans themselves are sound so I don't want to replace the whole set.

A If your pans are a standard size, try John Lewis. They sell a range of pan lids called Good Housekeeping. The 20cm (8in) one is £9.95, the 24cm (10in) one is £11 and the 28cm (11in) one is £15.50. Call 020 7629 7711 for your nearest store.

Q Do you know of a firm that can replace pieces of cutlery? I have lost a fork that was part of a set bought in 1966. I can't remember the name of the set but on the back of the forks it says 'Wostenholm Sheffield England 18/8 Stainless Steel R9886131'. The set was a wedding gift, so I would dearly love to replace the missing piece.

A The makers of your fork, Wostenholm of Sheffield, went out of business years ago, but there is a company called Nickel Blanks that can make up replica pieces of cutlery in many different styles. The only difference would be that it would not have the name of the manufacturer on the back. Unfortunately, the numbers you quote are quality numbers and not pattern numbers so you would have to send one item of cutlery or a photograph for them to have a look at the pattern. Call Nickel Blanks on 01142 725792. The rough prices for making up are £2.69 for a table fork and £2.34 for a dessert fork. Silver plated costs a little more - £4.94 for a table fork and £3.54 for a dessert fork. Good luck!

replacements

147

Q I am still using Kilner jars from 1939-48, both 1lb and 2lb size, but now I find the rubber rings have reached the end of their working lives. Can you advise me where I can obtain replacement rings? Modern Kilner jars use a different size of ring.

A Although I am totally into conservation and recycling, perhaps it is time, dare I say it, that you thought about buying some new ones. I think you will find it incredibly difficult to find any rubber tops that will fit the jars as all the measurements are now metric. Divertimenti kitchen shops, which do mail order as Cucina Direct on 020 8246 4300, have a range of Parfait jars from France that come in 500ml to 3 litre sizes and the replacement rubber tops are 30p each.

Q I hope to redo my kitchen in the summer, because I need new work surfaces. I have been advised that Corian is the best but it is very expensive. Is there anywhere or anyone who I can go to, to get it at trade price? Or is there something similar?

A My first question is, who is advising you on buying Corian? They may have a vested interest in selling it to you. Often kitchen shops who design your kitchen for you get a rake-off for using certain products and you should be aware of this. It might be worth phoning Corian direct to find local dealers they work with to check on a better price for your kitchen. Call 01442 346776. People suggest Corian because it is non-porous and hygienic for kitchen use. However, it does scratch and once scratched is susceptible to germs, as is any other surface that is scratched. You can have it professionally re-sanded and light scratches and stains can be removed with something called Bar Keeper's Friend, which you can get from most department stores. However, you should also think about other options for your kitchen surface. What about granite? I have used it and it makes a great surface in a kitchen. It is generally cheaper than Corian and doesn't scratch. There are lots of different colours to choose from: only the black type would be as expensive as Corian. My advice is to shop around when deciding on who is going to redo your kitchen. If you are good at DIY, you could make your templates for work surfaces yourself and get your local merchant to cut it for you. You would, of course, have to fit it yourself or employ a local tradesman, but it will be cheaper.

decorative details

Q Could you please tell me where I can obtain a kitchen pulley, the sort of thing that my mother hung her washing on and pulled up to the ceiling?

A Argos does one called an Edwardian-style airer, which costs £9.99. It has four natural wood slats that you can stain, paint or varnish if you wish. The ends are hand-cast iron, and pulleys, sash cord and cleats are supplied. Call them on 0870 600 3030 for your nearest stockist.

Q I would like to refurbish a wooden cutlery box but I am having trouble finding material for the lining. Do you know of anyone who could supply such material in wine red or royal blue?

A Most cutlery canteens are lined in velvet or baize. Velvet is available in a wide range of colours from department stores such as John Lewis (tel: 020 7629 7711) but it stocks baize in green only.

✳ Tessa's tip

Having spent two years searching antique markets to try and match up and add to my bone handled knives at home, I now realise there is an easier way to go about such things. If you like old-fashioned real bone knife handles then the only route is the antique one as they are not made now. But you can get excellent synthetic bone-handled knives with stainless steel blades, and they come with either square or rounded ends. The latest mail-order catalogue from Cucina Direct includes some that can be ordered via the Internet (the website is at www.cucinadirect.co.uk) or tel: 020 8246 4300 for a catalogue. This catalogue used to be the Divertimenti mail-order catalogue but now the retail shop Divertimenti and the mail-order business have separated with the setting up of Cucina Direct. Four bone dinner or dessert knives – square or rounded ends – cost £39.95. Cucina Direct also does steak knives for the same price.

Baize is made in other colours, however, mostly for specialist upholsterers. It might be worth ringing round local upholsterers to see if they have any baize offcuts in the colours you require. Be warned: refitting a canteen is a highly specialised and very fiddly job. It might be simpler to send yours to a specialist silverware firm such as Langfords for repair. Call the company on 020 7242 5506 for details. To give you an idea of what it would cost Langford charges about £35 to refit a canteen that holds a dozen pieces.

Q **I am re-decorating my kitchen and I'm looking for ceramic tiles and table mats with sunflowers on them. I've had no luck so far – any ideas?**

A No problem with sunflower tiles: Pilkington's Accents and Satins ranges, both have them. Each is charming but Accents are vibrant in colour while Satins are more subtle. Tiles are £1.79 each, or ten for £10.71. Call 0161 727 1000 for a local stockist. As for the table mats, go to Watchet Products of Somerset (tel: 01984 631207). They do a set of six sunflower mats for £19, as well as floral-pattern trays, coasters, and chopping boards.

❋ **Tessa's tip** Take a look at the mail-order catalogue from a company called Sala. They specialise in funky and unusual homewares from around the world. I especially like their rough-cast aluminium vessels. Chunky forms with polished silvery insides, these are very versatile – complementing Eastern or arty-crafty looks as well as modern minimal. Sala also does a beautiful range of stone vases, and glass hurricane lamps to put candles in so wax doesn't end up on your table. Call 01935 827050 for a catalogue or try the website, www.sala.uk.com

❋ bathrooms

At last, bathrooms are being taken seriously. I hate white clinical bathrooms. To me, the bathroom should be an indulgence and somewhere to be able to relax and take some hard-earned leisure time. Too many people still see it as a purely functional space, but the interior designers are working on it. Every area from the floor and the shower curtains to the bath itself, the toilet seat and accessories for the bathroom have been studied and modernised. No surface is safe. Mosaic floors and walls are hugely popular and easy to do yourself. You can reclaim your old tired bath and make it look gleaming new. As for dreaded limescale, it is possible to remove it and the DIY stores also sell all kinds of products for gleaming grout, polished glass – some better than others. I hope I have been able to direct you to the good ones.

Flooring in bathrooms has taken a turn for the better – no longer just cold tiles (I have never understood why people use tiles). You can have wonderful rubber or Marmoleum that is warm underfoot. There are also great photographic cork tiles, easy-to-paint wood floors – all kinds of ways to warm up the usually cold British bathroom. For those building new homes, there is the luxury of underfloor heating too.

And then there's paint. Some of you still can't believe that you can paint over bathroom tiles and it will work. The paint that is available now does remarkable things, but remember that paint is never going to be as sturdy as a fired tile colour, so you should take care when cleaning. In fact, in bathrooms altogether you should take care when cleaning. There are lots of nasty chemical products around that are no good for you or your bathroom. Stick to non-abrasive and gentle liquid cleaners and you will be fine.

baths

Q I am afraid that our bath was ruined by a cleaning product we used in error. Can you suggest anything we could apply to make the bath more presentable?

A There's a firm called The Lab on 020 7372 2973 that supplies bath refinishers all around the country with a specialist resurfacing kit from the States. It's suitable for all baths – acrylic or cast iron. Just phone them and they will put you in touch with someone in your area. They will redo the bath in situ, masking off the taps and plumbing etc and, 24 hours after it's finished, you can have a bath. All colours are available and a total rehab of your bath will cost in the region of £200: much cheaper than buying a new one and with no costs for new plumbing or tiling. Smaller chips can be treated, starting from about £70. The special kit can also be used on basins and tilework, but it is not recommended for the inside of the lavatory where strong chemicals are used.

Q I am doing up my 1930s' house and have come to the bathroom. I have a cast iron bath but I am not sure what to use on it as it is very rusty from being

baths

153

❋ Tessa's tip

Well, these aren't really my tips on how to remove limescale, but instead some invaluable tips that I have received over the years:

❋ This was given to one of my readers by a Spanish lady many years ago: use a pumice stone with a slightly rounded and pointed end. It gets into most corners and will clear the taps and base of a ridged shower.

❋ Alternatively, use an old toothbrush and a paste of the generally available Barkeeper's Friend.

❋ Or use Astonish, from Kleeneze (tel: 0870 333 6688), Akata, from Boots, or Powerbath or Viakal. Both of these last two are available from most supermarkets.

blocked in for many years. I realise the temperature has to be taken into consideration. Should I be using a special kind of paint for it?

A The best paint to use on a cast-iron bath is something like Hammerite that will withstand the heat of the water. What you need to do is to strip the bath right back to get all the rust off. Rub it back with wire wool or a wire brush to get rid of any flakes or rust. Then degrease using Hammerite degreaser and wash off any residue. Then you can use a primer if you have a really old pitted surface on the bath. This will even it out and give a good base for the top coat but you don't need to do this if your bath looks OK. For the top Hammerite coat, it is best to use a spray gun if you can as you need to work quickly with this paint or it gets a candy floss stringy texture to it. If you are using a gun, then use 2 parts paint to 1 part brush thinner and cleaner. You will need to do two coats. Each coat will be touch dry in about half an hour. If you do use a brush, make sure you use a large one. The Hammerite comes in 26 colours, 12 hammered finish and 14 smooth. They also do a satin black. Around £17 a litre.

Q I have just painted my bathroom tiles with an oil-based paint. Is it possible to paint my cast-iron bath in the same way?

A Use Hammerite paint in either a smooth or a hammered finish. If your bath already has a coat of paint, check that the new paint won't react with the old. Paint a 5cm (2in) square of Hammerite on it, leave for an hour and if there's no reaction it'll be fine. Then roughen all the old paint on the bath with sandpaper and wash with detergent and water. Rinse again with water. Then use two or three coats of Hammerite – you'll need three if you're going from a dark to a light colour. It dries very quickly, so always follow the instructions. However, professional bath restorers (try Yellow Pages) will often produce a superior finish with sprays.

Q Our enamel bath got badly chipped when a shelf (that my husband put up!) fell into it recently. Can I retouch it myself or leave it to the professionals?

A If it's just one chip and you're not too fussy, fill the dent with an epoxy resin filler, sand it down and coat it with enamel paint. You will always be able to see the patch, however good the repair. If that will bother you, get it done professionally now, rather than later. It will be much cheaper than a new bath!

Q I am about to redecorate my bathroom. Instead of buying a new bath, I was thinking of having my old one re-enamelled. Do you know of any firm that specialises in this?

 A There is a company called The Lab that can put you in touch with bath refurbishers that use its special method of resurfacing baths. Call them on 020 7372 2972. To have your bath done will cost you in the region of £200 and baths made of cast iron, ceramic, acrylic, pressed steel and plastic can all be resurfaced. They can also do a colour change for you for another £20 or so. The product they use is very tough and will withstand normal bath use, but if you scratch it, it will come off. So make sure you use non-abrasive cleaners – a neutral detergent such as Fairy Liquid. A general tip when cleaning any bath is to do it as soon as the water has run out, because once the bath has dried, you are much more likely to damage the surface.

Q Two of the six chrome plug-holes in our house have discoloured and peeled. Apparently they cannot be replaced, so what can be done to improve them. They make the whole sink/shower look grubby.

A You can replace them. Some are easier than others. If yours has a screw in the middle of the plug-hole it is easy: simply unscrew and refit. If it doesn't, it will have a screw underneath the bath, which means you may have to take off the bath panel and fiddle around. If you are not much good at DIY, get someone in. If you don't fancy that idea, and want to wait a little, there is a product that The Lab are working on that should be available soon which is a thin insert, in nickel and chrome, that you simply stick on over the existing outlet. Call the company on 020 7372 2972 for details.

baths

155

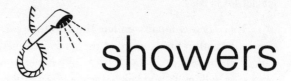 showers

Q We are urgently looking for a budget priced white shower tray and cubicle – we have found the Bette Caro, which is exactly the type we are looking for but it costs £3000 plus! It is a rectangular shape 900 x 700mm (35 x 27½in) with a cut out down one long side to give a wider walkway.

A I've never heard of the Bette Caro but it does sound very expensive. Try instead a company called Showeristic on 01352 735381. They specialise in making up showers to suit the space you have. Although they are based in Clwyd, they can cover the country. Talk to them, send them sketches and measurements. The measurements should be after the tiling has been done. Unless you are a dab hand at DIY, it is probable your plumber will do all the negotiation with them. They do have 90 x 70cm (35 x 27½in) trays and can fit whatever shape of shower enclosure you need. Their trend in their new catalogue is for less metal frames and more plain glass, so send for one and see the sort of work they do.

Q We are having problems finding a shower cubicle to replace our bath. Those on display are all 79cm (31in) at the base. Unfortunately the space available is only 68cm (27in). Do any manufacturers design cubicles to suit a smaller bathroom?

A First things first. Don't just look at what is on display in a shop – ask. A good shop should be able to help with such a request. A manufacturer called Selecta (tel: 01706 869988), definitely can help. Its new luxury range includes a door to fit 68-73cm (27-29in) shower cubicles that costs £159.99. A shower tray from the same source costs £69.99. Your nearest supplier is probably Rapid Hardware in Liverpool, but call Selecta to check.

Q I have been searching for a circular shower rail. Despite seeing them in homes magazines, I have been unsuccessful. Do you know where I can find one?

A Most bathroom shops sell contour shower rails, which you can almost bend into a circle, but if you want the real thing, try Ware

bathrooms

Bathroom Centre on 01920 468664. It sells circular shower rails in two sizes by mail order. The smaller one has a diameter of 60cm (24in) and costs £97 in chrome, £144 in white, and £152 in colours. The larger one (76cm/30in diameter) costs £104, £156 and £165 respectively. Ware also sells all the fittings you will need for the ceiling.

Q Can you tell me where I could buy a large-size shower base? I'm looking for one that's 120 x 90cm (4 x 3ft) wide, but my local suppliers seem only to do the basic size.

A I don't think much of your local suppliers! Try calling CP Hart, on 020 7902 1000. They have a shower base that is 120 x 90cm (4 x 3ft) wide, and 13.5cm (5¹⁄₃in) high. It costs £189 plus VAT and comes in white only. CP Hart recommend that you have the tray on site before tiling, as the measurements are approximate.

Q Can you suggest a way to hang a shower curtain in my bathroom? The bath is under a window at the tap end so there's nothing I can attach a rail to.

A Try Contourail by Jendico. This is a flexible curtain rail that will bend in a 90-degree curve, so you can fix one end to the wall opposite the window and the other end to the side wall. The rail is supported at the bend by a ceiling strut. Contourail is available in silver, gold and white finishes; call Jendico on 0116 277 0474 for your nearest stockist. The company also sells an extra-long, 220cm (7ft 3in) shower curtain – something that many readers have asked me about.

Q We have had our bathroom renewed and now need a non-standard size shower curtain. I have tried all the curtain and DIY stores but no one seems able to help.

A Try Croydex on 01264 365881. They do most lengths and widths of curtain, but as the business is relatively new the colour range is limited to peach, white, ivory, pink and whisper pink (the range should be expanding soon). They will also make the rods and rails. Delivery is available nationwide.

showers

157

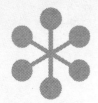

decorative
details

Q I want to update my bathroom, which is more than 20 years old and has one of those coloured bathroom suites that were in fashion in the seventies. I want to start from scratch and install a new white suite. My dilemma is this: do I employ a local plumber, joiner, plasterer, tiler, electrician, etc, or do I choose a firm that will do the whole job?

A First things first: removing the bathroom suite and replacing it with a white one needn't cost a fortune. But if you are going to give the whole room a makeover, then how you go about the job depends on your time, budget and whether you enjoy getting involved. Bringing in a series of people to do the work is likely to be much more of a headache than having one firm do everything for you, as work will only run smoothly if you are around to coordinate it. I'm not sure that it even ends up being cheaper and, if something does go wrong, you may be faced with a lot of people making excuses. Employing one firm makes it easier to sort things out. See if anyone you know can recommend a building company that has done satisfactory work for them. Then ask it to quote a price for the work you plan. Get another firm to quote too, in order to give you something to cost it against. But don't always go for the cheapest quote – there are lots of shortcuts less scrupulous builders can take, and you could well pay the price for them later.

Q I have moved into a flat where the bathroom suite is the dreaded avocado. Short of completely replacing it, what can I do?

A Well, the cheapest option is to try to disguise it by changing the surrounding paintwork, but if you really hate the colour that much, you need The Bath Doctor (tel: 01233 740532). This company specialises in recolouring bathroom suites in situ. They use a treatment

bathrooms

called cold cure enamelling, which requires a lower temperature to fix than vitreous enamelling, but leaves you with a durable finish. They will mask-off taps and tiles and spray your bath the required colour. They can even successfully respray the inside of the toilet bowl if you choose to do the whole suite.

Q I am trying to locate a minute hand basin to fit in a small toilet room. It really does have to be just big enough to wash hands. Can you help?

A Call a company called Colourwash on 020 8459 8918. They specialise in anything for bathrooms and have a small basin of 50cm (20in) wide by 22cm (8½in) depth – the depth being the critical measurement for you. If this is small enough, it would cost you about £50 plus carriage. They deliver nationwide.

Q We have recently renovated our bathroom, using an aquatic theme throughout, and would like a loo seat in a blue-green colour with a fish motif. Can you tell us where to buy one?

A Finding just what you're looking for might be more work than doing it yourself. Either use the existing loo seat or buy a simple wood or plastic one. Paint it with Plasti-Kote spray paint – their Odds 'n' Ends range comes in 47 vibrant colours and costs £2.89 for a 100ml can and £2.69 for a 59ml pot from all good DIY shops. Once dry, find some fish pictures you like, and photocopy them. They may be painted with a thin wash of water-based paint as desired. Leave to dry and then stick them to the loo seat with PVA glue, which dries clear. Then coat the seat with polyurethane clear varnish to protect the design.

Q About two months ago, I saw a goldfish toilet seat advertised in a DIY programme. It had a white/transparent background and was decorated with goldfish. Do you know of a company that makes these?

A A company called Curious Pedestrians makes all kinds of weird and wacky toilet seats – call them on 01453 886482. They can make loo seats to order and will make up your goldfish in a transparent background for you. You should have a look at their web site on www.bogseats.co.uk to see the full range they do. Let's put it this way, your request will be easy compared to some of their seats. They cost £155 so obviously you will have to splash out on it.

decorative details

159

Q We have recently moved and discovered that the toilet seat in our new house was broken and needed replacing. However, when we measured it we discovered that no standard seat will fit. The make of the toilet is Georgio and we are told that it is probably Italian. The existing seat measures 41 x 38cm (16 x 15in). We have been advised to have one specially made but it will cost in the region of £150 and we can't afford to pay such a lot of money. Please help.

A One place you could try for starters is the Architectural Salvage Index (tel: 01483 203221). For £10 you can join their database, which lists items both wanted and for sale. Alternatively, local architectural salvage firms may be able to help. Try one in Manchester on 0161 839 5525 or Preston on 01772 334868.

Q How can I permanently remove spots of mould from my shower curtain? It is made of 100 per cent polyester and we have bathroom curtains to match, which do not seem to be affected. I have washed the curtain according to the instructions, but the spots soon return.

A One of the most effective ways of cleaning mould off shower curtains is with the sterilising solution you use for babies' bottles. Take down the curtain and soak it overnight in a bucket containing a solution. Shower curtain manufacturers swear by it. If the mould spots are really stuck on, use a scrubbing brush. Look at the ventilation in your bathroom too – you may need a powerful extractor.

decorative details

160

✳ heating

A subject close to my heart. I am always cold and I hate cold homes. I think having a fireplace in a room makes an enormous difference to your spirits and if you can put one in, it is money worth spending. Often you can simply reopen fireplaces that were closed off when they were unfashionable in the 1970s. Lots of you also ask me about restoring old fireplaces and where to find surrounds. It has become an expensive business and a market cornered by the architectural salvage guys. If you are lucky enough to inherit one when you move into a house and it needs attention, there are plenty of tips here to help you out.

Also many people have built-in fires – those where you simply turn on the gas at the plug – but their fires have become jaded and need restoring. It is possible to find new parts for these fires, but you are likely to be told you can't as no one makes any money repairing things these days. It is much better to sell someone a new one. But be persistent with these firms, they often have stock dating back at least ten years, and sometimes earlier if you push.

Whenever you are installing fires, particularly gas ones, do make sure you get a recommended Corgi engineer to do it for you. As we live in the frozen north, having an efficiently heated home is a fantastic asset and shouldn't be a luxury even though the costs involved often make it so.

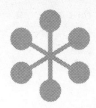

 fireplaces

Q We have a brick fireplace with a York stone hearth and mantel, which is dusty-looking and shabby. We can't replace it, so can you recommend a treatment to give it a much-needed facelift? I believe that at some time it has been sealed and varnished.

A The first thing you should do is remove any varnish with a paint stripper. Once the stone is back to its raw state, try using a range of products from a company called Liberon. Its Stone Floor Cleaner, which is water-based, will remove old wax, grease and grime on porous stone surfaces and is fine for both your mantel and the floor. Then you should apply Stone Floor Sealer, which will protect the porous stone. This product is also useful for terracotta and slate flooring. Finally, depending on the look, you want to achieve, you could use Stone Floor Shine, which you just brush on and leave to dry. All three products cost £9.29 per litre each, and should be available in good smaller DIY stores. Call Liberon on 01797 367555 for your local stockist.

Q I have just moved into an old house with a very beautiful fireplace in the sitting room. I want to make a real feature of it and I wonder if you could suggest where I might find an unusual fender?

A First, measure the width you need and keep these figures in your wallet at all times. Scour the reclamation yards in your area and any of the growing number of old fireplace shops. However, interesting fenders are hard to come by. I have been looking for ages and not found one. There are some brass ones that have extendable front pieces to fit most fireplaces but usually you find one you like and it is the wrong size. If you really want to go to town, you should think about commissioning your very own piece, which would make a real

fireplaces

163

statement. Contact Robin Gage at Original Club Fenders on 07000 286722. They also have an illustrated catalogue that shows their standard range of hand-made fenders if you're not feeling quite so adventurous.

Q My daughter has a sandstone fire surround that has become dirty and dingy. She would like to paint it, but is not sure what sort of paint would be best, and whether it would be successful. Any suggestions?

A She should use an oil-based primer first, and then an oil-based undercoat. The top coat should be eggshell or gloss, depending on the look she wants: it's a similar job to painting exterior masonry.

But think carefully before getting the paintbrush out. Old stone fireplaces are highly sought after, and they can be relatively easy to clean. Start with a heavy scouring pad or sandpaper to rub it back and remove the dirt. Then clean with basic household bleach. When dry, wax with a clear polish because the wax soaks into the stone, you will need to repeat the process.

Q My neighbour has installed a fireplace in his lounge. The surround is medium-coloured oak, 150 years old and lightly carved. He wishes to colour it bronze. Do you have any advice?

A I would suggest using a bronze gilding cream from Paint Magic, who have a mail-order service (tel: 01225 469966). It is called Fontainbleau gilt cream and costs £3.85 for a 15ml pot, which I am told will be enough to do the fireplace. The cream should be rubbed gently into the wood. It will probably need two coats. You can leave it matt or buff it. It is turps-based, so will take a day or so to dry, but will give a hard finish.

Q Our old marble fireplace looks so dirty and grey. We have tried things like washing it and were told we could sandpaper it down for a good clean look. Is this true? Can you tell us how we can get it to look good?

A You can achieve a glorious fireplace with a bit of elbow grease. Sand the marble down with medium sandpaper. Then use smoother grades of sandpaper until you reach 320g paper. To take out any scratches try a scouring pad with bleach or cream cleaner. Leave it to soak for a few minutes, then rinse with cold water. Polish the marble with marble polish or furniture polish depending on the shine

fireplaces

164

you want. You can also use a bleach clay, available from specialist suppliers, which acts as a sort of marble face pack. But this is best left to the experts as it can leave sooty black deposits. Contact Chesney's (tel: 020 7627 1410) for details of specialists in your area.

Q We are stripping many layers of paint off the fire surround in the dining room of our 1903 house, hoping to get down to white marble as in the two bedrooms upstairs. We now find the surround is a black material like slate but softer. Have you any ideas what this might be and any tips for this difficult stripping?

A It sounds to me like it would be slate given the period of the house but it could be wood! I would advise you get a local fireplace person in to have a look before you go any further because depending on what it is, you will need to treat it in different ways. It could even be cast iron but that would have pitting in the iron and you would probably notice this. With slate you could clean it up using WD40, the general household oil, but if it was wood, steer clear of oil. A good quality polish should clean wood up but you may just prefer to dust it and leave it natural.

Q I have a Victorian cast-iron fireplace that has a nasty crack in it. Is there anything I can do to repair it or do I have to replace the whole thing?

A This is really a job for one of the many antique fireplace shops around. It needs to be welded – this is easier than it sounds, can be done in situ and need not cost a fortune. Make sure you find a firm that knows how to weld cast iron and get a quote for the work. Cracks near the fire are more difficult because the cast iron deteriorates with heat. It's definitely worth doing: the prices of replacement Victorian inserts have rocketed in the past ten years.

Q I have a bedroom-sized cast-iron fireplace that I would like to install in my living room. The problem is that although it has an integral basket, it does not have a front and, at just 30cm (12in) wide, is not a standard size. Where can I obtain a front piece for it?

A Start by looking in local architectural salvage yards. If you have no luck there, try specialist fireplace shops, which may have something to suit. My one reservation is that your fireplace sounds a little small and may look swamped in a living room. See if the salvage yards have one that would fit the room better. You may be able to sell the one you have to them and do a swap.

fireplaces

165

Q My daughter's terraced house has cast-iron fireplaces in the bedrooms. How can she remove 90 years of paint to restore them to their original state?

A Having just done an item for *Home Front* on the dangers of lead paint in the home, I would strip such a fireplace with the utmost care as lead paint probably was used. You can test for lead paint with a small kit available in DIY stores. If there are traces of lead I recommend you remove the paint with an alkali-based solution from Strippers (tel: 01787 371524). It comes as a poultice that you paint on, cover with plastic bags or clingfilm for a couple of days, then peel off. Any remaining paint can then be washed off safely. They do two sizes: a 25-litre pot for £37.50 or a 5-litre pot for £8.85, exclusive of VAT and postage. The 5-litre pot should be enough for your needs.

Q I found an old Victorian fireplace in a skip and thought it would look fantastic in my house. But it has been badly painted, it's gone rusty from being left outside and, worst of all, several parts are broken. Is there any hope for it?

A Take heart, Focal Point restoration specialists south-west London (tel: 020 8769 5496) can achieve miracles. Olan and Ben Shorten, the owners, have been collecting old fireplaces for years and, like many in the same business, always have plenty of spare parts. Ben says the first thing he does is to determine whether the metal has any cracks by tapping it. If it sounds dull, then you have to hand-strip it, rather than blast the paint off, which would simply accentuate the cracks and blow the whole thing apart. Spare parts are then welded back on where pieces are missing and the metal is primed and polished with graphite to give, in this case, a stove-black appearance. Give Olan or Ben a call or look up fireplace restoration specialists in Yellow Pages, and good luck.

Q We have moved into a flat that has a horrible grey, beige and brown gas fire. We don't have the money to replace it and I doubt that we can get rid of it, as the boiler is located behind. Is there any kind of paint we can use to make it look more attractive? Also, can we use normal emulsion to paint the wood-look melamine surround?

A For the gas fire, try something called Hot Paint by Plasti-Kote. It comes in four colours – black, white, aluminium or blue (£7.35 for 400ml from most DIY superstores). If you have any difficulty finding it, call Plasti-Kote on 01223 836400 to locate your nearest stockist. For the melamine, you need a melamine primer – International do one (£9.99 for 750ml) or there's one called ESP (£11.99 for 1 litre), both from B&Q call 020 8466 4166 for your nearest outlet.

Q I have just had my gas fire serviced and there are a few chips on the front. The engineer suggested I use some gloss black Hermetite heat-resistant paint. I have looked in a few DIY stores, but I've yet to find any. Do you have any ideas?

A You can buy a small tin from Halfords for £3.69. It is designed for engines, so it should be heat resistant enough for your needs.

Q *Home Front* once featured a living flame gas fire created from black fire-resistant geometric shapes in a simple grate. Can you provide me with the name of a supplier for the shapes?

A The Platonic Fireplace Company (tel: 020 8891 5904) sells contemporary grates made in either chrome finished steel with a black tray inset, and black steel grids, or a black steel grate and inset tray. Prices range from £220 to £400. To complement the grates, they supply cast geologs (geometric shapes) which come in six varieties – sphere, tetrahedron, cube, cylinder, cone and prism. The company has recently started producing shapes in colours as well as the original dark grey. Shapes cost £180 for six. Both fires and geologs are British and European safety approved. If you are fitting a gas fire, make sure you get a registered fitter to instal it – call 01256 372300 for a Corgi fitter in your area.

Q I hate my 1950s-style fireplace which currently houses a gas fire. I can't afford to have it removed so wondered if I could at least paint the tiles?

A The tiles are far enough from the heat to make it an easy job to renovate them without incurring huge expense. First clean the tiles thoroughly, including the grout. You'll need two coats of tile primer – a litre should be plenty and costs about £7. Then paint the tiles the colour of your choice or, if appropriate, you could even stencil a design on to them. It's probably best to use an oil-based paint as it is very hard-wearing, though it takes about 12 hours to dry.

fireplaces

167

Q I wonder if you could give me the name of stockists of brass and copper heat-resistant paint. We have a lovely gas fire that is spoiled by a worn canopy. We have tried the usual B&Q, Halfords etc, but no luck.

A It depends how hot your gas fire gets. The paint I suggest is one from International and is heat resistant up to 200°C. It can be applied directly on to iron and steel and gives a smooth, glossy protective finish. However, you asked about brass and copper. These are non-ferrous metals and if you use this paint, you must first use a Special Metals Primer that International also do. It works well with aluminium, galvanised metal and chrome. It comes in 250ml and 750ml at £4.29 and £8.49. It takes 30 minutes to be touch-dry and is overcoatable in six hours. The heat resistant enamel paint also comes in 250ml and 750ml sizes at £5.29 and £9.99. It is touch dry in six hours and overcoatable in 24 hours. Call International on 01962 711177 for local stockists. It's not suitable for temperatures of 200°C or more.

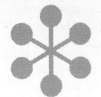

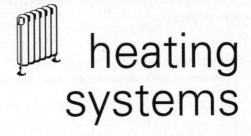

heating systems

Q Where can I purchase radiator covers? The sort I've seen are white, with fretwork in the front.

A The radiator covers you have seen may have been white, but they are simple MDF fretwork and can be painted any colour to match your room. Hundreds of firms make them. Don't forget local suppliers when you are thinking about items like radiator covers. They can often suggest individual little touches that will transform a room. Look in the back of homes magazines to find radiator-cover makers in your area.

Q We have some unsightly radiators that we need to cover. Can we make decorative wooden covers? Where can we find a pattern, or can we buy DIY kits?

A If you want to buy simple and inexpensive covers, then all the DIY superstores do them to fit most standard sizes. There are lots of

heating systems

169

✳ Tessa's tip A company called Cachet has casts metal radiator covers. It has created a range of 13 different pictures that can be incorporated in them, ranging from birds and dragons to Chinese calligraphy and musical instruments, and you can even design your own if you wish. The company says they give out much more heat than MDF covers: those apparently absorb between 20 and 25 per cent of the heat. The metal covers have a heatproof backing cloth behind the casting that creates a convection effect, forcing the air to rise and flow out of the front of the casing. Hundreds of different variations in design are available. The tracery range is cheaper, being made of punched aluminium, and starts from £100, while the average price of a cast one is about £400. Colours can be matched to fit your decor, too. Call Cachet on 01903 756534 for details.

radiator cover specialists who will send you a brochure, but for starters try The Classic Radiator Cover Co. on 01443 477824. If you fancy being a bit more adventurous, why not design a cover and have it made up by a local joiner?

 Q Can you advise me on how to treat a badly rust-stained radiator. I painted it twice with radiator enamel but the stains have reappeared.

A You don't say when you painted your radiator. What you should do if it is rust stained is to make sure any paint on it is six months old and therefore hard before attempting to repaint it. Any newer than this and you could find you get a reaction with the paint you are putting on, so do a test patch first. Any reaction will happen in a few hours. With a stained radiator, you first need to use paint remover to get the radiator back to its original state. Then lightly abraid the surface with sandpaper, wash with detergent and give it a fresh water rinse. Dry thoroughly, then use Hammerite No 1 Rustbeater (£5.15 for 250ml: 1 litre will cover 12 sq m/14 sq yd). This is a primer containing zinc phosphate that will keep the rust at bay. When it is dry, you have two options. You can use Hammerite 'smooth-' or 'hammered-' finish top coat (£5.29 for 250ml: 1 litre will cover 4.5 sq m/5⅓ sq yd). There's a choice of 26 colours. Or you can use Hammerite radiator enamel, which comes in a stain or gloss white finish (RRP £5.69 for 250ml). If you have copper pipes that need painting, Hammerite also makes a special metals primer in red or grey. The red is available at £4.19 for 250ml; the grey comes only in larger sizes. Hammerite products are available in all the DIY superstores and independent hardware stores.

 Q I have recently moved into a new flat and want to colourwash my lounge – but I have a problem with the ugly storage heaters. Can I paint them to blend into my scheme?

A You can paint storage heaters, but you must use a paint that stands up to the heat. Hot Paint by Plasti-Kote withstands up to 650°C, and can also be used on ranges and Agas. It comes in black, white, blue and aluminium, price £7.35 a tin. Super Enamel, also by Plasti-Kote, stands up to 150°C – which should be sufficient for your heaters – and this comes in 39 colours at £4.99 a tin. Most of the big DIY and independent hardware stores sell both paints, but you can call Plasti-Kote on 01223 836400 for your local stockist.

Q I am re-doing the kitchen in my new flat and I have heard of some new type of heating system that doesn't require radiators. Because the kitchen space is very limited, this system sounds like the answer. Can you tell me how it works?

A A system called Kickspace might be what you have heard about. It heats a whole room and is connected to an existing hot-water central-heating system. Giving out the same amount of heat, it can directly replace a radiator. It is a convector heater, so works by blowing out heat, and has two settings, including a boost switch. Kickspace would take up far less space than a traditional radiator and comes in three sizes of grille fronts. Contact Myson Kickspace on 0345 697509.

Q My conservatory is very chilly in the winter, and I am thinking of buying a wood-burning stove for it. What types are available and how much should I expect to pay?

A Unfortunately, because you live in a city, you can burn only smokeless fuel – so no wood, I'm afraid. But don't despair: there are some fabulous multi-fuel stoves on the market in just about any style you could want. If your taste is for modernist loft living, you'll like the amazingly trendy designs by Austroflamm. These come in a wide range of brilliant colours but they are not cheap: expect to pay £1,600 upwards. For a more traditional look Stovax does a range of cast-iron stoves that burn smokeless coal, starting from around £460 including VAT. You will need to install a chimney for these, however, and that could double the cost. Even if you are using an existing chimney, you may need to line it, as these stoves burn fuel very slowly and the smoke corrodes brickwork more than a standard fire grate does. You must have a chimney professional to install a stove, but whichever company you choose should send someone round to assess your needs and give a quote. Stovax are on 01392 474000 and Austroflamm Stoves on 01392 474060. Other good companies to call are Clearview Stoves on 01588 650401 and FrancoBelge on 0121 706 8266.

Q Where do I find out about underfloor heating systems? There is nothing in my Yellow Pages and I don't know where to start looking. Can they be used under 2.5cm (1in) thick slate floors or would that stop the heat travelling through? Also, can they be used upstairs on top of pine floorboards, underneath a carpet?

A Try two companies: Kampmann (tel: 020 8783 0033), and Thermo-Floor (tel: 01243 822058). Thermo-Floor (GB) Ltd supply two types of underfloor heating: electric and low-pressure water. Their electric heating is suitable for a small area such as a bathroom, where you could

heating systems

171

have it fitted for as little as £200. Underfloor water heating is designed for larger areas, and the minimum charge for installing it is £600.

Hard floor surfaces, such as slate, stone or tiles, are ideal for underfloor heating systems as they retain and maximise the radiated heat. Softwood floorboards and carpets are less efficient, radiating about one third less heat for the same amount of power consumed. Also, if you install heating under carpet, make sure you don't have underlay or any rubberised undercoating to the carpet, as this will act as insulation and prevent the heat from rising. The water underfloor heating is at its best when laid in a concrete base, because that retains the heat well. There is much to be said for this type of heating – especially if you are building from scratch and not having to rip up existing floorboards: no radiators to get in the way, no cold spots, just heat rising up through the floor. So, for your slate floors, go for it. But for your upstairs carpeted and floorboarded area, I don't think it is going to work.

Q **I saw some underfloor heating pads somewhere on the television instead of heating pipes. Have you heard anything about them and where can I find them?**

A Have a look in some of the self-build magazines for companies that do underfloor heating. *Build It* magazine is a good start and will give you lots of ideas. Try a company called Warmup who do a taped system that you tape on to the subfloor and then tile over with ceramic or stone tiles. Unlike pipes, you do not have to dig into the subfloor to put it in as the heating element is only 2mm ($\frac{1}{10}$in) thick and absorbs into the tile adhesive. The heater is controlled by a thermostat that maintains the floor temperature you want. Remember that underfloor heating is more expensive to run than gas central heating. But for a bathroom or conservatory floor where you are going to be using tiles, it certainly takes the chill off them. Often people use it in conjunction with radiators rather than instead of. See their website warmup.co.uk or phone them on 0800 318360.

❋ lighting

I still think lighting is one of the most difficult areas to advise people on and the one that most people get wrong all the time. Lighting designers make a fortune advising people on how best to light their rooms and there are all kinds of ways of achieving a good result. Most of them are expensive because lighting is. Some of the high street shops do occasional lights that work well but you have to know what kind of light they will give off.

There are different types of lighting – ambient, task, decorative, accent and kinetic. Ambient gives a general soft glow; task is for specific jobs like reading and sewing; decorative is for fun; accent lighting is when you shine a light on to something specific for effect, and kinetic is natural light from sources like candles. You can choose a crown silvered bulb that throws the light down instead of up. You can go for a halogen light that gives a natural white light; you can go for eco lights that give off a dimmer light but last for hundreds of hours. You need to go into a good lighting shop and ask or buy a lighting book and study it. Unfortunately, most of us inherit any wall lights and the sockets in our homes and have to make do as rewiring is costly and disruptive.

light fittings

Q I'm looking for a supplier of old-fashioned green-shaded reading lamps. I'm not sure what they're called, but you see them all the time on TV. I have looked in lots of lighting shops in the North West, but I can't find the sort I want anywhere.

A The lamps you are thinking of are called directors' lamps. Christopher Wray Lighting does one in solid brass with a green glass trough shade, price £131. Call 020 7736 8434 to find out your nearest branch, or call 020 7384 2888 for a catalogue. Christopher Wray also sells antique lamps and light fittings through its antiques shop (tel: 020 7786 8434), and this sometimes has original directors' lamps for about £400, as well all kinds of 19th- and early 20th-century domestic and ecclesiastical light fittings from Britain and abroad.

Q I like fairy lights all year round, but not of the twinkly, pastel variety. I have seen sets of chilli lights in several home decor magazines but have not been able to find out where I can obtain them. Can you help?

A Call 020 8748 6918. This company sells fairy lights by mail order all year round, unlike the shops that get them in only for Christmas. They have multi-coloured chilli lights called Fiesta and they also come in all red, purple or orange. A new range of nail varnish pink chillies has just come out. The lights cost £28 plus p&p.

Q I saw a light-fitting featured on television for use in a kitchen. It was of the pull-down type with a manufacturer's name starting with Marco. I have made some enquiries locally in lighting shops but they do not know the name. I think the switch had a chrome finish. Can you supply me with more details?

A Call Lighting 2000 on 020 8731 8601. The unit is from the Varco range, is called Marco Decorative and costs £87.50. It is 12 volt and is a single pendant drop fitting that is easy to raise and lower over a kitchen sink or a table. The shades come in three shapes: champagne flute, stepped glass and conical, and is available in blue, yellow, green and frosted. Postage is about £10.

Q We have a lounge-cum-dining room that has an outside window at the dining-room end only. We have lots of lamps but the room is still rather dark. Any bright ideas?

A The sketch you have sent me shows that you have a conservatory at the end of your dining area where all the light comes from. This may seem a radical suggestion, but why not turn your room around and have your lounge in the dining room/conservatory? Logically, a dining room is more likely to be used at night – when you don't need daylight – and the lamps you have will add ambience. Conservatories are no longer just that cold, leaky bit at the end of the house. Move your sofa into it, add a rug and it becomes a bright and cheerful lounge.

Q I am fed up with the lighting in my sitting room: whatever I try to do to create 'mood' never seems to work. When I think I've got a nice soft glow, I suddenly find I want to sit there to read and need a stronger light. Do you have any suggestions?

A You could try the simplest option which is to replace your master switch with a dimmer switch. It's also worth experimenting with different light bulbs – crown-silvered bulbs throw light down on a particular area. For individual lights, uplighters can give a general background light to a room. Small halogen lights carefully positioned to light up a favourite object are also good for creating mood. Try to avoid central ceiling lights, which allow you to see the bulb glaring at you as you sit on your sofa. It is also possible to get all your lights wired to the switch just inside the door, so that when you come into the room and turn on the switch, lights come on all around the room.

Q At the top of my house there is a small, windowless box room. I have tried all kinds of ways to brighten it up, but it still looks dingy and depressing so we

✳ Tessa's tip I saw some chandeliers recently, which I thought extremely pretty. They're from a company aptly called Delusions of Grandeur. The largest one they make – and it's huge – costs £275. But they also do a small size at £38, a medium for £52, and a large, two-tier one for £90. They are hand-made of bent wire with different coloured beads by a husband-and-wife team. They are about to launch two new ranges in the medium size (one tier): one made from a random selection of coins and one made from recycled glass with the opaque look glass has when it's washed up on the beach. They are the same price as the bead ones. Call 01233 750177.

never use it. Have you got any suggestions for ways in which we can overcome this sad state of affairs?

A There is a gadget called Solatube that can bring natural light into any room that has a roof directly above it. It consists of a clear dome attached to a tube with a highly reflective lining; the dome fits on the outside of your roof, and the tube hangs down into the room. Obviously it is only as good as the brightness of the day, but the makers claim that, in ideal conditions, it casts as much light as a 300-watt lamp.

Solatube is easy to install – no more than a couple of hours' work for a competent DIYer – but you have to be prepared to get on the roof so it may not be for everyone. The clear dome will fit most roof surfaces, including composite shingle, Spanish tile, cement tile and slate. You simply remove one tile and replace it with the dome, which is sealed to the roof with flashing. Alternatively, the manufacturers will install it for you. Approximate costs are £250 (plus £100 installation fee) for a 25cm (10in) diameter dome with a 180-210cm (6-7ft) tube. Call 01908 585840 for stockists.

Q Have you any suggestions for some fun lighting for my bathroom? The sight of the bare bulb poking through the present lampshade isn't very relaxing.

A I saw a light shade in a shop the other day that I thought was pretty unusual. When I contacted the company that made it, Columbia Glass, I found they had all kinds of surprising lights. Take, for example, their light called Sputnik. When lit, the light from within the sphere shines out to the glass spikes at the edges, illuminating the tips. If you put a coloured bulb inside, the light is seen as tiny points of colour. Handmade from crystal glass, it measures 340mm (13½in) in diameter and is available as either a table lamp or ceiling light. The company also makes a light called Medusa that has the same crystal

light fittings

177

✳ **Tessa's tip** This tip is for anyone with fluorescent lighting who fancies softening it up a bit: use a coloured tube called Cocoon. All you do is remove the existing fluorescent tube, fit the coloured sleeve over the tube and replace the light. The ambience of a room changes immediately. Originally sold only to shops, it is becoming popular in domestic settings. You can use it equally well underneath wall units in kitchens for a dramatic new look. There are 300 different colours to choose from. It is pretty inexpensive and when you compare it with fibre optics and coloured lights, it is positively cheap. A 120cm (4ft) sleeve costs £9.85; 150cm (5ft), £10.65; and 180cm (6ft), £12.25. Call Formatt Filters on 01685 870979 for more information.

circle with coloured twisted spikes sticking out of it. The spikes come in a host of colours. Call Columbia Glass on 020 7613 5155 for more information – they are constantly coming up with new and unusual designs that would look great in any bathroom.

Q I have a lava lamp from which some of the liquid has leaked. What is the liquid and can I top it up?

A Lava lamps are simply wax in water but I would not recommend trying to repair yours because it is electrical and could be dangerous. However, you can buy a replacement bottle from Mathmos Direct, mail order 020 7549 2700, for £23.95 including p&p, which will fit almost all types. To dispose of your old bottle, make sure the contents are cold and pour the liquid down the drain – the wax will be solid – then throw away the bottle.

Q Where can I buy low-energy light bulbs to fit into ordinary light fittings? Ones I've seen are rather big and ugly.

A The old-style energy-saving bulb is a heavy, rather unattractive thing that doesn't fit easily into many wall light fixtures. Now Osram have introduced the Dulux El Classic that looks the same as an ordinary bulb, fits most fittings and offers the same savings as the old style energy-saver. Available from Waitrose and Somerfield supermarkets and all good lighting stores, they cost £9.99 each. That may seem a lot for one bulb but, over time, the saving is immense. Energy-saving bulbs use 74 per cent less power and can last 15 times longer than conventional ones.

 decorative
details

Q My daughter has imitation brass oil lamps with glass shades in her house. Is there any way of making the brass bases of the lamps look old?

A A product called Tourmaline from Liberon (tel: 01797 367555), is used to age brass, copper and bronze. It is available in brown or black. First use Liberon's cold patination pre-treatment which cleans all the grease and oil off the item. Then dilute the Tourmaline with cold water and dab it on with cotton wool until you get the colour you want. The cold patination treatment costs £3.09 for 125ml and the Tourmaline costs £4.69 for 125ml.

Q I am desperate to find a supplier of brass, dome-shaped light switches. Can you help?

A JD Beardmore is the company you need to contact. If you are struggling with light fittings, it has a huge range to choose from – as well as countless knobs, knockers and other fitments – and the staff are incredibly helpful. The switches that you want are called ZB switch

decorative details

179

✳ Tessa's tip There are some amazing lights from Christopher Wray that you can style for yourself. They are made of thermo-plastic rubber and you can curl them or fold them to give a darker edge to the light. Available in five colours – lime, red, blue, orange and yellow – they are 33cm (13in) tall, and take 25-watt bulbs that give out a soft glow. The lights cost £23.50 each from Christopher Wray (tel: 020 7736 8434). Postage and packing is extra – the amount varies depending on where you live.

Christopher Wray produces a mail-order catalogue showing its huge range of lighting – some 6,000 lights in a wide variety of styles. The catalogue costs £5, plus £2.95 p&p, but it does include a £5 gift voucher. To order a copy, tel: 020 7384 2888.

plates and cost £21.83 plus VAT each. Beardmore also does the wooden block that was traditionally used to mount them on for £7.34 plus VAT. The block comes in either beech or maple. Call Beardmore on 020 7670 1000.

Q **I live in a house built in 1952 and have recently decorated it. I now need new fascia plates for certain light switches but have been unable to find replacements. They are double switches and the plates have circular holes. Is there anything I can do short of rewiring?**

A I think you will have to change the fittings, but it would not mean rewiring the place. I don't think you will be able to find new plates that will go over your old switch fittings as the sizes have all changed. Try a company called A Touch of Brass (tel: 020 7351 2255), who will send a catalogue to you. They have a range of brass and chrome switch fittings in Tudor, Georgian and Regency styles, so there should be something there for you. The only other thing I could suggest is that you look in some of the architectural salvage yards where they may well have some old fittings.

Q **I am renovating an old house, which includes rewiring the whole place. I don't mind some basic new sockets in most of the house but I would like to have something more in keeping with the place where they show in the room. Do you know of any firms that make socket switches that aren't white plastic. I have seen some stainless steel ones, which I like, but they are too modern.**

A I agree with you, especially in sitting rooms or bedrooms, the white plastic fittings can look garish in an old property. Call Period House Group for their catalogue on 01759 373481. They do a whole range of forged iron work from curtain poles, to doors, door and window furniture and even old style nails. Their forged steel plate switches and sockets start from £19.39 plus £4 p&tp and they have every combination you could want, including telephone sockets.

Q **Do you know of any unusual shades for both ceiling lights and tables? I find these most difficult to buy locally as everything seems to be so similar. Where could I find something a little bit different?**

A I agree with you that lampshades are extremely difficult to get right. You could try customising a standard shade by embroidering it with blanket stitching around the edges, painting it or sticking paper cut-outs on it to create a découpage design. But if you want to buy something, why not try one of textile designer Isabel Stanley's sweet

lighting

lampshades, above right? These are made with coloured ribbons of petersham, satin or velvet, and start from £34. Call her on 020 7209 2101 for details.

Q **I am writing to see if you can give me any help regarding fly marks on lampshades. We live on a farm where the cattle buildings are close to our house and flies come in through the doors and windows. I have three fabric lampshades that are badly marked and I have tried to clean them without success.**

A I too have failed to get marks off fabric lampshades. I assume you have tried using the froth from a gentle detergent but, if this doesn't work, I can only suggest that you cover the shade in some way. What you do will depend on the look of your rooms and where the lampshades are. For example, you could try your hand at fabric painting – Dylon Colour Fun Soft Fabric Paints might jazz your shades up a bit. You could also try stitching buttons to the shades to cover the marks. Then there's découpage – gluing pictures that you like to the shade. PVA glue is best for the job and you can use a coat of clear matt varnish once the glue is dry. However, I have a sneaky feeling that none of these ideas will be what you really want. You can get good quality lampshades at quite reasonable prices these days – BHS has a good selection. I suggest you might try some parchment shades, which will prove a lot easier to wipe clean. The only other thought for cleaning lampshades – baby wipes – they do lift stains from carpets sometimes – so have a go.

decorative details

181

❋ Tessa's tip Coming home from a week in the country, I saw the most beautiful crystal hanging in a friend's window. As the morning light came through, it refracted through the crystal and sent amazing rainbow colours splashing all around the room. I've never been susceptible to the power of crystals before, but the light from this one gave me a real lift. So my tip this week is to find a crystal – or a group of them – and hang it where it will catch the light. All you have to do then is to admire the effect. The more facets on the crystal, the better, as it means there are more angles for the light to spin off. Devotees of feng shui believe that light is a powerful way of activating the chi energy in the home and you can buy them through the Feng Shui Catalogue. Call 020 8992 6607 to order.

Q Is there a store in the London area that sells unusual standard lampshades? Department stores all seem to carry plain, 1950s styles.

A Ann's Lighting (tel: 020 7937 5033) is a great shop that makes lampshades to order in silk, parchment, card or laminated fabric. Its staff can also re-cover old frames and copy original frames and fittings. The shop has a selection of designs and fabrics to choose from, or you can provide your own fabric and trims. If you want to come up with your own design, they will make it for you. Price obviously depends on size and fabric chosen. Allow 4-6 weeks for orders to be made up.

Q Where can I find lampshade frames for making my own lampshades? I have looked on the Internet but can only find suppliers in the US.

A Fred Aldous is a company I have mentioned before because it is excellent for all kinds of craft items. It does a full range of lampshade frames: as an example, coolie frames cost from £3.32 for a 250mm base; the drum shape starts at £1.22 for a 140mm diameter and 115mm height. It also stocks empire, bowed empire and bowed tulip styles. If you are interested in crafts in any way, its catalogue is a must. Call the company on 0161 236 2477.

✳ storage

People write endless books about storage –

indeed, I have written one too. Storing your stuff has become hip and trendy and the items you can buy for storage is hip and trendy too. Whether you are into baskets, boxes, plastic containers, dividers, trunks, built-in fancy wardrobes for your shoes and clothes, pop-up televisions that appear from a chest at the end of the bed, shelving or filing systems, there is something for you out there. Most of us need to be organised to survive the clutter that we generate in our lives. Many of us work from home and need to have efficient systems to survive.

The market has changed so dramatically in the last ten years and you really can get storage in any colour or material to suit your taste. I still think that some of the more inexpensive products on the market work just as well as the pricier versions, but it depends on the look you want to achieve.

The stylists in the magazines are responsible for making us believe you should have everything in lines and neatly stacked, but is that what you want to achieve? It is all attainable and I must say that when you live in a tidy house, it does make you feel better. I always fall short – three small children don't understand neat lines – so my advice is to try not to be too obsessive about it or you will constantly feel you are failing. Remember that when you see the photos in the magazines, they tidy up before they take the pictures. And they don't live in it afterwards.

184

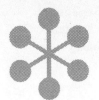

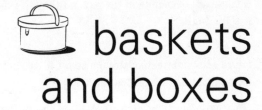 baskets
and boxes

Q Have you got any good tips for sorting out washing? I have a permanent mess in my laundry area which looks horrible and I would like to tidy it up.

A It's best to have your laundry basket in the bedroom so that it's nearby when you're changing clothes and bedding. I like the idea of linen baskets because they're not only attractive but can be folded up when not in use, so are space-saving too. They are available in two sizes: divide up into three sections for different coloured washes.

Q We are both in the media and by the end of the week our flat is strewn with magazines and newspapers. Can you suggest a practical, stylish and unobtrusive method of storing them?

A I know exactly what you mean – and magazine racks are back in the shops. The Conran Shop (tel: 020 7589 7401) has plywood ones in soft blue, green or natural. I recently bought a great fifties' cane and plastic basket in a junk shop for my papers. It has a handle which reminds me I have to take the papers to the recycling bin each week.

Q I am saving newspapers one for each of my grandson's birthdays until he is 18. I wonder if you could tell me how I could store them to ensure that they don't go yellow-brown colour?

A As paper is made from mechanical wood pulp you should keep it away from sunlight. The best method to vacuum pack them as it is the oxygen in the air that turns them yellow coloured. Lakeland Plastics do a vacuum pack for storing clothes and I don't see why it wouldn't work for your newspapers. They do two sizes: large which is 56 x 84cm (22 x 33in) for £5.95 and jumbo 90 x 120cm (36 x 48in) for £9.95. All you do is put the papers inside the bag. Then attach your vacuum cleaner nozzle to the hole in the top of the bag and suck out the air. Then put a stopper on the hole. Call Lakeland on 015394 88100. Remember it is the humidity in the air that attacks paper so always keep it below 70 degrees. Make sure that you don't fold the newspapers as the folds create weaknesses over time in the paper. I think it's a great idea for a present. Fascinating!

Q **I need some interesting storage boxes to add colour to my room, which is mostly black and white. Can you help?**

A Your local branch of Habitat should have plenty of colourful boxes. Alternatively, try mail order. The Holding Company (tel: 020 7610 9160) and Paperchase (tel: 020 7467 6200) both have an extensive range of brightly coloured storage boxes suitable for all your needs. There's no excuse for dullness and clutter!

Q **We have very little cupboard space. Can you suggest some cheap and cheerful storage ideas that won't take up too much room?**

A Look at the space you do have and work out what is wasted. First, throw away anything you don't use. Separate your summer and winter wardrobe and store what you aren't using in clear, zippered bags (to stop moths) in high spaces or under the bed. Buy a set of thin hangers for the wardrobe – bulky ones take up valuable room. Or make a feature of a pile of attractive storage boxes – Habitat do a great range in all colours. A useful tip – have a special place for everything and remember to use it.

baskets and boxes

---

* Tessa's tip I love baskets and have hundreds of them at home for every conceivable thing. I've just discovered someone who is as nutty as I am about them. Nick Smyth of Chairworks has 20,000 sq ft stuffed full of baskets of every sort. His laundry basket is just one of the shapes he does that I like. It costs £49.95 and is made of plastic wrapped around grass. I was also particularly taken with a potato basket that Nick saw being used while out in China and had made up. It costs £22.95 and also comes in chocolate colour. Chairworks do an extensive range in their mail-order catalogue, which you can get by phoning 020 7498 7611. Basket making is one of the few crafts that has remained unchanged for centuries and a basket in your home lasts for years. Nick's baskets come in willow, rattan, wicker and bamboo and range from traditional shopping bags to a whole host of storage containers. The garden range has wood flower trugs in several sizes. Carriage costs £3 for two items.

---

storage

Q I am making some small boxes for storage and have been unable to obtain any small, high-quality hinges and clasps. Can you help me locate a supplier?

A A fast-growing superstore called Hobby Craft is devoted to everything you could want in the arts and crafts world. Their range is huge - 40,000 items for more than 150 crafts. When I spoke to them, they did have the hinges and clasps you're looking for, but it's best to check before you go as their stock is ever-changing. They also organise demonstrations and workshops in store that will suit all grades of workers from beginners to experts, and these cost between £5 and £7. The workshop programme changes every four months, with seasonal activities during half-terms and other holidays. To check the whereabouts of your nearest Hobby Craft, call Freefone 0800 0272387.

Q I have moved into a rented flat and I want to find a stick on soap tray for the shower. I can't start drilling holes in the tiles and there isn't room for those huge things that go over the showerhead for everything. I can't find one anywhere. Do you know where I can get one?

A There are all sorts of brightly coloured plastic soap dishes that stick on the shower, but most of them don't work. It is extremely irritating when products that are designed to do something specific don't do their job, but I can recommend on extremely stylish soap dish that will work perfectly for your shower. Go to Muji. They have a chrome basket that has two suckers that stick through the chrome dish and attach to the shower. It is very simple and it works. It costs £5.50 from all Muji stores. Call them on 020 7437 7503 and they will tell you your nearest store.

baskets and boxes

187

❃ Tessa's tip I have had many inquiries about where to find attractive, practical vessels to suit modern as well as traditional interiors. I think Karamica's metallic vases fit the bill. As well as curved shapes, Keramica also produce square-sided vases that can be postioned flush against a wall to save space on narrow shelves and mantelpieces, and are shortly introducing a tableware range. The company designs and manufactures all its own styles, and they have some amazing glazes. Prices are from £30. Call the company on 01782 207206.

hanging and hiding

Q Do you know where I can buy a clothes airer? I live in a flat where outdoor clothes lines are banned, but I have found an airer invaluable. My old one came from a mail-order firm that no longer sells them.

A You need the Lakeland Ltd storage catalogue. They do all kinds of storage products, including the Capri drying rack in white metal at £14.95, which is like a fold-up ironing board with a horizontal wire top for hanging jumpers. They also do the traditional concertina clothes dryer in wood for the same price. Call them for a catalogue on 015394 88100.

Q My son has a collection of more than 400 CDs, which is still growing. They are kept in a motley array of storage units that hold various numbers of CDs from 20 to 64, and take up valuable floor and surface space. Is there shelving for CDs, preferably horizontal, which would not be too expensive or difficult to install?

A There are all sorts of CD storage systems around but many of them can take up too much space if you have a serious collection, as your son does. I would get your son to put up some simple shelves –

✳ Tessa's tip

I don't know what to tell you about first in the new Ocean catalogue - I think so many of the products in it are just plain gorgeous. Order a copy and browse through it and you will definitely find something you need and love – especially if you are looking for storage ideas. I am rather partial to the beech hanging stool, which is a good example of the stylish and practical designs they offer. It costs £49 and it is a useful item that can be easily accommodated into anyone's decor. Check the catalogue's garden furniture range too - there are some beautiful slatted benches and chairs that fold up easily for winter.

Of all the mail-order catalogues around at the moment, this one is especially well thought out. It has a wide range of prices, too, with items from £10 to £1300. To order yourself a copy, call Ocean on 0870 242 6283.

---

make sure you get good strong brackets. Keep the space between the shelves to a minimum. Some simple 18mm (¾in) thick pine or plywood should do the trick. If you decide vertical storage really isn't beyond the pale, Ikea do a more capacious type. Try the Skallid range – £19 lacquer and black; colours £26 – which hold 112 CDs.

Q I live in a one bedroom, first-floor flat that is overdue for a spring clean and redecoration. I have so much clutter and furniture, but no garden, spare room or even a passageway in which to store it. Is there a company that would crate and store some of my belongings for a short period and then help me put it back again?

A Most removal firms provide a storage service too. In your area try Crispins on 020 7739 0303. Without seeing the contents of your flat, the prices are only estimates but for a first-floor flat expect to pay in the region of £300-£400 for crating your possessions and removing them, and then another £20-£25 per week for storage. All prices plus VAT. Insurance costs £1 per £1,000 of goods. For anyone with a similar query in other areas, try a national firm like Pickfords. It's always worth getting a couple of quotes. Obviously it will cost you more per week to store for a short time rather than for a year or so. And the price depends on what you are crating up – antiques and delicate items cost more to store.

Q I have a very small kitchen and no room for a bin in it. I have seen something that can be attached to the back of the kitchen sink door which you can put a plastic bag on and use as a bin, but I can't find one anywhere. Can you help me?

A Yes, try a company called Betterware on 0845 143 1010. They do a carrier bag bin which you simply screw on to the back of the

hanging and hiding

189

❋ **Tessa's tip** If you want something a little different and very stylish to hang your hat and coat on, try the latest hook design from Coexistence (tel: 020 7354 8817 or www.coexistence.co.uk) for all the amazing furniture and accessories they offer. I know a coat hook could be seen as a purely functional item but, when it doesn't have coats and hats on it, it's very nice to see a good-looking one. And it is usually one of the first things you see when you come into the home. The one hook offers lots of options for storage – smaller children's coats at the bottom and a large rounded hook to hang a couple of adult coats on without destroying their shape. And with the shelf above there's a perfect safe place at the top for hats. It comes in a painted black, white or aluminium finish and costs £45.

door. It is basically a ring which you then fit your plastic bag into. The bag is the bin effectively. Theirs is 33cm (13in) across by 18cm (7in) wide so make sure you have 18cm (7in) deep behind the door to allow it to close properly. The actual ring is 8.2cm (3¼in) high. It costs £4.99 and can be ordered on a Freephone number – 0500 555667.

Q My attic is soon to be converted into a spacious bedroom with en-suite bathroom, for my six-year-old son. Can you suggest practical and inspired decorating and furnishing ideas for the new room or recommend a good publication for children's rooms?

A Lucky six-year-old is what I say! En-suite bathroom. I'm not sure that anything I can suggest will match up but here goes. Having a six-year-old myself, I know that the most important things are not what you want. They want hidey holes, spaces under the bed for crawling in with their friends, lots of cushions to throw and make dens out of. They need storage and I recommend lots of plastic boxes that can be stored full of Lego, Duplo, farm animals, space equipment, plastic food and implements, not to mention all those dressing-up clothes. Then they need somewhere to put shoes so they can find them.Ikea do very good shoe racks for £9. Then they need book shelves. I suggest you do not go for anything built in as children's needs change as they get older. Think of the room as totally moveable. If you are putting electrical sockets in, put in plenty to allow them to change the position of their bed, desk and everything else. i would paint it in a neutral colour and let their own art and possessions – posters, photos, memorabilia – inhabit the walls, rather than what you would probably prefer; a tasteful colour. Children should be allowed to express themselves and where better than their bedroom, so don't expect it to look like your sitting room. Buy jolly duvet colours, get lots of brightly coloured cushions, use fairy lights to make it magical and you can't go far wrong. As far as books go, I would just hunt in a good bookshop and browse through the magazines – the styles vary so much – it is what you can bear and what your budget will allow. Just remember that your child will be eight in two years and want something totally different.

✳ outdoors

The outdoors is just as important as the indoors.

No self-respecting garden would be without its water feature, unusual bench, mosaic table – oh and, of course, some plants! Many of you want to know how to fix hammocks, put in ponds, stop the herons from eating the goldfish, colour the concrete patio, and that eternal question – can you paint white UPVC furniture a different colour? Well I think the answer to that question has to be no, it will look terrible even though many of you have told me you have done and it looks great – I'm still reserving judgement.

People also want to know how to get the old ivy suckers off the wall, how to clean mortar and oil stains off the ground, how to stop sleepers oozing tar and where to get willow fencing. It seems that the outdoors presents as many problems as inside the home.

If you have an old house and you are renovating it, I am passionate about doing it properly. Check with the local council and get names of recommended craftspeople. You need the right materials – from the lime mortar to the paint. People also ruin the look of houses by putting in the wrong type of windows. There is a wealth of information around and your local council's historical buildings department is the first call you need to make. For most of our houses, we still need to use the right products because you will save yourself money in the long run. Preparation is the key to everything in the decorating world. Do that and it will last.

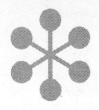

 furniture

Q I have a bamboo garden sofa and chair that have been left lying around in the garage. A combination of grandchildren bouncing on them and the attentions of our cat means the cushions are no longer usable. Can you tell me if it's possible to buy replacement ones?

A If you want cushions that fit the shape exactly you will have to have them made up, but it shouldn't cost you too much. Get an upholsterer to make up some foam cushion seats for you. I take it you will be using them in the garden, so you won't want feather. Or you could just buy a whole host of white scatter cushions. Never throw what is basically good furniture like this away – you can usually revamp it.

Q We have a three-seater teak garden bench that is 25 years old but still in good basic condition. Initially we used teak oil at regular intervals, but after a time the colour changed. We sanded it down and put on what we thought would be an ideal protection – varnish – but this flaked off. Last year we had it stripped, but have done nothing with it since. How can we get it back into good condition?

A Teak furniture does weather well, but you probably went wrong by putting varnish on your bench and possibly the teak oil in the first place. You would have done better to have let it weather naturally to a silver/grey finish. If you use oil you should apply it to a clean surface before it has started to weather, and wipe away any surplus oil immediately.

Q How can I polish out the scratch marks on my plastic patio table?

A Why don't you try using Brasso. It sounds strange, but it takes off the top surface of the plastic paint and lessens the scratch marks. The other thing to try is T-Cut, which is used to polish cars. It also takes off the top coat, but to be honest this is the only way you're

furniture

193

going to be able to reduce the scratches. T-Cut is available in Halfords and most supermarkets.

Q I have a set of white plastic garden furniture which, although in good condition, defies cleaning. I would like to paint it, but have been told that this cannot be done. Can it?

A There's nothing to stop you painting anything – what it would look like is a different story. The mass market garden furniture you see is heavily plasticised UPVC. It's specially made to be flexible and smooth and no paint on the market is going to stick to it for long. Try light sanding, then undercoat and put a gloss paint on top. But as the chair heats up and cools down, it will start to crack off. If you really hate the white chairs, splash out and buy another colour. They come in all sorts of colours including green and blue. Painted plastic chairs would turn your relaxing rest in the garden into irritation. Don't do it!

Q I have a circular patio table with a latticed top made of some sort of plastic or resin. This used to be white, but it has weathered badly – even though it's stored away in winter – and is now grey. Can you suggest a white paint suitable for plastic, or some other way of renovating it? I have tried a PVC cleaner and a few other products, but with no luck. If I paint the top, it needs to be with something durable.

A So for all of you with tired tables and chairs, I suggest Plasti-Kote all-purpose spray paint. This is solvent-based, which makes it extremely durable. Clean your table thoroughly before spraying, then put at least two coats of polyurethane varnish over the top, and your table should look like new. The Plasti-Kote range comes in 39 colours and costs £4.99 a tin. It's available at all the DIY superstores – but if you have any problems getting hold of it phone the manufacturers on 01223 836400 and ask for your local stockist.

Q I have a lovely, old metal bench that has deteriorated badly during the winters it has been left out in the garden. Can I restore it or do you know someone who can do it for me?

A After recent press reports about the potential dangers of removing lead paint, I would send your bench away for restoration. Oxley's Furniture Restoration Services (tel: 01386 840466) will send a written quote for collecting, restoring and redelivering if you send them a photo of your bench. The process includes shot or blasting to remove old paintwork, dust and grease. The new metal is prepared, primed and resurfaced in either stove enamel or polyester powder, depending on its future use. They can match colour samples or even do a verdigris finish.

Q I used to have a deckchair with a canopy – great for enjoying a sunny day without getting burned. Are these still made, and do you know where can I get one?

A John Lewis's Steamer deckchair has a canopy and a footstool – so you can really relax in the garden! Priced at £95, it is made of wood and covered in green canvas. Call John Lewis on 020 7629 7711 to find out where your nearest store is.

Q Do you have a simple solution for cleaning the green mildew off my white-painted aluminium garden furniture?

A The best tip for cleaning any garden furniture is to make sure you do it at least once a year. That way, the general grime and grease from the air doesn't have time to destroy the paintwork. To clean mildew, I would suggest a mild detergent in warm water and, if it doesn't come off immediately, keep battling away.

To restore flaking paint on aluminium furniture. First clean the surface and remove all the old, flaking paint. Then apply a Special Metals Primer, available from International. Allow to dry for six hours, then use Japlac, from the same company, which is a high-gloss enamel paint suitable for exterior use. A 750ml tin of primer costs £8.49 and a 500ml tin of Japlac is around £7.49. Both products are available in most DIY stores but if you have any difficulty finding either call 01962 711177 to find your nearest stockist.

I've also had a similar enquiry about removing green mould from the Perspex roof of her conservatory. As with garden furniture, you should use nothing stronger than mild detergent in warm water. If the mould is still there after repeated cleanings, add just a touch of bleach to the soapy water and leave it to soak into the mould. Only use a soft cloth to clean the Perspex, otherwise you'll scratch the surface and only succeed in providing an even happier place for the mould to live. There are no suitable chemicals for this problem I'm afraid – just good old elbow grease!

furniture

195

Q My wife and I were married last August and as a wedding gift a relative kindly agreed to buy us a mosaic table for outdoor use. However, we are still unable to find a company that will deliver or make one to our specifications. The table needs to be big enough for two people to dine at and our budget is roughly £250. Those we have seen have a wrought-iron base and a round top. Any ideas?

A You will not find a company to make a mosaic table to commission for your budget, I'm afraid. What I suggest you do is make it yourself. I have made a mosaic table in a weekend with someone helping me. Designing it yourself would be much more fun and far more romantic than getting it made for you. Simply get a blacksmith to make up the iron base to your design. You will also need an MDF base for the table-top, which you can get a timber merchant to cut to size for you. The tiles can be bought from the Mosaic Workshop on 020 7263 2997. They have a mail-order catalogue of all the tiles that they stock. They have a vast range of colours and sizes for you to choose from. Otherwise, you can break up floor tiles and make a random pattern, which is even cheaper. The basic ingredients should cost you about £150. For the pattern, call the Dover Bookshop on 020 7836 2111 for a catalogue. They have books with Roman designs, Arab designs and patterns on Victorian tiles. Once you've chosen a design, sketch it out on the MDF and then test out your pattern with the tiles. If you are happy with it, use a PVA glue to stick the tiles to the base. It is best to work from the middle out. You will need tile nippers to cut your tiles to the correct shape. Leave the table to dry for four hours before grouting. Use grey grout as this has a more subtle appearance. Wipe away the excess grout with a damp cloth before it dries.

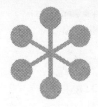

 walls

Q The previous owner of our house spilled paint in several places on the exterior brickwork – which is stock brick. Is there anything we can use to remove the paint?

A Try a spirits of salt solution (made with hydrochloric acid). This is often used on patios, and you can get it at builder's merchants. Paint stripper may work but, because brickwork is uneven, it's sometimes difficult to get it into all the cracks. One product that will definitely do the trick is called Peel Away. It's like putty and you can squeeze it into all those tricky spaces. You spread it over the surface and cover it with a special tissue, wait until it dries, then peel it off. There are three types available, for alkaline, solvent-based and whitewash/cementwash paints. You can also use Peel Away for removing paint from wood, plain plaster walls, wallpaper, cornicing, cast iron and even car bodywork. Make sure you speak to the company first about your exact requirements, and always follow the instructions on the label. Peel Away is made by Palace Chemicals Ltd, Langlow Division, on 0151 486 6101. It's also available from Focus Do It All.

Q We have a corrugated iron garage, built about 45 years ago. It was originally a dull black and we repainted it forest green two or three years ago. This paint is now peeling off and the whole garage needs repainting. What do we use?

A You need to get the old paint off first. Once you have removed this with wire wool, buy a two-pack etch primer, mix it together and paint a thin layer over the garage. This gives a good base for paint to stick to. It's probably what you forgot to do the last time you painted it. Then paint with a good-quality, oil-based paint. It should last longer than your previous attempt.

walls

197

Q I want to smarten up the outside of my house, which, at present, is a mixture of grotty render and unsightly mismatching brickwork. Any suggestions?

A Just paint it. We painted the back of a rendered and pebble-dashed house in a deep lilac for *Home Front in the Garden.* It's so simple to do. The major drawback, of course, is that paint is hard to remove if you later decided you don't want it. Dulux (tel: 01753 550555) suggest Weathershield for both brickwork and pebble dash.

Q The rendering on the outside of my house looks drab and grey. What type of paint can I use to brighten it up?

A That depends on the age and style of your home and where you live. The first rule is: be sympathetic to the architecture. For rendered houses, limewash is ideal because it does not seal the surface of the masonry and also retains the character of the place. Limewash comes in a range of colours. Try Anglia Lime (tel: 01787 313974), Potmolen Paints (tel: 01985 213960), Rose of Jericho (tel: 01935 83676) or Farrow & Ball (tel: 020 7351 0273). For newer houses, masonry paint is the usual choice. Check out Dulux's Weathershield range or Sandtex's textured masonry paint – both available in DIY stores.

Q My daughter has bought a lovely old terraced house in North Yorkshire. It needs lots of work both inside and out, and the first job she wants to tackle is to remove the flaking white paint from the exterior brickwork. What could she use for this purpose? Money is tight and she would be prepared to tackle it bit by bit.

A I admire your daughter's determination but I'm not sure this is a job for an amateur. Why not repaint? Simply clean down the flaking areas and use exterior emulsion paint and a rough surface paintbrush. Section the house in vertical strips and finish each painting session at a feature such as a window or door so any variations won't be too noticeable.

If your daughter is determined to clean off the paint herself, and has masses of time on her hands, she'll have to hire scaffolding and a hot-water pressure steamer. A company called Strippers (tel: 01787 371524) will identify the paint on the house if you post them a scraping, and they can send you the correct stripper. To have the job done by a professional will cost you between £25 and £60 a square metre, and a small house front is about 25 square metres. I'd say it was money well spent!

Q I am plagued by youngsters spraying graffiti on my garage door, and repainting it just seems to offer them a blank page to start again. Are there any preparations or paints I can use that will stop their paint adhering to mine?

A Try a company called Coo-Var (tel: 01482 328053). They sell an anti-graffiti coating called Coo-Var P101, which you can apply over water-based paint, gloss or varnish. It comes in a two-pack that you have to mix together carefully. Simply paint your garage door in the colour of your choice, then apply the coating over the top. It is a very high-gloss varnish that allows graffiti to be removed by using a special aerosol or gel, also made by Coo-Var. Simply spray, or spread the gel, over the graffiti and it breaks down the paint. Coo-Var stresses that it works with most graffiti but there may be some paints that are resistant. If you have to remove graffiti constantly, the aerosol may eventually start to break down the high-gloss finish and then you will need to rub back the area with wet-and-dry paper and recoat the whole garage door once more. The coating costs £27 for 1kg and £109 for 4.5kg. The aerosol and gel cost £5.50 each. You can order these products at a decorators' merchant; call Coo-Var to find your local stockist. Dulux also make an anti-graffiti product but it is very expensive. It would take you about three days to apply and involves putting on a two-coat sealer, a two-coat primer, a two-coat topcoat and then an anti-graffiti remover. Unfortunately, they all come in minimum amounts of 5 litres and the total price of the set amounts to around £280. If you decide to use the Dulux product, it may well be worth getting a painter/decorator in to do the job for you.

Q We recently removed a carport from the side of our house but the work has left a very unsightly layer of bitumen on the brickwork. Any advice on how to remove it?

A Use something called Stain-Away, an alkaline solution that lifts and softens hardened layers, making them removable with water. It will work on bitumen, although the job might require a few goes, and will also remove glues, oils, grease, paints on concrete, varnish and other stains. Stain-Away is lethal stuff so do take care when using it as it will melt your wellingtons. A litre of it costs £16.58, plus VAT. In your area, Clewer Cleaning Services (tel: 01923 268139), stocks Stain-Away and will do the job for you if you want. For details of local stockists elsewhere in Britain, call Casdron, the UK suppliers of Stain-Away (tel: 01962 732126).

walls

199

Q We have just had a beautiful new kitchen fitted which I love. The only problem is, the window above the sink and food preparation area overlooks the garage wall. The other window and outside door look into our lovely garden and I'm getting a crick in my neck just trying to get a better view. Can you suggest some way of making the garage wall more pleasing to the eye?

A My first thought is whoever planned and designed your kitchen for you should be shot. When installing a new kitchen, the top rule in my book is, make sure the washing-up area overlooks a window. Sadly you are now stuck with a brick wall. However there are a couple of solutions you could opt for. You could paint the wall a more attractive colour: Dulux do a range of colourful paints suitable for brick, called Weathershield Waterseal. Or – and this is the one I would prefer – get a mural artist to paint you a beautiful trompe l'oeil landscape so at least you can imagine you are looking at a garden. Commissioning an established mural artist starts in the region of £800, but you would have a fantastic talking point for your home and a treat for your eyes.

Q I recently cut down an ivy that had grown to about 2.7m (9ft) high on one of my outside walls. Although the area now looks much neater, the brickwork is badly marked. I have tried wire-brushing and scraping the bricks but to no avail. Do you know of any method or material to clean the brickwork?

A Try using masonry cleaner or paint stripper in a diluted form. You should check the instructions first to make sure the product will not dissolve your bricks – some of these strippers are very strong. Treating your bricks in this way will remove some of their colour, but there is a product called Brickmatch that will restore it. You can buy this from the Brick Centre (tel: 01246 260001). They say it's a bit like dirt in a can, and you just paint or sponge it on. Brickmatch comes in light, medium and dark tones and costs £26 plus VAT for 1 litre, which is enough to cover about 400 bricks or 6.6 sq m (7³/₄ sq yd) of wall. Incidentally, if you have graffiti on your walls, the same techniques can be applied to remove it.

floors

Q In front and behind our house are paving flags that need a good clean. How can I bring them back to their best? Any suggestions?

A Once you have tried scrubbing off all the surface dirt and debris that builds up on these slabs, you can buy a patio cleaner from any DIY store. There are various kinds of makes but any should lift the mould and algae deposits. Seal with a patio sealer. Alternatively, hire a high pressure jet spray and attack with that. The best way to keep dirt at bay on patio slabs is to clean them regularly so the dirt doesn't have time to build up.

Q My garden path is laid with paving slabs, and when wet it is like a skating rink. How can I make it safer?

A Keep the path clean and avoid the build-up of mossy, slippery deposits: for a thorough hosing down, hire a high-pressure water jet. Alternatively, clean paving stones with a warm solution of soda crystals.

Q My patio is suffering from old age. The slabs are alternate pink and white, but they're worn and stained with lichen and dirt from passing traffic. I can't afford to have the area re-paved and would appreciate any renovation ideas.

A Precast concrete slabs can start to look pretty tired. Try the cleaning products available in DIY stores for concrete slabs – there are plenty around. See how much dirt comes off with scrubbing. Car accessory shops such as Halfords also have detergents for grease, tar and oil removal. I've read that cat litter can lift recent tar stains – worth a try. Alternatively, try to distract attention from the slabs. Buy some large terracotta pots and fill them with trailing ivy and cheerful flowers such as pelargoniums or daisies.

floors

201

Q What do you suggest I lay on top of concrete slabs that are beneath slide/swings/climbing frame for your children. And where can I purchase it?

A Try a company called Park Leisure (tel: 01233 733782). They do a recycled tile made from shredded car tyres in various thicknesses from 20mm to 80mm (¾in to 3¼in)- obviously, the higher the equipment, the thicker the tile you will need to – heaven forbid – break any fall. They come in 1-metre squares and start at £17.50 a tile for the 20mm (¾in) thick version. There's a £50 delivery charge, plus £27 for the glue you will need to stick them to concrete. These tiles can only be laid on a concrete surface.

Q I want to make a Japanese style garden but I can't find the right sort of gravel. I'd like to use a light creamy colour but all I ever see in garden centres are pinks and greys. Do you have any suggestions?

A A company called Natural Collection (tel: 01952 254101) does a whole selection of coloured gravels, including an almost white one called 'cream spa'. This is in their more expensive range, which costs £110 per ton (as against £49.99 for the cheapest), but there are discounts for bulk purchase. The best grade of gravel for drives and gardens is 14mm (½in), and it should always be laid on a flat surface over a weed-proof membrane.

Q We would love to decorate our garden with really bright stones or pebbles, or special glass. Do you know where we can get anything like this from?

A Garden centres now stock all kinds of brightly coloured gravels and pebbles. Phone your local one to see what they have. There's also a company called House of Marbles (tel: 01626 835358), that

❋ **Tessa's tip** Decking, as we've found so often on *Home Front in the Garden*, instantly transforms the most ordinary patch into something a bit special. Even a small patio, perhaps with pots, can encourage you to make more use of your garden. If you have children, a deck can provide a mud-free play space in winter. Be aware, though, that it may become slippery after rain, so take care with small children. Provided a deck is scrubbed occasionally, it should weather well and age beautifully. You can colour the wood too – Ronseal does 12 deck colours as well as deck sealer, oil and cleaner to help you look after the wood. Many garden centres and DIY superstores now stock decking so start by having a look there. Call the Timber Decking Association (tel: 01977 679812), for advice on the best type of wood for your garden.

floors

202

specialises in all kinds of glass nuggets for your garden. They do a mail-order range of lustre or clear glass in green, light blue, dark blue, turquoise, black, peach, gold and plum. A pyramid pack containing 25-30 nuggets costs £1.99-£2.99, small tubs with 40-50 nuggets in them cost £1.99-£2.99 and large tubs with approximately 180 nuggets are £3.99-£5.99. Add £3.95 p&tp for orders under £50 (orders over £50 are free).

Q A concreted area at the back of our house looks cold and drab. I would like to brighten it up with paint, but my husband insists that concrete paint would flake and look even worse. Any suggestions?

A Standard concrete paints do not 'breathe', and this is what your husband is probably thinking of. Even when used on internal floors, it can start to peel if exposed to water. Try instead an acrylic matt paint by Potmolen Paint (tel: 01985 213960). Available in a wide range of colours, it gives a smooth finish to concrete, cement, render or stucco. For best results, don't begin work on frosty or damp days. Fill any holes in the concrete and clean it thoroughly first. Then apply a thinned coat of paint and leave to dry for about four hours. Finish with an undiluted top coat. Four hours later, the transformation should be complete.

Q Leading up to our front door there are seven steps made of cement slabs. Over the years they have become mottled and stained, and no amount of scrubbing with bleach, or powerwashing, seems to improve them. Is there some sort of paint I could use on them – or have you any other ideas?

A There's really only one paint that I would recommend for this sort of job. It's a microporous acrylic matt made by Potmolen Paints. One litre of white costs £11.37 and colours cost £11.44. You can use it not only on cement but also on concrete, stucco and even old paintwork. Don't apply it during damp or frosty weather, and leave it at least five hours before allowing it to get wet. If there are deep holes in the cement, fill them first with lime mortar. Any mould should be treated first with Potmolen's Neutralizer. Call Potmolen on 01985 213960 for your nearest stockist.

floors

203

Q Do you have any advice on how to remove moss from Tarmac? Someone suggested Jeyes Fluid. Also, a film of moss is building up on the roof of our house. We have had it scraped but the moss has come back and is spreading rapidly. Is there anything we can spray on the moss to kill it without damaging the tiles?

A There used to be a moss cleaner you could buy, but it has been taken off the market because it was found to be carcinogenic. That is the trouble with many powerful agents. Whoever told you about Jeyes Fluid was correct. It is definitely worth trying as it is a gentle but tough cleaner. It is widely used in dog kennels for cleaning so safe to use. More specialised cleaners, such as Pathclear, that are designed to clear weeds from Tarmac, paths and patios, are also available. If you have small children and animals, I would not let them near the path until the stuff is dry and even for a few days after that. If it can kill weeds, it probably contains chemicals that are best avoided. I am always cautious about any product for the garden that kills things as you don't know where it will end up. I would go for scraping and a high pressure water jet to loosen the moss first. If anyone has any environmentally friendly ideas, I would welcome them: this seems to be a common problem.

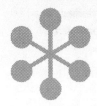 decorative
details

Q I want to make some cushions for our garden chairs, but most of the practical 'outdoor' fabrics seem to be rather shiny and unattractive-looking. All the fabrics I like best would spoil in the rain – and I'd worry about food stains every time we had a barbecue. Any suggestions?

A I think I can help. Try Scotchguard Protector for Fabrics – an aerosol you can spray on furnishing material that gives it an invisible waterproof coating that will repel showers and greasy fingermarks. It is available from Sainsbury, Tesco, Savacentre, and some branches of B&Q, at £4.99 for 400ml. So you can go ahead and make your cushions in the fabric of your choice.

Q I have just returned from holiday in Spain. I found an old parasol in a second-hand shop. The owner said it dated from about 1810 and it is in need of re-covering. Can you give me the address of any company that specialises in this work?

A Call a very nice man, Mr Benattar from Benattar Brollies on 020 8539 5967, who says he will do what he can to mend your parasol. It is very difficult to let you know the cost as it is completely dependent on what he does to the parasol. Although you bought it in Spain, it may in fact come from anywhere and be of any age, so the best thing to do is to contact him and talk him through what it looks like. He may well be able to make you up a new cover. What we think of as a 'spoke' is called a rib in the trade, so count them and give him a ring. While his main business is manufacturing men's and women's classic English umbrellas, he obviously loves umbrellas and has lots of bits that might just fit your treasure from Spain.

decorative details

205

Q My garden is a bit of a suntrap and I just wish it could be a bit more shady at midday. As it is, I tend to retreat inside when I would most like to sit out. Any ideas?

A I suppose you have thought of the obvious solution, which is a parasol/umbrella in the middle of a wooden table. These can look very attractive. Alternatively, why not try an awning, which you can pull out when the sun gets too much? A company called Thomas Sanderson sells awnings in different colours and in lots of fabrics, all of them fade-resistant. Call them on 0800 220603 and they will send someone to your home to measure up and help you choose. They install the awnings themselves, and offer a five-year guarantee. The awnings can be attached to brick, hard wood and most UVPC fixtures. They can be particularly effective on a balcony or a roof terrace and the really clever thing is that they open and close automatically, depending on how bright the sun is.

Q In one of your TV programmes you used a child's umbrella to make a topiary table decoration. I thought it was very unusual and great fun. Do you know anywhere I can buy other interesting frames for my conservatory and patio?

A The Wadham Trading Company (tel: 01367 850499) does all kinds of wonderful topiary frames from penguins to giraffes to lop-eared rabbits and frogs. They're made of galvanised steel wire and suitable for indoor or outdoor planting. Prices start from £15 plus p&tp. They all come with instructions on planting. For indoors, the tiny ones look great planted with moss and creeping figs or variegated ivy. The larger outdoor pieces work well with ivy or box. You'll get two or three growths a year so it should take only a couple of years to achieve a talking point for your patio. Wadham takes special commissions too.

Q I saw some amazing water sprinklers at a show recently but I have lost the details. They sprayed water in a really unusual way and looked very impressive. Can you track down the manufacturer for me as I would love to buy one?

A I know of some garden sprinklers that are certainly different. They come in all kinds of shapes, from orchids to bells – and something called Shoot the Moon, which looks like a spiral. They all throw out water over an area of up to 6m (20ft), with a maximum water pressure of 2.2kg (5lb), and attach to your hose via a connector. Made of copper, they stand in the ground with a double prong to keep them sturdy and gradually develop a verdigris finish. They cost £199, including carriage, from Waterdance on 01279 876055.

Q The submersible pump I have in the garden pond has to be replaced. I have been looking for a new one but without success. Can you please let me know where I can get another? The one I have used is an Otter and has pumped water up to a height of some 180cm (6ft) to the top of the waterfall.

A Fountains Direct on 01932 336338 does fountains for all kinds of sites and certainly has something for your garden. The Nautilus 3000, priced £115, is made by the German company, OASE, the European market leader in pond pumps. The company is a water display specialist and can create any kind of fountain you can imagine. Simply phone to discuss your ideas. The largest one it has ever installed was 110m (120yd) high!

Q I have always loved water features in gardens. Dabbling in pottery, I have just completed a stoneware bowl to match a fish that I made last year. I would like to set both of them up outside with a water pump, but have no idea how to go about it. They also need to be raised up from ground level and I wondered whether a plinth made of brick or stone would be suitable.

A Focus Do It All stock a wide range of water features, including pond pumps, cascades and spray fountains. Pick up a copy of their garden catalogue in a store or phone Freefone 0800 436436 for a copy (they can also advise you on how to install the water feature). A low-voltage bubbler kit costs around £59.99 and contains a pump and reservoir to feed the fountain. A log-and-pebble surround might

❋ **Tessa's tip** How about a hammock for the summer? In fact, you can have a hammock all year round, as I have just discovered. I was given one for a wedding present six years ago, but I could never find the right place for it in the garden. The solution was to put it up indoors! Inside, all you have to do is find a joist in the wall and securely fasten the hooks. It gives us endless fun with the children and you can take it down easily when you want the room for another use. The Mexican Hammock Company (tel: 0117 972 4234), does mail order and supplies all the fixing instructions you will need for both out or indoors. The largest model costs £59.95, plus £5 p&p. The company also sells a special hammock frame that is made of steel and easy to erect, and it even has instructions on how to get into a hammock successfully. You may not want to spend the whole night in one, but for relaxing at the end of the day, there's nothing better.

decorative details

207

be a good way of raising your fish and bowl off the ground. The log border costs £7.99 for 20 x 15cm (8 x 6in) and £12.99 for 20 x 30cm (8 x 12in). A bag of pebbles costs £6.79.

Q Is it possible to obtain the acrylic tubes that are used for the popular vertical displays filled with water with air pumped from beneath? I am aware that these displays can be purchased complete, but I would like to make my own if there are suppliers who can supply the tubing in different sizes.

A Bubble tubes are available from GP Plastics Ltd on 0121 772 0033. If you want to buy the tubing alone (it comes in 2m/2¼yd lengths), prices start at £60.58 for the 100mm (4in) diameter version. Ring GP Plastics to find out prices for other diameters. The company can supply the water pumps too but it would be cheaper to buy one from an aquarium. Do make sure that when you are making it you use extremely strong glue, as the water will be very heavy.

Q Herons have taken some of the fish from my garden pond. Can you suggest a way to protect them without spoiling the look of the pond?

A One solution is to fix a mesh screen just below the surface of the water. If your pond is concrete-lined and not too large, this is a reasonable DIY job. Get a sheet of galvanised metal mesh from a builder's merchant and have it cut to the right size and shape. Drill holes in the side of the pond lining and screw in fixings for the mesh. Then seal the fixings and holes with silicon (pet shops sell this for mending fishtanks).

Underwater mesh isn't a perfect solution, however. Fish can get through it and be stranded out of the water, and birds can land on it and get at the fish. An alternative way of deterring herons is to stretch fishing line around the edge of the pond to form a fence. Set up some bamboo poles and stretch fishing line between them at heights of 15, 30 and 45cm (6, 12 and 18in) above the ground. That should do the trick.

Q What kind of paint could I use to paint terracotta and plastic flowerpots?

A Let's start with the terracotta ones. Basically, most paints will work on terracotta, so it depends on the look you want to achieve. You can use gloss paint if you want them bright and shiny, or vinyl matt for less of a sheen. Once you've painted them: try Waterseal, normally used on walls if you've got damp, or – a cheaper option – PVA glue. Although this is white when you paint it on, it will dry to a clear finish. For plastic flowerpots, you might try Plastikote, a spray-on paint that is even supposed to stick to plastic loo seats! Realistically, over a period of time the paint will start to peel, but as we're talking pots and not large items of garden furniture, you should get a good season's worth of wear out of them and they are fairly inexpensive to replace. You could also try the melamine tile primers that are now available. These, once applied to your pots, will allow almost any paint to stick to them.

Q I am starting to think of unusual Christmas presents for my husband and I wondered if you know anywhere I can get a weather vane made.

A Dorset Weathervanes can design and make any weather vane you like. Their standard designs include motorbikes, golfers, beekeepers, animals, witches on broomsticks, dolphins and trains, but they will happily design anything else you can think of. Made of mild sheet steel, which is then zinc plated and coated to be hard-wearing, they are easy to attach to any gable end, chimney or pole. The full size designs are 60cm (24in) but smaller sizes are also available. You can get them made up in copper, brass, bronze or full colour. Prices start from around £70. Call them on 01258 453374 for more details.

Q I have found a large log, with the bark still on it, that I'd like to display in my garden. I want to give it a weathered, bleached look. What's the best way?

A First you must remove the bark. The best tool for this is an adze, which is a bit like a pickaxe. You'll then need to have the wood sandblasted: the driftwood effect is created by eating away at the soft grain, leaving the hard grain to show through. Your local Yellow Pages should list firms which can do this for you; it shouldn't cost much more than £40. Then paint the wood with limewash to give it a bleached look. Once you've done that, coat with anti-woodworm treatment and then paint with an oil-based undercoat, slightly diluted with turpentine, to allow the grain to show through. When that coat is dry, paint with a matt polyurethane varnish to protect it, paying special attention to the end grain, as water will seep into this first. Don't leave the log resting on the ground, or it will rot. Put it on blocks, and it should last for years.

decorative details

209

Q We saw some rather beautiful stone balls on *Home Front*. Where can we buy one?

A Haddonstone does a range of reconstituted stone balls from 18 to 53cm (7 to 21in) in diameter that look great on their own or on top of gateposts or columns. The smaller balls come with a base. Together they weigh 10kg (22lb) and cost £36.10. A 53cm (21in) ball costs £148.18, plus £72.58 for a collared base to sit it on. The company has more than 150 UK stockists. To find your local one, call 01604 770711 or write to Haddonstone, The Forge House, East Haddon, Northampton NN6 8DB.

Q I am looking for something a bit different to put in my garden. It is not a particularly big space – it's a standard fenced-in garden with a bit of lawn and a tree – and I would like to make a focal point in one of the corners. Have you any ideas?

A Well, where do I begin? It depends how much work you want to put in and how much money you want to spend. Paint is always a good bet – use it to make the fence a different colour. Or you could try digging the flowerbeds wider, splitting the garden into sections, or using different types of products – maybe gravel, some decking, a water feature, a large, beautiful terracotta pot, something more modern in concrete, a sculpture, new lighting, more plants . . . I could go on. I think that the woven willow fences, from Focus Do It All, are a fun idea. You could use just one or two to make a corner feature and add a different texture to the garden. They cost £29.99 for a 180 x 180cm (6 x 6ft) panel and are made from a pressure-treated softwood frame with interwoven strips of willow wired into place. Call free on 0800 436436 to find your nearest store.

❋ **Tessa's tip** Marc Kitchen-Smith came to making mosaic pots via writing film scripts and advertising. Wanting a change of career, he was walking along the Thames one day and saw lots of old pottery lying in the mud. Keen on salvage, he started to think what he could do with it and came up with mosaic pots. All the pottery he uses is recycled from the river and, because his pots are handmade, no two are alike. Call Marc on 020 7488 3270, tell him the colour scheme you want and he will make you a pot to order. Prices start from £90 so they are not cheap, but they will grace any balcony or patio and can stay out all winter. So while there is little colour in the garden in winter, a gorgeous pot will add some glamour.

Q Where can I purchase a Union Jack flag? I'd like not a hand-held one, but a large one on a pole.

A What a great question! Elpees Entertainments on 01634 297708 does flags for every occasion in every size. Its custom-made range starts at 180 x 90cm (6 x 3ft) (£47.50 including VAT). These are hand-sewn and come with rope and toggle ready to attach to the flagpole. They are made from Admiralty-approved fabrics by traditional methods. It also does a standard range of Union Jacks from £1.99 (34 x 30cm/18 x 12in). It is promoting a 21st-century flag; the 180 x 90cm (6 x 3ft) version with rope and toggle is £45 inc VAT. If you want your own logo stitched below it, it will cost £24 extra. Call for a free colour brochure.

Q I have been trying to find somewhere to buy brass letters as opposed to numbers to screw on my front gate to show the name of my house but so far I have had no luck. Do you know of a supplier?

A Call Danico Brass on 020 7483 4477. They do brass letters that are 5cm (2in) high and they come in two styles. They do the sand cast ones at £2.50 each and the die cast ones at £4.40 each. The sand cast are cheaper because the letters will come up in slightly different sizes as they are not set in a metal die, while the more expensive die cast ones will match exactly, so unfortunately for you, you will probably want the more expensive ones! They can also offer a customised service and will lazer cut any type face you want for a price, including scrolls and seraphs.

Q I want to put down some wooden decking in my garden. Is it possible to incorporate some lighting to add interest in the evening, and can you recommend someone who makes lights for such projects, or anyone I can ask for advice? I am no electrician!

A When installing lights in a garden, keep it simple and low-key – you want to see the effect, not the lighting. A company called Outdoor Lighting (tel: 01372 848 8000), offers a full range, including various recessed uplighters that would sit well in your deck. One, called the Nimbus, has a 20-degree tilt so you can angle it at focal points in the garden; while another, the Weebee, is a smaller, cheaper model without the tilt. Both use a 12-volt fitting, so you would need to have a transformer. Prices start at £100 per light, and you should also get a honeycomb or grille (£14) to cut down glare. For a cheaper but still effective look, Outdoor Lighting also sells spike-mounted fittings that just push into the ground, price £57.50 plus VAT. Orders under £350 have a £15 delivery charge.

decorative details

211

Q **I recently read something about solar-powered lights for garden paths, but I didn't make a note of the details at the time. Now my daughter-in-law wants some for her new garden. Do you know anything about them?**

A I'm sorry to disappoint you, but most of the solar-powered lights on the market just aren't very good. The problem is that their solar cells don't generate enough power during the winter to illuminate a path. Your best bet is to buy a light that has a battery as well as a solar panel. Wind & Sun (tel: 01568 760671), makes a solar/battery lantern that works very well, but it is rather expensive at £100. The company has other ecologically-sound products, such as wind-up radios for £59.99, wind-up torches for £49.99 and solar-powered fountains. Why not think about buying your daughter-in-law one of these instead?

Q **I'm looking for some unusual garden lights. A couple of years ago I saw a string of them in the form of cacti: can you help me find something similar?**

A Are you thinking of electric lights or candles? I recommend candles: the light they cast is far more romantic for a garden party. Nice Irma's produce a good range: small candles cost £5.20 and large £8.20 (call 020 8343 7610 for mail order; free p&tp for orders over £35, otherwise add £3.95). The Conran Shop (tel: 020 7589 7401) sell night light holders, price £2.95 plus p&tp, that stick to the outside of your window panes. Conran also do a range of glass candle holders (£25) with steel spikes that push into the ground. Garden centres and DIY stores sell garden flares – candles on sticks that push into the ground – and these cost only a few pounds. Ikea do small metal lanterns that you can put candles in and hang from trees. Floating candles also look great in a bowl with some rose petals. Homebase have a pack of five for £2.49. Enjoy the party!

212

❋ **Tessa's tip** Have you ever thought about a wormery? Before you cringe with horror at the idea of a bag of worms being delivered to you through the post, think again. If you have a garden and want to manufacture you own compost easily, it is the ideal, easy-to-manage way of doing it. All you have to do is put your old peelings, etc. into it and the worms will turn it into liquid feed. You need never see the worms and it is odour-free, unlike many rotting compost heaps. It is environmentally friendly and will cut down on the amount of rubbish you have lying around. Phone The Garden Factory on 01543 462500 for a wormery that costs £59.95 plus p&p.

Q I want a French-style blue and white enamelled metal house number plate. Could you find me a stockist please?

A There is a company called Franco-File that makes them here (tel: 01884 253556). The plates are vitreous on steel, deep blue with a white border. French people buy them from the local mairie (the town hall). A two-digit number plate from Franco-File costs £17.50, a three-digit one costs £22.50. Signs such as 'WC' cost £14, 'Privé' is £17.50, 'Défense De Fumer' £22.50. The company also makes house name plates to order in French blue or English green. An 8.5 x 25cm (3½ x 10in) sign with a maximum of 12 letters/spaces costs £42.50. Sizes go up to 18 x 35cm (7⅛ x 13¾in). Prices include p&tp.

Q I am interested in installing solar panels for domestic electricity generation. Can you tell me what suppliers there are, and what technical jobs are involved?

A I suggest you call the Centre for Alternative Technology in Wales who will be able to help you with everything you need to know about suppliers and the technical side of installing solar panels. They can help with all sorts of inquiries, such as how to install a wind-powered generator, how to insulate your home in the most efficient and economical way, even how to deal humanely with slugs in your garden. They have a very good booklet called *Save Energy, Save Money* that costs £2.50 and gives you all sorts of hints, as well as details about grants for keeping your home warm. The centre runs courses on solar power, produces resource sheets, books and lists, and can advise you about people in your area who could install the panels for you. The centre basically acts as a middleman and I can thoroughly recommend speaking to them. Their number is 01654 702400. If you are thinking about going the whole hog and building your own ecological house in the future, look for a book called *The Whole House Book*, which is an invaluable resource on everything you will need to know. It costs £29.95.

decorative details

213

practicalities

Q We've noticed that open-air restaurants have started using outdoor heaters that look like giant parasols. We think these are a marvellous idea, letting you stay outside when the evenings get chilly. But where on earth can we get one?

A The heaters you've seen run off a gas bottle in the base, and burn it under a high hood that reflects heat downwards. They're very effective but quite expensive. The Fiesta range from Sovereign Distribution starts at £580 plus VAT and p&p, but there is shortly to be a cheaper domestic version for £400 plus VAT and p&p. Call 020 8386 5122. The DIY stores and garden centre also do a smaller version for around £200.

Q How can I clean a stone bird bath? I'm not sure what it's made from and I have tried washing it, but still can't shift the dirt.

A It doesn't matter whether it's natural stone or a composite, treat it in the same way. If you haven't yet done so, try a strong nylon bristle brush and a soapy detergent like a washing-up liquid. Failing that, hire a domestic jet wash from a tool hire store and 'power-wash' the bird bath. Or you could try rubbing a cloth soaked in methylated spirit into the really dirty areas. Wash the meths off afterwards. You could also try a patio cleaner, available from garden centres, but remember that stone is meant to weather and age gracefully. It's only when the birds reject it that you need to worry!

Q I wonder whether you could let me know where it is possible to buy a collapsible parking post! My son moved into a flat some months ago and has an allocated parking space. However as there are so few parking spaces he often arrives home to find that another vehicle is in his space. Any thoughts?

A I do get asked for some strange things in this column! Call a company called Broxap and Corby who make just what you want.

They are designed to unlock and lift up when you are not there and simply fold flat when you want to drive over it. It will not damage your exhaust pipe. It is 70cm (27½in) high and has a diameter of 6cm (2¼in) and costs £70. Call 01782 564411.

Q I have been looking for some swings and slides that will 'go' with my garden. Everything I've seen so far is made of plastic or metal. Is there anything more natural-looking available?

A Kiddie Wise (tel: 01538 304235) specialise in natural wood swings, slides and climbing frames. The firm's most popular model is: a set consisting of two swings, a slide and a climbing ladder delivered to your home for around £299.50. You have to assemble everything yourself, but the company assure me that most clients find this easy to do. All the wood used is pressure-treated and should last for years.

Q I have been searching for some thick bamboo to create an edge to a Chinese garden I am building. Any suggestions?

A Call the Cane Store on 020 7354 4210 or write to 207 Blackstock Road, London N5 2LL. Their bamboo ranges from 60mm (2¼in) in diameter to 150mm (6in). It comes in 3m (10ft) long poles, and the 60-70mm (2¼-2¾in) ones cost £14.50 including VAT. If you want the pole uncut, it will cost at least £15.50 for carriage.

Q Every year I have to repaint my garden gnomes because the paint has peeled off. Can you tell me if there's a special way to prepare them for painting, and if there is a long-lasting paint that I could use on them. The gnomes are made of stone.

A You say your gnomes are made of stone but I suspect that, like most gnomes, they are made of concrete. It is probably the alkalinity of the concrete that is causing the paint to lift off. To combat this, try using a concrete sealer and painting your gnomes with a floor paint that is tough enough for exterior use. A firm called International do both the sealer and the floor paint, and you can buy them from most DIY superstores. The paint comes in two shades of red, two greens, black, brown, grey, terracotta and blue – enough colours to spruce up your gnomes. For more information call International's helpline on 01962 711177.

practicalities

215

Q The original conservatory on our home – a listed building – is in a very bad state. We want to build a new one, but we're anxious that it should be in keeping with the house. Is it best to rebuild or should we try to patch up the original?

A If your conservatory really is in a bad way, it would be cheaper to have the whole thing rebuilt rather than to keep patching it up. A company offering a bespoke service will give greatest flexibility. Ask to see a building firm's references and try to take a look at something they've built. The Glass and Glazing Federation (tel: 020 7403 7177) offers a free advice service on choosing a conservatory and will advise you of its members in your area.

Q I am looking for a small, solar-powered fan to keep the air circulating in a conservatory where grapes are growing. Do you know of a firm that manufactures such a fan?

A The only company to supply them in the UK is Solar Solutions Fountains Ltd (tel: 01544 230303), which has the perfect fan for you: it costs £200 plus VAT, measures 12.5 sq cm (5 sq in) and comes with a finger guard. It works off two panels and they say it is so powerful that if you pick it up, it nearly jumps out of your hand. You can buy the fan by mail order. The company also specialises in solar-powered fountains of all sizes.

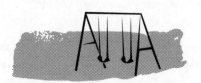

❋ Tessa's tip If you've got a garden, I think you should have a shed. You can store garden tools in them, but some can be used as a summerhouse or playhouse, too. A company called Walton Garden Buildings has a large range of sheds, summerhouses, log cabins, and beautiful children's playhouses. Remember, if you are going for a children's playhouse it should have the safety CE code on it (which the Walton children's ones have). These will have had the timber sanded to avoid splinters, Perspex windows, hinges that can't trap a child's hand and air holes. Most of these are suitable for five-year-olds but if you want a 'family' type shed, the company does lots with verandahs, windows and doors to suit. They come flat-pack, and you can even custom design one. Call 01636 821215 for details of your local dealer.

✳ cleaning
and fixing

The questions that have appeared on my desk to do with cleaning over the last few years have been brilliant to answer. I find it very satisfying to try and find solutions for basic daily cleaning chores. You have helped me in many of the tips. One really good one is to use baby oil to keep your stainless steel gleaming. Some if these simple tips remind me of the traditional books that used to appear to help the 'housewife' with her battle with stains in the home. Of course, we now have a huge mass of products that are available – some better than others – and I try to find the good ones.

As for repairing items, I do believe that we should try to repair something before we throw it away. Our culture shouts 'Buy another', but often the thing that is broken is better quality than that which you buy to replace it with. A lot of you ask me how to restore old buildings – everything from banister spindles to whole houses. With every repair – be it on a small glass item or a large building – I would take advice before making any decisions. There are always experts available to talk to who can direct you to the right person. Don't just make a botch job of something – you may find you have ruined a very nice rug, mirror, knife handle or whatever. Write to me first!

 cleaning

Q I have a Le Creuset casserole that I use every week, but the inside is very stained and looks unsightly. I have tried soaking it with bleach to no avail. Do you have any suggestions?

A The Le Creuset range has a creamy enamel that will discolour over time – usually from cooking mushrooms and onions – and can wear thin to show the cast iron underneath. Steradent tablets, normally used for cleaning false teeth, may help. Alternatively, ring 0800 373792 for a special Le Creuset Pots and Pans Cleaner, £3.75 including p&p. By the way, the discoloration makes no difference to the final taste.

Q I have a beaten copper cooker hood that I naively thought would – after a little maintenance – become shiny again. Needless to say, it blackens quickly and needs constant cleaning. Is it possible for me to get it gleaming and then put a varnish on it to keep it that way?

A If only! This sounds like the perfect solution, but the trouble is, you'd need a heat-resistant varnish and I know of no such product that's available. If you find it impossible to clean, then the only thing I can suggest is to give up on your copper finish and paint it. If you do this, use a special metal primer and then a heat resistant enamel over the top. Call International on 01962 711177 for a local supplier of these paints. Otherwise, it's back to good old elbow grease.

Q I have a polished stainless steel cooker, and I cannot find a cleaning agent that works without leaving streaks and watermarks on it. Someone suggested product called Astonish but this says on the label that it's not to be used on polished steel. Any suggestions?

A I have checked with Astonish and they say their Oven and Cookware cleaner is fine for your cooker, as long as you don't

cleaning

use a scouring pad and a heavy hand. That might dull the surface, which is why there is a warning on the label. Used gently with a soft cloth, however, it should work a treat. Astonish is also suitable for use on pots, plastic garden furniture and UPVC products. It costs about £1.99 and is available in most supermarkets (or phone Astonish on 01132 625206 for stockists). The company do a whole range of other cleaning products so it might be worth getting a brochure.

Q **What can you recommend to clean my stainless-steel saucepans? I have used some wonderful white powder that worked wonders, but unfortunately it no longer seems to be available. Please help.**

A Try Scrubs (tel: 01306 743868), which is a multi-surface metal and fibre-glass polisher. A resealable pack of 18 cloths, each 20 x 28cm (8 x 11in), costs £8.95 plus VAT. They are impregnated with an ammonia polish and contain no harsh abrasives. You could also try a powder called Hollywood stainless steel cleaner, available from John Lewis branches at £5.79 for 200g. The store also does its own gel for cleaning stainless steel, which costs £1.45 for 300ml.

Q **In a lapse of concentration, I put a hot pan down on a plastic mesh mat and now have plastic stuck to a heavy-based, ridged bottom, stainless steel pan. Have I ruined my best pan?**

A The plastic is probably polyethylene. It's fairly innocuous and will eventually burn off with a bit of use. If you have a gas cooker, heat the pan very gently over a low flame, just to soften the plastic, then scrape it off with a piece of wood. Stainless steel and plastic are not compatible, so it should come away quite easily. Remove the residue with a pan scourer. I am sure you have not ruined your pan.

* **Tessa's tip** Here is a tried-and-tested method for making your windows sparkle. First add vinegar to the water when cleaning windows with a chamois leather. (Vinegar is also good for wiping finger marks off furniture before polishing.) After you have cleaned your windows, give them a finishing touch by crumpling a newspaper and polishing over the window surfaces. It will remove any persistent smudges.

cleaning and fixing

Q Is it possible to renovate the bone handles on my set of knives? Over the years they have become discoloured and look unattractive.

A Many of you have written in with this problem. Someone even asked me how to clean a discoloured Mahjong set! Abbey Horn of Lakeland on 01524 782387 will buff knives and lift their grubby appearance. Call first, then send the knives for a quote. A rough guide is about £30 for bone salad servers. Or try it yourself with a small polishing mop, plus brown lustre cutting compound and lots of advice from Southdown Abrasives (tel: 01273 463677). Or there's the old-fashioned remedy – stand the knives in a glass of half water, half bleach for 12 hours. Rub the handles with toothpaste, then dry and polish with talcum powder. And, to treat the Mahjong set, if it is ivory, try rubbing it with lemon juice. Don't get hot water near it as it turns ivory yellow.

Q I have recently been given some pieces of silver plate, beautifully designed but heavily tarnished. Silver polish will not clean them. Can you tell me what might?

A If the silver is not coming up at all, then it has probably been lacquered and you will need to get professional help. Call Langfords on 020 7242 5506 for advice. It could also be that there is no plating left and you are polishing bare metal. If, on the other hand, you are just having difficulty cleaning the fiddly bits of the decoration, try Goddard's Silver Dip. Simply immerse your silver in it for a short time and it will bring up the shine. To get into the nooks and crannies, use a very soft toothbrush or nailbrush.

Other Goddard's products that might help are its foam polish sponge it on, rub it on and rinse it off), and the same company's polish-impregnated gloves. Both are available in good hardware stores. Alternatively, you could get a butler.

Q How can I remove the white film that builds up in glasses through constant washing in the dishwasher? Is there any way of preventing it in the first place.

A The white film that builds up is usually caused by lack of salt in the dishwasher. The simplest way to stop it happening is to make sure you always keep the salt full or if you forget such things in the chores of daily life, you can get dishwashers that remind you – Miele do one. Once you have got the white film deposit on the glasses, the worst thing you can do is to try and get it off by washing the glasses again. This simply bakes it on harder than before. What you have to do is to soak them in liquid detergent and scrub with a rough scourer until you

cleaning

221

get it off. I speak from experience – once you have carefully scrubbed all your glasses, you don't forget the salt again!

Q After years of arranging flowers in my treasured cut-glass vase, the bottom half is looking decidedly murky. I have cleaned it regularly using limescale remover and meths, but to no avail. Please can you help?

A There could have been a chemical reaction within the glass, in which case there will be very little you can do to get rid of the markings. If, however, the staining is caused by plant and water residue, it may be worth trying Magic Balls. They are little copper-plated ball bearings that you can swoosh around a vase, perfume bottle, etc, and they act as a mild abrasive. You can buy them by mail order from Presents for Men (tel: 01295 750100) at £3.99 plus p&p. Even if they won't shift the stain in your vase, they're a useful thing to have in the cupboard.

Q I wish to avoid using cleaning products from companies that have conducted experiments on live animals as part of their research and development process. Can you please advise me of any suitable alternatives?

A Try a company called Ecover. Their products certainly fit your requirements. None of their products are tested on animals and all their lines are biodegradable, causing minimum damage to the environment. They tell you exactly what is in the products so you can be sure of what you are buying. Ecover does quite a wide range of products, including washing-up liquid, fabric conditioner and multi-surface polish.

Q I have unearthed an old marble washstand from the back of our shed and find that the marble has numerous patches of what looks like iron mould. I

✳ **Tessa's tip** Here are two wonderful ways to keep metal gleaming.

✳ Polish chrome with a little bicarbonate of soda on a damp cloth. Then rinse and dry thoroughly. To keep chrome taps gleaming, rub them occasionally with a cloth dipped in paraffin.

✳ To clean tarnished forks and spoons, roll up some aluminium foil into balls. Put the cutlery and foil balls into a pan of water and boil gently until cutlery is shiny.

cleaning and fixing

understand marble is porous and don't know whether these marks can be removed without doing some damage.

A   The best way to deal with these marks is to soak them out. Buy a small bag of Carlite, a finishing plaster available at any DIY store. Mix a small amount of it with some strong liquid bleach such as Izal (not a greasy one such as Domestos). Paste it over the iron marks and leave to dry overnight. The stain will lift and attach itself to the plaster. When dry, wash the plaster off with cold water using a sponge. You will have lifted the shine off the marble and it will look pitted, so use a hard furniture wax such as Johnson's Clear Polish and lightly buff it up. Don't use straight bleach without the plaster or you will spread the stain into the marble.

Q   After using a new iron for a while, I find the ironing plate develops a rough area a bit like limescale. Nothing seems to remove this without also removing the smooth surface of the iron. I've ruined two irons trying to solve this problem, and I don't want to spoil a third. Do you have a remedy?

A   An iron cleaner is available from most department stores. It is a bit like a rubber and costs just £1.75. You rub it on to your iron when it's hot and then rub it off with a cloth, taking the film with it. Irons with stainless-steel plates generally mark less than those with galvanised-steel ones. Although most steam irons are now designed to take ordinary tap water, I find that you still get dirty marks on the bottom of the iron. If you heat up the iron and then iron some brown paper, it should remove some of the dirt, but I'm looking to readers to provide other ingenious solutions to this problem.

Q   For many years we have used Blu-Tac to attach our Christmas cards to the brick wall surrounding the fireplace. Because the bricks are quite rough, there are now a large number of Blu-Tac bits that we can't get rid of. How can we remove them and clean the bricks at the same time, as they are rather dirty looking?

A   Try to remove as much as possible with fresh Blu-Tac. Then get some lighter fuel and rub it into the brickwork with a small brush. Let it dry and use another fresh piece of Blu-Tac to remove any leftover pieces. Repeat the process several times until your wall is back to normal. May I suggest that when you're displaying Christmas cards this year, you try hanging ribbons on either side of the fireplace and stapling the cards to that?

cleaning

Q We want to clean a copper chandelier. It is a family heirloom that my great nephew wants, but it needs a clean and I would like to be able to do this before he gets it.

A Apparently it is quite unusual to have a pure copper chandelier – more likely it is copper-plated. If you want it cleaned and replated, call a company called Verdigris London Ltd on 020 7703 8373. They specialise in brass, copper, pewter and bronze restoration and will also gild and lacquer. To get an idea of cost, send them a picture of your heirloom as they need to see how ornate it is. Cost is dependent on the number of arms it has and its detail. Once they have cleaned it, you can lacquer it yourself, which will protect it for the next 20 years, but you must not use varnish. Call a shop called Foxell and James who are experts in lacquers. Their number is 020 7405 0152.

Q We have a Baxi Bermuda coal-effect gas fire, about ten years old, with a glass screen. Over the years the glass has become cloudy, and now looks rather unsightly. The fire still works perfectly well, but we have been told that the glass can't be cleaned and will have to be replaced. Do you know of any cleaning method that would work?

A You could try a ceramic cleaner called Hobrite, which you can get from any hardware store. This will remove surface discoloration but I doubt that is the problem: the clouding is probably caused by years of heat-stress, as the glass expands and contracts when the fire is turned on and off. It might be worth having a professional fitter look the fire over – just to make sure that there is no other cause of the discoloration – but sadly I think you will have to buy new glass. The original manual should list the part number you need.

Q My young son recently knocked over a glass of milk on the newly laid natural coir flooring in his room. I've cleaned it numerous times, but there still seems to be a slight sour milk smell. Any ideas?

A I assume you've been using warm water, soap and detergent. Try again, putting a little ammonia in the warm water. If that doesn't do the trick, one of the largest suppliers of coir matting, Crucial Trading recommends and supplies a cleaner called Klanz (£16). If that doesn't work either, call in a professional carpet cleaner. Spills are inevitable with small children – floorboards might be a better bet.

cleaning and fixing

Q Could you please tell me if there is anything that will remove the residue left on our house walls after removing climbing ivy. When it was pulled away, the tentacles were left behind. Wire brushes make no impact.

A There's a special brick cleaner called Disclean Brick Cleaner that you can buy at builder's merchants and places like Jewsons. It costs around £6 a bottle and will definitely get off those toughened ivy suckers that are a devil to remove. If you can't find it easily in your area, ring the manufacturers on 01352 741919 who will tell you your local stockist. Disclean will also remove mortat stains, rust stains and calcium deposits. It is easy to use – use neat or dilute with water. If you are diluting, remember to put the water in the bucket first. Wear rubber gloves and have adequate ventilation. Put it on with a natural fibre brush or spray and leave for five minutes and then rinse with water.

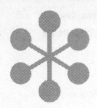

fixing

Q The fabric sun-canopy over my lounge window has acquired some nasty dark green stains from nearby trees. Do you know of a special cleaner that would solve the problem?

A There are a number of things you could try. You might take it off its frame and have it dry cleaned and reproofed, as you would a raincoat. Or you could put it in the washing machine on a cold wash with standard washing powder, put it back on the frame while still wet and leave to dry. You could soak it in the bath, again using cold water and a capful of bleach. Leave until the marks go, then stretch it back on the frame while still wet. Or you could just leave it alone. Sometimes these garden accessories look more in keeping with their surroundings when nature has worked its spell.

Q I have been sent a very fine bone china tea set that belonged to my grandmother. Unfortunately, on its travels from South Africa, two of the pieces arrived broken. This tea set was originally bought somewhere in Europe in the early 1900s. There are no markings or names on any of the pieces. Do you know of anyone who can piece the set together again for me? I have looked in vain for somebody in the Manchester area.

A Skilled people for this type of job are few and far between, and most of them seem to be in London. But before you think about the repair remember that bone china is translucent and the repair is going to show and, to be honest, probably not look very good. Besides, you wouldn't be able to drink from a teacup that had glue anywhere near the rim. But, if you do still want a repair, call China Restorers on 020 8444 3030, who have been mending china for 40 years. You will have to hand deliver it to them, and they are in London. So maybe you should consider a company called TableWhere on 020 8361 6111.

cleaning and fixing

They find obsolete and old pieces of china for people in exactly your position. They have a huge range of china and could probably locate what you need. Send them the photographs you sent me and they should be able to help. I have mentioned this company before on this page, and it always attracts a great deal of interest.

Q I have some broken china that, although not of great value, I would like to stick back together. I already have the Araldite glue, which has been recommended to me, but I am finding it difficult to get hold of superfine white Milliput and marine filler. Any suggestions as to where I might find a supplier?

A I have checked with several professional china restorers and they haven't heard of marine filler, so I wouldn't bother with it. Milliput, which sets rock-hard, should be enough to sculpt in where china is missing. It surprises me that you've had trouble finding this – any good hardware store should stock it, and the superstores certainly do.

Q Can you recommend a good adhesive to stick hard plastic to hard plastic, for minor repairs to fridge trays, vacuum cleaners etc?

A Evo-Stik do a plastic adhesive that should do the trick for all the repairs you list.

Q What's the best way of sticking material to wood? I want to replace the fabric lining of an Edwardian cabinet.

A The best type of glue to use is latex-based, something like Copydex. Spread the glue on both the material and the wood surface and allow to dry. When it is touch-dry, stick the surfaces together. With a latex-based glue you will not get the bleed-through into the material that you get with petroleum-based glue. If you want to remove the material at any time, it will also not be damaged by latex-based glue. Try General Woodworking Supplies on 020 7254 6052. A 125ml jar of Copydex with brush will cost you £3.

Q Do you know of any repair material to fill in a small chip out of the lid handle of my dinner service vegetable dish? This is not a crack, just a chip.

A Try Evo-Stik's Squeezy Decorative Filler, applying it in layers and allowing each to dry. It's heatproof, waterproof and can be painted. Or try waterproof white tile grout, both from DIY stores. For

fixing

a small fee, the Museums and Galleries Commission (tel: 020 7273 1444) will send a nationwide list of ceramics restorers.

Q Recently I spilled some Bostik All-Purpose adhesive on the upholstery of my car and have been unable to remove it. Do you have any suggestions on what I can use?

A This is one of the few glues made by Bostik that is solvent based, so you'll need acetone, which you can buy at the chemist. Nail varnish remover contains acetone so give this a try first, although it may not be strong enough to remove the glue. If possible, remove the upholstery and take it to a dry cleaner.

Q Our house is a Grade Two listed property dating from the 1750s that we would like to restore in keeping with its period. Where can we find information about period doors, woodwork, wall colours and furniture?

A Just a few thoughts to get you started. Remember that you can claim back VAT on any improvements you make to a listed property. This will save you an enormous amount of money. Redoing an old property is a labour of love and, if you are doing it over time, make sure you enjoy living in unfinished houses before you start. One of the things I would advise is to get in touch with the Royal Institute of British Architects (tel: 020 7580 5533), and the Royal Institution of Chartered Surveyors (tel: 020 7222 7000). They will be able to recommend someone locally to oversee your project. You might think this will be expensive, but it will probably save you money in the end. It is usually advisable to have someone between you and the builder unless you go for a highly reputable firm such as St Blaise (tel: 01935 83662), which specialises in historic house repairs. An organisation called Acanthus (tel: 0117 977 2002), is also worth contacting. It is a group of independent architects who specialise in restoring old houses. Potmolen Paints (tel: 01985 213960), offers extremely helpful advice on painting historic buildings. Also Farrow & Ball (tel: 01202 876141), has a paint range that includes National Trust colours. Don't forget the local library for research, too.

cleaning and fixing

Q Could you please tell me how to restore an old mirror? Should I just paint something on the back of it? And if so, what is it and where can it be obtained?

A It is not quite as simple as just painting the back of the mirror. It is a skilled job that is best left to the professionals. You didn't mention where you live but there is an excellent firm I know of in London called Gray & McDonnell (tel: 020 7739 4022) who specialise in glass restoration, bevelling, engraving, sandblasting and in silvering mirrors. They will resilver your mirror for you but it must be taken out of its frame and delivered to them in London. If you do not live in London, you could try calling a local specialist glass restorer who may be able to refer you to someone in your area who does this type of work.

Q We have an antique mirror with a carved frame. The glass is very marked with little circles of brown. I would like to re-silver it myself if possible. Can I?

A This is a job for a specialist. Your local glazing shop can tell you if re-silvering is possible – in some cases it only highlights scratches. If it is, they can send the mirror to Gray & McDonnell in London (tel: 020 7739 4022) who will resilver for £4.50 per 30 sq cm (12 sq in). Remember, though, that antique marks are fashionable, and the mirror may be worth more as it is.

Q I have found a wonderful old gilt frame in a second-hand shop. It was a real bargain but a few bits of the moulding have broken off. Do you have any tips before I start to repair it?

A It is quite a straightforward job to mend a stucco frame with some modelling clay and a modelling tool from an art shop. First, clean the frame using vinegar. Then simply take a small piece of the clay, warm it up in your hands and push it on to the damaged area. Using your modelling tool, carve it into the shape that's missing. When it is dry, you can use a nail file to shape the intricate parts. Paint the new moulded parts with a red oxide undercoat and then rub on a gilt cream to match the rest of the frame. You can have lots of fun 'knocking back' the frame to its original antique look. Use wire wool to rub back colours that you try. Paint Magic does mail-order creams on 01225 469966.

fixing

229

Q When I retired, my family clubbed together to buy me a model of a Thames barge. However, 15 years later I have only just managed to complete the hull. Is there anyone who can help me complete this project, as it seems such a shame to leave it unfinished?

A Fortunately for you and the many other people with unfinished models languishing in the attic, there are skilled modelmakers around who will build models to order and will also consider abandoned projects, for instance John Bertola.

Presented with your barge, John begins by taking apart your previous work. He then re-starts from scratch, painting the parts as he goes along, using mainly aerosol paints and touching in with a similar-coloured pen. John can be contacted at Superyachts.

Q I have an early upright piano, with walnut inlaid in a tulip design and two brass candle holders. It has been in the garage for four years and I'd now like to have it repaired and tuned (a hammer is broken). I thought it might be good for a millennium party. Where can I get this work done?

A While they are lovely to look at, pianos can be prohibitively expensive to repair and recondition. Unless it's a Steinway or a Broadwood, it really isn't worth touching. However, if you do want to go ahead, look in the Yellow Pages for someone who can do tuning and repair work for you.

Q We have two oil paintings, about 50 years old, which have darkened over the years. Is there an easy way to clean them?

A The simple answer is no. Every painting is different and there is no method safe for an amateur to try. The best thing is to

---

❋ **Tessa's tip** I get a lot of letters asking where to find period pieces to replace broken or lost fittings in homes. All over the country there are reclamation yards that specialise in everything from antique floorboards to 18th-century baths and Georgian fireplaces. It's shocking to find how many valuable items we still throw away – do you know that three-and-a-half million bricks are made every year, and that two-and-a-half million are thrown away? Or that more than 33,000 tonnes of reusable materials are sent to landfill sites every day? For details of your nearest reclamation yard, or for help in locating a particular item, call Salvo on 01890 820333.

fixing

230

phone the Association of British Picture Restorers on 020 8948 5644. They will direct you to an expert restorer.

Q I have a candelabra with glass holders for the candles, two of which are broken. Could anyone make me some new ones if I sent them the pattern?

A You're in luck. I know the most amazing place where you can get all sorts of things like this repaired. It's a firm of glass restorers in London called Wilkinson and Son (tel: 020 7495 2477). They stock countless pieces of period glass from old chandeliers, so may have a suitable match for a lost piece. If they haven't, they can make a new piece for you, though expect a slight variation in colour. They do many other types of repair work, such as mending chips or snapped stems on wine glasses. Prices for this kind of work start at £10 plus VAT. Take them all the pieces of broken glass and bear in mind that the join will appear as it does when the pieces are held together up to the light. That said, their results are staggering. Call Wilkinson and Son for advice about sending glass items to them for repair. Larger pieces need to be delivered by hand; smaller ones, suitably wrapped, may be sent by post.

Q My problem may not be strictly DIY, but I wonder if you can help? I have an old hairbrush that is made of ivory, but the bristles are very worn. Do you know anyone who would be able to restore it for me?

A The people you need to call are Facets on 020 8520 3392. You can contact them only on Monday and Tuesday between 1pm and 5pm, but they can rebristle any brush or rebuild it entirely if there are no bristles left. For an ivory brush, prices start at £50 (£40 for other brushes). Call them first for a quote. The service should take no longer than a month. They can also fit new teeth in silver and silver-plated comb backs.

Q My mum has left me an Edwardian terraced cottage that I want to give to my daughter to live in. My mum let it go, and it has no central heating – just open fireplaces – and no double glazing. The electrics will need attention too, and my daughter doesn't know where to start. Are there grants for this sort of work, and should she get an architect or a builder? She loves her nan's house but she needs ideas!

A Isn't your daughter lucky? It can be very satisfying to refurbish a house from scratch. The cottage may be eligible for a grant for improvements (such as rewiring, central heating or a new roof) and/or

fixing

231

energy-efficiency measures (such as double glazing or insulation). Either way, it is essential that she does no demolition or other work until the cottage has been assessed. To find out which type of grant, if any, applies, your daughter should call the local authority. They will also be able to tell her if the cottage is in a conservation area and, if so, strict rules will apply when selecting building materials and styles (such as colour of brick, type of window-frame).

Local conservation societies may be able to suggest names of good suppliers and builders. Whatever the situation with grants, I advise getting two good local builders each to quote for the job (ask them if you can visit other houses they have worked on).

Employing architects can be helpful, too. They can suggest ideas about space and light that you may not have thought of, and they needn't cost a fortune. I know of one refurbishment project where architects were employed for just a few hours right at the beginning, and they made an enormous difference to the result. To find an architect, call the RIBA Clients' Advisory Service on 020 7307 3700.

Q Running along the top of our skirting boards are electric wires for the burglar alarm and the phone. They can't be hidden because we have a tiled floor. Is there any way of disguising them – they get on my nerves and they're awkward to dust.

A The simplest thing to use is mini trunking. This is hollow square tubing that sits above the skirting board. It comes in various sizes, sometimes with compartments to keep cables separate. Or you could go for more expensive hollow skirting that fixes over your original skirting and the wires. This is available in different veneers and you attach it with glue.

Q My loft is insulated with fibreglass. Every time I go up there I get choked by the fibres and dust. Is there a product I could spray on to the insulation to permanently suppress this?

A That's a tricky one. Your loft certainly sounds like something of a health hazard, but as far as I know there isn't a spray that would do the job for you. I think your best bet might be to remove the old insulation and replace it with the modern type, called glass fibre roll. This comes with a sort of nylon sock around it to keep fibres and dust from escaping, and you can buy it at Jewson or Travis Perkins. You could lay boards over the existing insulation, but the expense would only be worthwhile if you want to use your loft as a room rather than just a storage space.

cleaning and fixing

Q We are three students preparing to move into a ground-floor flat. Our problem is that one of its rooms has only bare brick walls, with no covering or paint of any kind. We would like to do something to keep the cold out, but we're not sure what material to use for simple insulation. We don't have a lot of money to spend and we would like to tackle the problem ourselves. Are we facing a chilly winter, or could you give us some advice?

A What you do depends upon how much work you want to take on and whether your landlord approves. You don't want to do a major insulation job only to find that your handiwork gets you thrown out. In any case, I think bare brick walls look great – they're very fashionable and might not be cold at all. Perhaps it would be better to go for a quick, easy and temporary solution such as hanging thick fabric or rugs from the walls.

If you decide to do a permanent job, you could cover the walls with thermal board. This can be stuck straight on with glue recommended for the purpose, and you can make it extra-fast by screwing it in. Or you can fit wooden battens round the walls and nail the board to these. Put fibre blanket over the battens before nailing on the boards. This is a major job that might mean moving skirting boards, light switches, radiators, etc, and you'd have to plaster over the boards afterwards. Unless you are all decorating students and this would be practice, I don't recommend it!

Q I hope to buy a flat in a converted Victorian villa where I know the soundproofing is not very good. As a musician, I don't want to disturb my neighbours and would like to soundproof a room that measures 3.3 x 3m (11 x 10ft). Would this work, and who could do the job – or is it a DIY project that I could tackle?

A A company called Ecomax Acoustics (tel: 01494 436345) can advise you on what soundproofing the flat would entail. The first thing to say is that total silence cannot be achieved; soundproofing can only reduce the noise level, and the more sound insulation you want, the more expensive it is going to be. You would need to put down acoustic flooring or lift the floorboards and insert special slabs between the joists. For the walls, a heavy plasterboard with a special acoustically-absorbent layer between the old and new wall would help. Simply putting up egg-crate foam on walls helps only with a room's internal acoustics. You could replace the door with either a fire door that has fire seals or a more expensive timber acoustic door. A secondary ceiling could help and would only reduce the ceiling height by 5 to 25cm (2 to 10in). Or you could use dense plasterboard or fit a new ceiling on separate joists with sound-

fixing

233

absorbing material between the old and new. Approximate prices per square metre: for floors, between £25 and £50; walls, between £35 and £45; secondary ceilings, between £25 and £35. It is possible to do the work yourself, but check with Ecomax that your DIY skills are sufficient for the work involved. It would be a pity to get it wrong.

Q **The dividing wall between my semi-detached bungalow and my neighbour's has very little sound protection. How can I improve the sound-proofing? The wall is built from 23cm (9in) thick concrete blocks laid flat, then painted.**

A It's impossible to stop noise from adjoining houses – it travels through the walls, ceiling and floors. The best solution is to stop at source. If you are still speaking to your neighbours, ask them to move speakers and televisions off the floor and away from party walls. Get them to insulate their walls with polystyrene sheet, insulating board or cork. If that's not possible, try building a second interior wall. Put wooden battens on your wall, stuff the gaps with heavy-duty mineral wool and fix heavy-duty plasterboard over it. Then replaster. Much easier to make friends with the neighbours.

Q **I am writing to ask if you know any companies that specialise in producing made-to-order internal air grilles. If so, I would be grateful to receive any publications/information available and a list of stockists.**

A Try a company called Chris Topp on 01845 501415 who specialise in restoring historic metalwork. They are based in North Yorkshire but if you send them a sketch of what you want and specify whether you want it in steel or wrought iron with the size you need, they can send it to you. Do remember that steel is cheaper to work in than wrought iron. Wrought iron is the best material outside but, as your grilles are for the inside you have the choice.

Q **Do you know where I could buy a high-pressure air blower for blowing dust and dirt out of brick air vents inside our house, and for window vents and electric fans as these also suffer a build-up of dirt. The air vents cannot be removed.**

A I'd contact your local hire shop and ask for a compressor and an air line. This ought to do the job and shouldn't cost you more than £40 for a couple of days hire. These shops have all kinds of useful tools for those one-off jobs and their prices are usually pretty competitive.

Q Could you please advise me of stockists for coloured glass and coloured tile seconds in my area? Also, what bonding agent would be best for joining glass pieces about 12mm (½in) in diameter?

A Go to James Hetley at Schoolhouse Lane, London E1 9JA (tel: 020 7790 2333). They sell all types of coloured glass. If you are making a Tiffany lamp, for example, you can buy 450g (1lb) of broken coloured glass for £1.88 plus VAT, or 450g (1lb) of antique glass for £3. They also do tools, bases and various leads and copper foils for bonding the glass. A mail-order service is available for tools and accessories. Glass can be delivered by courier for £11.25, or £15 for orders over 10kg (22lb) (orders over £150 are delivered free).

As for coloured tile seconds, you should definitely take a trip to Fired Earth at Adderbury, near Banbury (tel: 01295 812088). They have fabulous coloured tiles at discounts of 20-60 per cent. They also have offcuts of natural flooring and some beautiful Persian rugs in a room display – alas, these are not on discount.

Q I'm very interested in using some thick glass bricks as a screen to separate my kitchen from the dining area. Where can I get them?

A Glass bricks are becoming very popular and can be used both inside and outside the house. They're most commonly used in bathrooms, but I've also seen whole houses built from them! The bricks come in all shades from rose to grey to turquoise, they reflect the light beautifully and are easy to clean. Luxcrete (tel: 020 8965 7292) does a modular system of different-sized units that you can put together easily.

Q Is there a simple, effective way to stop hammering in the water pipes of my house? It is unpredictable, worrying and driving us mad!

A There is no simple cure to this nightmare. It's caused by too much pressure in your pipes. You can buy a pressure reducer to put on to the main incoming water supply but if you have a power shower, this is not an option. Alternatively, try to find the source of the knocking. Often these are on bends in the plumbing – the pipes knock against joists. Clip the pipes and insulate round them to lessen the noise. Of course, it usually means taking up the floorboards.

fixing

235

Q My daughter and her husband have recently moved into a Victorian house. When they tried to put up bookshelves in the children's bedrooms, they found that the plaster just crumbles away and will not hold screws, rawlplugs, etc. Does this mean that the wall has to be completely replastered? They can't afford to replaster at this stage.

A It's not the plaster itself but what's behind it that supports the screws you are putting in. So, first of all, make sure you are using long screws. Check what the wall behind the plaster is made of. It is likely to be brick or a framework of timber supports and either of these is fine to drill into. Make sure you get the correct fittings from your DIY shop. If the plaster keeps falling off, you do have a problem because it isn't going to look very good but you could put up temporary shelves if you don't mind flaky plaster. Otherwise, use freestanding bookshelves until you are ready to replaster the room. There are lots of perfectly good cheap bookshelves around: try stores such as Habitat, Ikea and even your local auction house. It is sometimes good to leave things freestanding in a child's bedroom because you may want to move things round as they get bigger.

Q On *Home Front* recently you helped to redesign a kitchen for a couple on a limited budget. You used some glass shelving that appeared to have small self-adhesive brackets fixed to the wall. Could you tell me where these came from? We are currently redesigning our bathroom and they are exactly what we need.

A The brackets you saw on *Home Front* came from a company called Hafele (tel: 01788 542020) that specialises in components for all kinds of shelving, kitchen units and sliding doors, as well as lots of door furniture, kitchen carousels, decorative hinges and unusual ironmongery. The glass shelf supports we used in the kitchen were made of zinc alloy and are available in three different finishes – polished chrome, polished brass and white. Prices start from £1.21 each depending on the size you require for your shelves. They are suitable for glass up to 6mm thick. As for the glass itself, simply buy the required length from your local glass merchant, which you can find in Yellow Pages. Remember that glass shelves are very heavy, so check with the glass merchant on the correct size of bracket. Hafele supplies large companies directly, so phone them to find a local stockist of the brackets you need.

cleaning and fixing

Q We want to improve the security of our basement flat. Friends have recommended grilles for the windows and doors and folding gates for the French windows. Are there any we can buy that won't make us feel like we're living in prison?

A All kinds of craftspeople are getting into security these days – unfortunately business is booming. If you have a local blacksmith he may be able to make up your own design.

Q We would like to build a small holiday home and someone told us of a wooden barn you can buy, which has one side that drops down to form a patio. Do you know where we can find this type of building or have you any other suggestions?

A You certainly can buy a tiny wooden retreat for your weekends. Let me stress it wouldn't be suitable for permanent living but for £30,000 you can buy a 7.6m (25ft) long by 3.6m (12ft) wide by 4.6m (15ft) high cabin, glazed on two sides, with a deck that opens exactly as you wanted. At one end there's a double bed, a separate room with a bio loo and wash area (for a little more you can have a shower fitted), an open-plan area at the other end of the cabin and a two-person sleeping platform. Phone Carpenter Oak on 01225 743089 for details. The cabin is made to full building regulations and the price includes erecting it on the buyer's site. For a fraction of the cost, they also sell the Shepherd's Hut, which is insulated entirely with sheep's wool and is only 2.4 x 3.6 x 4m (8 x 12 x 13ft) high, for those ultimate cosy weekends.

Q We are converting our loft into a bedroom and would like the bannisters and spindles for the loft stairs to match our existing ones, which we believe to be original, and are square shaped rather than round. Our house was built around 1910. None of the local companies we have tried can match them. Is there a company that can do this?

A There's a company called Gifford Mead (tel: 01278 453665) that is based in Bridgwater, Somerset and they specialise in exactly this sort of work. They do replacement spindles, newel posts, hand and base rails to your specification. For spindles, send one to the company to use as a template and they will make you a true copy by machine. Their prices depend on how many you have made. They can make them up in any wood you want but normally people want soft wood as they are often painted.

fixing

Q I live in a tall semi-detached Victorian house. It's beautiful and filled with features, but the halls and landings are very narrow and dark. I want to brighten them up, and I'm happy to paint like mad, but I dread finding it all looks wrong – the house has already been done out in many paint effects, none to my taste. Cost is relevant as I've just become a single parent. Any advice?

A Start by concentrating on the one place that you see the most – the entrance hall. Make it a room and not just a walk-through. Clear it of all the shoes, bikes and other debris. Whatever is on the floor, give it a good clean. You could also add a colourful rug – diagonal patterns give a feeling of space. Choose a colour that will lift your spirits when you open the door on a dark, gloomy day – a soft yellow perhaps. Add mirrors to brighten the walls. Cover or paint an ugly radiator. If there's enough room, put up a shelf and display something you love. Look at your lighting: new shades and different wattage bulbs may help. Once you've done the hall, the landings may not seem so depressing. But even if they are, I'm sure your new hall will inspire you to tackle them.

Q I'm interested in acquiring an inexpensive spiral staircase for a loft conversion that wouldn't require building regulations approval. Do you know of any suppliers that would fit the bill?

A There's a company called Kensington Traders (tel: 01582 491171) who do everything from small loft conversion spiral staircases to much bigger installations. If you want to keep the cost down, it's best to have it made from a combination of wood and steel, as a wooden handrail alone could cost as much as £700. As a rough guide, a metal/wood staircase for a small domestic space would cost between £450 and £1,200, while a wooden one would start at £1,200 and go up to £2,000. Kensington Traders say it's advisable to comply with BS5395, part 2 1984, category A, if you're going ahead with a conversion, otherwise you may encounter problems when it comes to selling the property. Loft conversions can add substantially to the value of your house, so it's worth doing it properly.

Q **Can you tell me of anyone that makes spiral staircases?**

A   You don't say what you want the staircase to be made in. You can get wood, stainless steel, mild steel, concrete, glass – obviously what you choose depends on what your budget is. The company to phone first is Safety Stairways who have been making spirals for 35 years and are the biggest in Europe for this type of work. They can make anything you want – they have the equipment on site to make it directly. If you want to be counted among the rich and famous, they have done spirals for the likes of Ginger Spice, Liam Gallagher, David Seaman, Noel Edmonds and Richard Curtis. That doesn't mean that they don't have smaller ones too. Their prices start from £800. Phone them for a catalogue on 0121 526 3133.

fixing

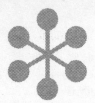

tessa's tool kit

Dynagrip knife

These retractable blade trimming knives are incredibly useful in your tool box. They are simple to use and come in handy for all kinds of little jobs. With a normal duty blade it is useful for craft work, where you may be cutting rubber or leather, slicing plastic and polystyrene. The heavy blade is great for stripping wiring and cutting things like plastic floor tiles. Then there are angled blades for getting into small spaces and finishing off jobs, neatening up edges. There is a special linoleum blade for cutting tiles and wood and metal saw blades for more specialist jobs. There is no end to the uses of this clever little knife. Stanley make it on 08701 650650.

 Tessa's tip There's a new tape available here that they've had in the States for ages. It's called Duck Tape and it can repair almost anything, so it's worth getting a roll to keep for emergencies. You can tear it by hand and it's completely waterproof. You can use it for endless jobs – sealing leaky guttering, mending dripping radiators, fixing torn car seats, holding up broken bumpers, repairing tents and wet suits, binding hockey sticks, mending split watering cans … I could go on!

It is available in large 50-m rolls down to 3-m flat packs for storing in the car. The small sizes come in lots of colours, which make it suitable for labelling luggage. The big size comes in silver. The company say it can even be used as an emergency tow rope, but I hope you never have to use it like that. It is available in all DIY shops and costs £1.99 for the small size.

Electric drill

It doesn't matter how much or how little DIY you do, everyone needs a good drill. The choice is bewilderingly vast, so decide what you want to do with yours before you buy. For most ordinary DIY tasks you don't need a heavyweight monster with loads of features. I use one which is exclusive to B&Q. It's cordless – which is a huge advantage – and takes only five hours to charge the battery. It's well specified, with six power settings, forward and reverse modes, a battery charging base and three-pin charger unit. The case is a bit lightweight for heavy-duty use, but for most household jobs you'll find it's your flexible friend. Available at B&Q stores around the country and quite a bargain at £23.97.

Folding workbench

This must be the most useful tool of all. A folding workbench will make almost any job easier – it can even clamp something as big as a door. It won't take up too much space either, because it folds up so cleverly. A good one will cost you about £100 but in my opinion that's money well spent – it is taking short cuts using inappropriate equipment that causes slips and injuries. The latest Black & Decker Workmate has a one-handed clamp action so that you can use your other hand to secure objects in place. I'd say that something like this is an essential – but if you are serious about DIY, you probably have one already.

Hammer

Every tool kit should have a hammer – having said that mine is without one at the moment. People walk off with them. I like a hammer that is heavy but not too heavy and I like it to have a rubber handle for good grip. I think you need to try hammers out personally as every one has a different action and you need to feel which weight you prefer. They start from 75g (3oz) for fine hammering and go up to what you want, but most people go for a 450g (16oz) or 600g (20oz) standard one.

Hot knife

There's a company called Fred Aldous based in Manchester which sells these. It is called a Weller hot knife and costs £23.80 plus £2.50 p&p. The company has a great mail-order catalogue full of art and craft materials – as well as some of those items that don't seem to be available

tessa's tool kit

241

elsewhere. It can also supply equipment for rug making, lampshades, lacemaking, weaving and patchwork. It also stocks cane for chairs, candlemaking moulds, materials for batik and silk painting and they have a large range of stencils too. Call 0161 236 2477 for a catalogue.

Low-tack masking tape

When you are buying masking tape, try and get hold of the low-tack variety. It seems to be harder to get than you think, which is odd as it is the best stuff around. Normal masking tape can be quite difficult to remove from carpets and window panes whereas the low tack stuff makes decorating easy and clearing up very quick. It is also very good for stencilling work.

Multi-ratchet ladder

Decorating can be fraught with danger, especially where ceilings are concerned. I have heard of so many accidents that happen when people overstretch while standing on an unstable or unsuitable surface. That's why a multi-ratchet ladder is brilliant – it offers you all kinds of configurations for decorating. There are lots of different models available but I think the one from B&Q is a good price. It has four different sections, which means you can create a stable platform for yourself while decorating. It also turns into a step-ladder and extends to a 3.75m (4yd) straight ladder, and it stores very neatly, which is a bonus. It costs £49.97 – a bargain when you consider you're getting two different ladders and a decorating platform in one.

Multi-tool

I love this neat little gadget from Gerber – it is so small yet it does lots. Sturdily made in stainless steel, the Compact Sport has pliers, scissors, wire cutter, serrated blade, flat and Phillips screwdrivers, bottle and can opener, wire crimper and steel file. It's cleverly designed so each item rotates and locks into place for use. It comes in a small pouch that fits on a belt or in a handbag. Some multi-tools have so many components that they are too complicated to use, but this one is easy to operate. The Compact Sport costs £49.99 and is available in Halfords, Homebase and DIY stores.

cleaning and fixing

Nail gun

This is a larger than usual tool for me to feature and suitable only if you do a lot of DIY carpentry. But if you are putting down floorboards or putting up dado rails, fencing or panelling, a nail gun could come in handy. It is a far more efficient way of nailing than using a hammer and it doesn't damage the wood, unlike a hammer which can splinter it. A nail gun takes nails between 31 and 63mm (1¼ and 2½in) and the nail cartridge is at a 45-degree angle so you can get to awkward places easily. It has an adjustable depth setting for precise nailing and countersinking, and with no cord, battery or compressor, is very easy to use. Nail guns can be hired from shops such as HSS, or Rutlands have a limited number of reconditioned models from the US to buy at £200. Call the company on 01629 815518.

Paint roller

Everyone who has done a bit of decorating needs one of these. This is a sturdy design with the birdcage centre made of metal. You simply slip whatever roller you want on to it. They usually come in two sizes – 4.5 and 4cm (1¾ and 1½in) and cost around £4. Most people use a medium-hair roller for general painting work but short-haired ones are better for oil-based finishes and flat surfaces. The longer lambswool ones are very soft and suitable for rougher surfaces where you need to get the paint right in. They also give a smoother finish than some of the others so it is worth experimenting when you start to decorate. They all only cost a few pounds and are available everywhere. Foxell and James do an Acorn one (tel: 020 7405 0152).

Staple gun

If you work on a makeover programme on television, a staple gun is without doubt your greatest asset. They are fantastic at covering things at speed. I don't really like them for serious work but they are very useful as a general, all purpose tool. You can make a seat cover, cover a notice board with baize, in fact any job that needs a quick fix. You only need to use one hand so the other can hold the material in place and they are all designed now for easy action. The Stanley Sharpshooter costs around £24 and is available at DIY superstores.

tessa's tool kit

243

Tile nibbler

If you are following the craze for doing mosaics, then these little beasts are the business. They allow you to cut tiles to the pattern you want, even making small curvy shapes. They are called nibblers because that is exactly what they do. They allow you to nibble the tile to shape and give you total control over it. Some of the Roman style mosaic work is very detailed and you will definitely need them, but even if you are doing a more abstract, loose pattern, they help the shape and the flow of the mosaic by softening the edges of the tile. Don't forget to wear goggles when using them as tiny little pieces can often fly up into your eye.

Wire wool

If you do a lot of painting and decorating wire wool is a useful product to have around. It comes in all grades according to the job you are doing. Usually the medium/coarse grade is used for rubbing down old varnish on wood or metal before painting. It is much easier to use than sandpaper if you are trying to rub down awkward shapes like bannisters as it moulds to your hand and you can really get into the space you are rubbing back. Once the surface is ready for painting, you use the fine wire wool to work in the new varnish – it sands it back for a finer finish. There are lots of companies who sell it.

✳ directory

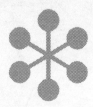

walls and ceilings

Action Products
270 North Road
Yate
South Gloucestershire BS37 7LQ
Tel: 01454 228702
(Tex Remover: removes textured coating and paint)

Anaglypta Advice Line
Tel: 01254 870137 for stockists of Lincrusta

Anglia Lime
PO Box 6
Sudbury
Suffolk CO10 6TW
Tel: 01787 313974
(limewash)

AS Handover
Unit 37H
Mildmay Grove North
London N1 4RH
Tel: 020 7359 4696
Website: www.handover.co.uk
(Mylar stencil sheeting and hot stencil-cutting knives)

B&Q plc
1 Hampshire Corporate Park
Chandlers Ford
Eastleigh
Hants SO53 3YX
Tel: 020 8466 4166
Website: www.bandq.co.uk
(ESP: a melamine primer)

Baer & Ingram
Dragon Works
Leigh-on-Mendip
Nr Bath BA3 5QZ
Tel: 01373 812552
Website: www.baer-ingram.co.uk
(wide range of wallpapers, especially those with characters, e.g. Wallace and Gromit)

Brick Centre
Brimington Road North
Whittington Moor
Chesterfield
Derbyshire S41 9BH
Tel: 01246 260001
Website: www.brickcentre.co.uk
(Brickmatch: restores the colour of brickwork)

Casdron
Wood End
Prospect Road
Alresford
Winchester
Hants SO24 9QF
Tel: 01962 732126
(Stain-Away: lifts and softens hardened layers)

Coo-Var
Ellenshaw Works
Lockwood St
Hull HU2 0HN
Tel: 01482 328053
Website: www.coo-var.co.uk

E-mail: info@coo-var.co.uk
(anti-graffiti paint)

L Cornelissen & Son
105 Great Russell St
London WC1B 3RY
Tel: 020 7636 1045
(distemper ingredients)

Craig & Rose
Unit 8
Halbeath Industrial Estate
Cross Gates Road
Dunfermline KY11 7EG
Tel: 0131 554 1131
(decorative paint finish)

Crown Paints
Crown House
PO Box 37
Hollins Road
Darwen
Lancashire BB3 0BG
Tel: 01254 704 951
Fax: 01254 774414
(oil-based eggshell and gloss paint to repaint Lincrusta)

Designers Guild
3 Olaf Street
London W11 4BE
Tel: 020 7243 7300
Fax: 020 7243 7320
E-mail: info@designersguild.com
Website: www.designersguild.com
(will help you find stockists of tartan wallpaper)

Dow Corning
Meriden Business Park
Copse Drive
Coventry CV5 9RG
Tel: 01676 528000
Website: www.dowcorning.com
(details on mastic remover)

Dover Bookshop
18 Earlham Street
London WC2H 9LM
Tel: 020 7836 2111
Website: www.doverbooks.co.uk

Dulux
ICI Paints
Wexham Road
Slough
Berks SL2 5DS
Tel: 01420 23024
(Heritage Hotline)
Tel: 01753 550555
(customer advice)
Tel: 01753 534225
(Weathershield range)
Website: www.dulux.co.uk
(Dulux range)

Ecomax Acoustics
Gomm Road
High Wycombe
Bucks HP13 7DJ
Tel: 01494 436 345
Website: www.acoustic.co.uk
(advice on soundproofing rooms)

Farrow & Ball Ltd
Uddens Estate
Wimborne
Dorset BH21 7NL
Tel: 01202 876141
Fax: 01202 873793
E-mail: info@farrow-ball.com
Tel: 020 7351 0273 – London shop
Website: www.farrow-ball.com
(paint range which includes National Trust colours; limewash)

Foxell and James
57 Farringdon Road
London EC1
Tel: 020 7405 0152
(lacquers)

walls and ceilings

Frieze Frame
Unit 2
Gordon Street
Wirral CH41 2JQ
Tel: 0151 650 2401
E-mail info@friezeframe.com
Website: www.friezeframe.com
(themed mural kits)

James Hetley & Co
School House Lane
London E1W 3JA
Tel: 020 7790 2333
(glass paints)

Homelux Nenplas
Airfield Industrial Estate
Ashbourne
Derby DE6 1HA
Tel: 01335 340340
Website: www.nenplas.co.uk
(tile transfers)

Home Free
Royal Avenue
Widnes
Cheshire WA88 1HF
Tel: 0990 748494
Website: www.homefree.co.uk
(tile grout cleaner)

HSS
Tel: 0845 728 2828
Website: www.hss.co.uk
(steam stripper stockists)

International
Plascon International Ltd
Brewery House
High Street
Twyford
Winchester SO21 1RG
Tel: 01962 711177
Website: www.plascon.co.uk
(full range of paints and primers for all surfaces: walls, floors, tiles)

James Mayor
120 Frazley Street
Birmingham B5
Tel: 0121 643 8349
Website: www.jms.uk.net
(ranges of dado wall panelling)

The Mosaic Workshop
Unit B
443-449 Holloway Road
London N7 6LJ
Tel: 020 7263 2997
Website: www.mosaicworkshop.com
(mosaic tiles, grout, glue)

Ray Munn
861-863 Fulham Road
London SW6 5HP
Tel: 020 7736 9876
Website: www.raymunn.co.uk
(HomeStrip: a stripper for stains and paints)

National Federation of Terrazzo, Marble and Mosaic Specialists
Tel: 0845 609 0050 for local supplier

Nu-Line
315 Westbourne Park Road
London W11 1ES
Tel: 020 7727 7748
(flexible mirror tiles with a peel-off backing)

Paint Magic
62 Walcot Street
Bath BA1 5BN
Tel: 01225 469966

Palace Chemicals Ltd
Spekehole Industrial Estate
Speke
Liverpool L24 4AB
Tel: 0151 486 6101
(Peel Away: removes paint from wood and other surfaces)

Paper Moon
53 Fairfax Road
London NW6 4EL
Tel: 020 7624 1198
*(wallpaper specialist who stock
Beatrix Potter characters and they
also do photo murals)*

Pebeo
305, Avenue de Bertagne
BP 106 - 13881 Gémenos Cedex
France
E-mail: info@pebeo.com
Tel: 02380 901914 – UK shop
Website: www.pebeo.com
*(products for decorative work, paints
for use on many surfaces)*

Pilkington's
PO Box 4
Clifton Junction
Swinton
Manchester M27 8LP
Tel: 0161 727 1000
Website: www.pilkingtons.com
(tiles with sunflowers on them)

E Ploton
273 Archway Road
London N6 5AA
Tel: 020 8348 2838(mail order)
Website: www.ploton.co.uk
*(bleached and unbleached natural
sponges)*

Potmolen Paint
27 Woodcock Industrial Estate
Warminster
Wilts BA12 9DX
Tel: 01985 213960
(distemper and linseed oil paint)

Pumex (UK) Ltd
Unit D4, Grampian House
Meridian Gate
Marsh Wall
London E14 9YT
Tel: 020 7363 5455
Website: www.pumex.co.uk

*(pumice stripping blocks for rubbing
down paintwork)*

JH Ratcliffe
135a Linaker St
Southport PR8 5DF
Tel: 01704 537999
Website: www.ratcliffepaints.co.uk
(lead testing kits)

Tony Roche
Website: www.tonyroche.co.uk
lemon@tonyroche.co.uk
*(stencils in traditional and modern
designs)*

Rose of Jericho
Westhill Barn
Evershot
Dorset ST2 0LD
Tel: 01935 83676
(limewash)

Sandolin
Tel: 01480 497637
(quick drying clear varnish for wood)

Shortwood Carvings
Bradlington Ltd
Rear of 133 Becontree Ave
Dagenham
Essex RM8 2UL
Tel: 0208 9838863
*(plastic carvings, e.g. cherubs, panel
designs, friezes)*

Paul Smoker
1 Lathan Street
Kettering
Northants NN14 3HD
Tel: 01536 373 158
Fax: 01536 373431
(ready-made distemper paint)

walls and ceilings

Stanfords
12-14 Long Acre
London WC2E 9LP
Tel: 020 7836 1321
Website: www.stanfords.co.uk
(biggest map shop in the world)

The Stencil Store
20-21 Heronsgate Road
Chorleywood
Herts WD3 5BN
Tel: 01923 285577
Website: www.stencilstore.com
(stencils, crackle glaze)

Stuart Stevenson
68 Clerkenwell Road
London EC1M 5QA
Tel: 020 7253 1693
Website: www.stuartstevenson.co.uk
(transfer metal leaf)

Strippers
PO Box 6
Sudbury
Suffolk CO10 6TW
Tel: 01787 371524
(paint stripping materials)

Stuart Interiors
Barrington Court
Barrington
Ilminster
Somerset TA19 0NQ
Tel: 01460 240349
Fax: 01460 242069
Website: www.stuartinteriors.ltd.uk
(period wood panelling)

Troika Architectural Mouldings
41 Clun St
Sheffield S4 7JS
Tel: 0114 275 3222
(custom-made cornicing)

Urchin
Tel: 01672 872872
Website: www.urchin.co.uk
(smelly paints, e.g. Gob Stopper, Banana Skin)

Vymura
Talbot Road
Hyde SK14 4EJ
Tel: 0161 368 8321
Website:
www.englewoodlimited.co.uk
(wallpaper with characters, e.g. Thomas the Tank Engine)

David Wainwright
Liberty plc
32 Kingly Street
London W1R 5LA
Tel: 020 7734 1234
(wallhangings made from wood)

Sebastian Wakefield
Camlaithe
Kettlewell
Skipton
North Yorkshire BD23 5QY
Tel: 01756 760809
(murals and trompe l'oeil work)

The Wallfashion Bureau
High Corn Mill
Chapel Hill
Skipton
N.Yorkshire BD23 1NL
(send an sae for a free booklet on how to wallpaper)

Zinsser
26 High Street
Pinner
Middlesex HA5 5PW
Tel: 020 8866 9977
Fax: 020 8429 3283
(Cover Stain: top-quality primer; primer sealer to seal knots)

floors

Fred Aldous Ltd
37 Lever St
Manchester M1 1LW
Tel: 0161 236 2477
E-mail: Aldous@btinternet.com
Website: www.fredaldous.co.uk
(rag rug materials)

The Alternative Flooring Company
14 Anton Trading Estate
Andover
Hampshire SP10 2NJ
Tel: 0500 007057
E-mail: sales@alternative-flooring.co.uk
Website: www.alternative-flooring.co.uk
(100% coir matting in a range of colours)

Alufloor
Unit 2B, Anchor Bridge Way
Mill Street West
Dewsbury WF12 9PP
Tel: 01924 461355 or 01924 450008
(aluminium floor tiles)

Behar Profex
The Alban Building, St Albans Place
Upper St
London N1 0NX
Tel: 020 72260144
(clean, mend and preserve rugs and carpets)

Berry Designs
157 St. Johns Hill
Battersea
London SW11 1TQ
Tel: 020 7924 2197
(patterns for bathroom floor design)

David Black Oriental Carpets
96 Portland Road
London W11 4LN
Tel: 020 7727 2566
(professional carpet restorers)

Casdron
Wood End, Prospect Road
Alresford, Winchester
Hants SO24 9QF
Tel: 01962 732126
(Stain Away: for removing marks from tiles and other surfaces)

Charltons World of Wood
Frome Road
Radstock
Bath BA3 3PT
Tel: 01761 436229
(bamboo flooring)

Crucial Trading
PO Box 11
Duke Place
Kidderminster
Worcester DY10 2JR
Tel: 01562 825200
(reversible mats made out of paper)

Dalsouple Direct Ltd
PO Box 140
Bridgwater
Somerset TA5 1HT
Tel: 01984 667551
Website: www.dalsouple.com
(rubber tiles)

floors

Evode Industries
Newtown
Swords
Co Dublin
Tel: 00353 1840 1461
(Stain Away: stain remover for flooring)

Fired Earth
Twyford Mill
Oxford Road
Adderbury
Oxon OX17 3HP
Tel: 01295 812088
Website: www.firedearth.com
(oils and sealers for wood floors; tiles and grout)

Forbo-Nairn
PO Box 1
Kirkcaldy KY1 2SB
Tel: 01592 643777
Website: www.forbo-nairn.co.uk
(Marmoleum: a natural lino, ideal for allergy sufferers)

Foxell and James
57 Farringdon Road
London EC1M 3JB
Tel: 020 7405 0152
(treatments for wood floors)

Guru
77-81 Scrubs Lane
London NW10 6QW
Tel: 020 8960 6655
(rugs)

Eva Johnson
Tel: 01638 731362 for information
Fax: 01638 731855
(oils and other treatments for wood floors)

Liberon Waxes
Mountfield Industrial Estate
Learoyd Road
New Romney
Kent TN28 8XU

Tel: 01797 361136
(floor sealer for cork tiles)

Harvey Maria
Trident Business Centre
89 Bickersteth Road
London SW17 9SH
Tel: 020 8516 7788
(cork tiles)

HG Systems
Tel: 01206 795200
Website: www.hginternational.com
(specialist floor cleaning products)

International
For details: See **Walls and ceilings**
(floor paints for vinyl and linoleum)

Johnson's
Frimley Green Road
Frimley Green, Camberley
Surrey GU16 5AJ
Tel: 01784 484100
Website: www.scjohnsonwax.com
(Traffic Wax Paste: high sheen wax for slate tile floors)

Lassco Flooring
41 Maltby St
Bermondsey
London SE1 3PA
Tel: 020 7237 4488
E-mail: flooring@lassco.co.uk
Website: www.lassco.co.uk
(reclaimed flooring specialist)

Liberon
For details: See **Walls and ceilings**
(Floor Protector: improves the appearance of slate and marble)

Lithofin
Tel: 01962 732126
Website: www.lithofin.com
(treatment for tiles, cleaners and primers)

floors

LTP
Tone Industrial Estate
Milverton Road, Wellington
Somerset TA21 0AZ
Tel: 01823 666213
(cleaners, sealers and polishers for all kinds of floors)

Luxomation
579 London Road
Isleworth
Middlesex TW7 4EJ
Tel: 020 8568 6373
Website: www.luxomation.com
(stainless steel tiles)

Morlands
Northover
Glastonbury
Somerset BA6 9YA
Tel: 01458 835042
(animal skin rugs)

Roger Oates Design
Tel: 01531 632718
Website: www.rogeroates.com
(anti-slip underlays for runners)

Original Features
155 Tottenham Lane
London N8 9BT
Tel: 020 8348 5155
Website: www.originalfeatures.co.uk
(original and reproduction tiles and fireplaces etc)

Oxfam
Tel: 01865 3136000
Website: www.oxfam.org.uk
(rugs and other household furnishings)

Paragon
Corbie Cottage
Maryculter
Aberdeen AB12 5FT
Tel: 01224 735536
(central vacuuming systems for underneath carpets)

Scotts of Stow
The Square
Stow on the Wold
Gloucestershire GL54 1AF
Tel: 0990 449111
(anti-slip mesh to hold rugs on to carpets)

Sealocrete PLA Ltd
Greenfield Lane
Rochdale
Lancashire OL11 2LD
Tel: 01706 352255
E-mail:
bestproducts@sealocrete.co.uk
Website: *www.sealocrete.co.uk*
(concrete paint suitable for interiors and exteriors)

Stairrods UK
Unit 6
Park Road North Industrial Estate
Blackhill, Consett
County Durham CH8 5UN
Tel: 01207 591176
(clips and rods for stair carpets)

Stone Age
19 Filmer Road
Fulham
London SW6 7BU
Tel: 020 7385 7954
Website: www.estone.co.uk
(stone floors)

Volanti
46-76 Summerstown
Tooting
London SW17
Tel: 020 8947 6561
(products to protect wear on carpets)

Helen Yardley
A-Z Studios
3-5 Hardwidge Street
London SE1 3SY
Tel: 020 7403 7114
(makes rugs for your wall or floor, large range in size and colour)

floors

furniture

Architectural Salvage Index
Netley House
Gomshall
Guildford
Surrey GU5 9QA
Tel: 01483 203221
E-mail: salvage@handr.co.uk
Website: www.handr.co.uk
(salvaged furniture, e.g. four-poster beds)

Armfield
191 Church Road
Benfleet
Essex SS7 4PN
Tel: 01268 793067
glass@armfield.com
(glass furnishings, innovative usage)

Artefact
36 Windmill St
London W1T 2JT
Tel: 020 7580 4878
(ornate framed mirrors)

Business Design Centre
52 Upper St
London N1 0QH
Tel: 020 7359 3535
Website:
www.businessdesigncentre.co.uk
Website: www.newdesigner.com
(contact for new designers/graduates)

Carpenter Oak
Hall Farm
Thick Wood Lane
Colerne
Chippenham
Wilts SN14 8BE
Tel: 01225 743089
(wood cabins large enough to contain beds/wash areas)

Coexistence
288 Upper St
Islington
London N1 2TZ
Tel: 020 7354 8817
E-mail: enquiries@coexistence.co.uk
Website: www.coexistence.co.uk
(furniture and accessories)

The Cornflake Shop
37 Windmill St
London W1T 2JU
Tel: 020 7631 0472
Website: www.cornflake.co.uk
(speakers in a range of colours)

Crafts Council
44a Pentonville Road
London N1 9BY
Tel: 020 7278 7700
Website: www.craftscouncil.org.uk
(showcase designers, e.g. flexible furniture)

Crewkerne Carriers
18 Buckland Road
Penmill Trading Estate
Yeovil BA21 5EA
(courier firm)

DICO Furniture Ltd
Constantine Street
Oldham OL4 3AD
Tel: 0161 665 1417
Website: www.dicointernational.com

Dragon Shed
The Gallery
56a The High Street
Ascot
Berkshire SL5 9NF
Tel: 01344 627748
Website: www.dragonshed.co.uk
(Chinese wooden screens)

Dylon International Ltd
London SE26 5HD
Tel: 020 8663 4296
Website: www.dylon.co.uk
(dyes)

Foxell and James
For details: See **Walls and ceilings**
*(Libnet Furniture Cleaner: removes
varnish and wax)*

Felicity Irons
Struttlend Farm
Old Ways Road
Ravensden
Bedford NK44 2RD
Tel: 01234 771980
Website: www.rushmatters.co.uk
*(rush products; designs and makes
headboards with a difference; works
to commission)*

London Wall Bed Company
430 Chiswick High Road
London W4 5TF
Tel: 020 8742 8200
*(fold-away and fold-down beds plus
add-on furniture)*

St Blaise
Westhill Barn
Evershot
Dorchester
Dorset DT2 0LD
Tel: 01935 83662
*(restoration firm specialising in fine
joinery)*

Taskers DIY
Unit G1-G3
Liver Industrial Estate
Long Lane
Aintree
Liverpool L9 7ES
Tel: 0151 525 4844
(felt pads for the bottom of furniture)

Wallbeds
Suite 662
Linen Hall
162-168 Regent St
London W1R 5TB
Tel: 020 7434 2066
(fold-away beds)

furniture

soft furnishings

Allied Carpets
76 High St
Orpington
Kent BR6 0JQ
Tel: 01689 895000
Tel: 0800 192192 for your
nearest branch
(range of soft furnishings)

Appeal Conservatory Blinds Ltd
6 Vale Lane
Bedminster
Bristol BS3 5SD
Tel: 0117 963 7734
Website: www.appeal-blinds.co.uk
(conservatory blinds)

Arthur Beale
194 Shaftesbury Avenue
London WC2H 8JP
Tel: 020 7836 9034
(yacht supplier who have canvas and large sized eyelets)

Harry Berger Cleaners & Dyers
25 Station Road
Cheadle Hulme
Cheadle
Cheshire SK8 5AF
Tel: 0161 485 7733
(dye cotton velvet curtains)

Borovick
16 Berwick St
London W1V 4HP
Tel: 020 7437 2180
(massive range of fabric)

Bute Fabrics
4 Barone Road
Rothesay
Isle of Bute PA20 0DP
Tel: 0800 212064
Website: www.butefabrics.com
(tough performance fabrics for upholstering)

Celestial Buttons
54 Cross St
London N1 2BA
Tel: 020 7226 4766
Website: www.celestialbuttons.co.uk
(wide range of buttons for clothing and also interior design)

Dainty Supplies Ltd
Unit 35
Phoenix Road
Crowther Industrial Estate
District 3
Washington NE38 0AD
Tel: 0191 416 7886
(craft and haberdashery materials)

DWCD
Tel: 020 8964 2002
(interior accessories, e.g. scented lavender bags)

Dylon International Ltd
For details: See **Furniture**
(dyes and Image Maker: transfers a photocopy on to fabric)

Early's of Witney
New Witney Mill
Burford Road
Witney
Oxfordshire OX8 5EB
Tel: 01993 703131
(replacement taffeta and silk edging for blankets)

Eclectics
Unit 25
Leigh Road
Haine Industrial Estate
Ramsgate CT12 5EU
Tel: 01843 852888
Website: www.eclectics.co.uk
(blinds and sliding panels)

Eiderdown Studio
228 Withycombe Village Road
Exmouth
Devon EX8 3BD
Tel: 01395 271147
(re-cover eiderdowns and duvets)

Joss Graham Oriental Textiles
10 Ecclestone St
London SW1W 9LT
Tel: 020 7730 4370
Website: www.cloudband.com
(wide range of fabrics)

Jersey Vogue Fabrics
14 Station Road
Edgware
Middlesex HA8 7AB
Tel: 020 8952 7751
(fabrics, fillings for cushions)

Keys
Stephenson Road
Clacton-on-Sea
Essex CO15 3AW
Tel: 01255 432518
(special size bedlinen, e.g. round beds)

John Lewis
171 Victoria St
London SW1E 5NN
Tel: 020 7629 7711
Website: www.johnlewis.com
(fake fur, feathers for pillows, combination duvets)

Liberty plc
Regent Street
London W1R 6AH
Tel: 020 7734 1234
Fax: 020 7573 9876
Website: www.liberty.co.uk

Lunn Antiques
86 New Kings Road
London SW6 4LU
Tel: 020 7736 4638
(specialise in antique linen and lace)

Ian Mankin
109 Regents Park Road
London NW1 8UR
Tel: 020 7722 0997
(large range of utility fabrics)

Melin Tregwynt
Castle Morris
Haverfordwest
Pembrokeshire SA62 5UX
Tel: 01348 891644
(blankets, bedspreads, floor cushions in numerous wools)

soft furnishings

Monkwell
10-12 Wharfdale Road
Bournemouth
Dorset BH4 9BT
Tel: 01202 752944
Website: www.monkwell.com
(fabrics for upholstery, accessories and curtains)

Natural Fabric Co
Wesson Place, 127 High Street
Hungerford
Berkshire RG17 0DL
Tel: 01488 684002
(natural upholstery and curtain fabrics)

Nice Irma's
Unit 2, Finchley Industrial Centre
879 High Road
London N12 8QA
Tel: 020 8343 7610
Website: www.niceirmas.com
(unusual covers for cushions plus range of curtains, lampshades, doorknobs)

Osborne & Little
304 Kings Road
London SW3 5UH
Tel: 020 7352 1456
Website: www.osborneandlittle.com
(furnishing fabrics)

PA Tex Ltd
Unit 1, Worcester Road
Evesham
Worcestershire WR11 4RA
Tel: 01386 442794
(convert eiderdowns to duvets and recover old eiderdowns)

Peacock Blue
201 New Kings Road
London SW6 4SR
Tel: 020 7384 3400
Tel: 0870 3331555 (mail order)
(bedlinen, bathrobes and towels)

Plasti-Kote
PO Box 867
Pampisford
Cambridge CB2 4XP
Tel: 01223 836400
Website: www.spraypaint.co.uk
(spray paints for different surfaces)

Portmeirion Group
London Road
Staffordshire ST4 7QQ
Tel: 01782 744721
Website: www.portmeirion.co.uk
(fabric)

Renaissance Weavers
Staple Court
Hockworthy, Wellington
Somerset TA21 0NH
Tel: 01398 361543
(recreates historic fabric and carpet designs)

Silk Shades Interiors
Tel: 0115 988 1846
(silk specialists)

Isabel Stanley
Unit W10
Cockpit Yard Workshops
Northington Street
London WC1N 2NP
Tel: 020 7209 2101(mail order)
(textile designer specialising in lampshades and photograph albums)

Tidmarsh & Sons
32 Hyde Way
Welwyn Garden City
Herts AL7 3AW
Tel: 01707 886226
(laminate materials and shaped blinds)

soft furnishings

directory

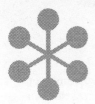

doors and windows

Aaronson Noon
Roxby Place
London SW6 1RS
Tel: 020 7610 3344
E-mail: adam@aanoon.demon.co.uk
Website: www.aanoon.demon.co.uk
(glass door knobs, coat hooks)

JD Beardmore
17 Pall Mall
London SW1Y 5LU
Tel: 020 7670 1000
Website: www.beardmore.co.uk
E-mail: beardmore@beardmore.co.uk
(selection of letterplates and other door furniture)

Philip Bradbury
83 Blackstock Road
London N4 2JW
Tel: 020 7226 2919
Website:
www.philipbradburyglass.co.uk
(specialist glass shop, provides glass panels)

Brats
281 Kings Road
London SW3 5EW
Tel: 020 7351 7674
Website: www.brats.co.uk
(beaded curtains)

Breezeway
Tel: 01234 781000 (mail order)
E-mail: info@breezeway.co.uk
Website: www.breezeway.co.uk
(US-style insect screens for windows and internal and external doors)

Clayton Munroe
Kingston West Drive
Kingston
Staverton
Totnes
Devon TQ9 6AR
Tel: 01803 762626
Website: www.claytonmunroe.com
(diverse range of door handles and door furniture)

Danico Brass
31-35 Winchester Road
Swiss Cottage
London NW3 3NR
Tel: 020 7483 4477
Fax: 020 7722 7992
(brass letter plates, offers a customized service)

Dartington Steel Design
Unit 3 and 4
Webbers Yard
Dartington Industrial Estate
Totnes
Devon TQ9 6JY
Tel: 01803 868671
Website: www.dartington.com
(range of door furniture)

doors and windows

Duwit
Unit 1
Orion Trade Centre
Guiness Circle
Newbridge
Manchester M17 1JT
Tel: 0161 872 0626
Website: www.specialistdiy.com
(chrome fittings including door handles and dimmer switches)

English Heritage
23 Saville Row
London W1S 2ET
Tel: 020 7973 3000
Tel: 01793 414910(to get free booklets re renovating windows)
Website: www.english-heritage.org.uk
(conservation of windows and their fittings)

Fashion Fun Kee
c/o Minit UK
Unit 5
Old Field Road
Maidenhead
Berks SL6 1TH
Tel: 0800 169 3161
(make keys in distinctive patterns)

Franco-File
PO Box 31
Tiverton
Devon EX16 4YU
Tel: 01884 253556 (mail order only)
(blue and white enamelled house plates, French-style)

Glass and Glazing Federation
44-48 Borough High Street
London SE1 1XB
Tel: 020 7403 7177 for nearest members
Website: www.ggf.org.uk
(free advice service on choosing a conservatory)

Glover and Smith
9a Winchester St
Overton
Nr. Basingstoke RG25 3HR
Tel: 01256 773012
Website: www.gloverandsmith.com
E-mail: sales@gloverandsmith.com
(door handles, cabinet pulls, pewter objects)

James Hetley & Co
School House Lane
London E1W 3JA
Tel: 020 7790 2333
(700 different types of glass plus copper tape etc)

Jewel Tools Supply Co
31 Hatton Wall
London EC1N 8JJ
Tel: 020 7242 8528
(rouge and salvyt cloths to help remove small scratches in glass)

Lead and Light
35a Hartland Road
London
NW1 8DB
Tel: 020 7485 0997
(stained glass suppliers who can add toughened glass to help make it more secure)

London Graphic Centre
16/18 Shelton St
Covent Garden
London WC2H 9JJ
Tel: 020 7240 0095
Website: www.lgc-unlimited.com
(glass paint)

Merlin Glass – Liam Carey Door Handles
Barn St
Station Road
Liskeard
Cornwall PL14 3AU
Tel: 01579 342399
Website: www.glassdoorhandles.com
E-mail:
liamcarey@merlinglass.demon.co.uk
(coloured glass door knobs in varying shapes)

Nice Irma's
For details: See **Soft furnishings**
(ceramic door knobs)

Nicholls & Clarke
3-10 Shoreditch High Street
London E1 6PE
Tel: 020 7247 5432
Fax: 020 7247 7738
Website: www.nichollsandclarke.com
(stainless steel letterplates)

North Western Lead
Newton Moor Industrial Estate
Mill St
Hyde
Cheshire SK14 4LJ
Tel: 0161 368 4491
Website: www.decraled.co.uk
(Decra Art Pack - coloured film for making stained glass-effect windows)

Period House Group
Fold Court
Buttercrambe
York YO41 1XU
Tel/fax: 01759 373 481
E-mail: info@phg-uk.com
Website: www.phg-uk.com
(forged iron work from doors to old style nails)

The Sash Window Workshop
Unit 8/9
Brickfield Industrial Park
Kilm Lane
Bracknell
Berks RG12 1NQ
Tel: 01344 868668
Website: www.sashwindows.com
(specialise in restoring sash windows)

The Society for the Protection of Ancient Buildings
Charity No. 231307
37 Spital Square
London E1 6DY
Tel: 020 7377 1644
Fax: 020 7247 5296
E-mail info@spab.org.uk
Website: www.spab.org.uk
(booklet in association with English Heritage re: windows)

doors and windows

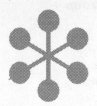

kitchens

Abbey Horn of Lakeland
Holme Mill
Holme, Nr Carnforth
Lands LA6 1RD
Tel: 01524 782387
Website:
www.edirectory.co.uk/abbeyhorn
*(buff knives and lift their grubby
appearance)*

Aga
Station Road
Ketley
Telford TF1 5AQ
Tel: 0345 125207
Website: www.aga-rayburn.co.uk
(Aga pans)

Argos
Tel: 0870 6003030 (customer
services)
(Edwardian-style airers)

Armitage Shanks
Ideal Standard Ltd
Bathroom Works
National Avenue
Kingston upon Hull HU5 4HS
Tel: 01543 490253
(automatic taps)

Paul Beck
Crosswinds
Happisburgh
Norfolk NR12 0RX
Tel: 01692 650455
*(vintage car supplier: may have
sealers for old fridges, etc.)*

Coachtrimming Centre
45 Anerley Road
Crystal Palace
London SE19 2AS
Tel: 020 8659 4135
*(classic car supplier who could have
parts, e.g. rubber seals for old
fridges)*

The Cook's Shop
Riverside Place
Taunton
Somerset TA1 1AG
Tel: 01823 271071
(kitchen equipment)

Corian
DuPont Corian®
McD Marketing
Maylands Avenue
Hemel Hempstead
Hertfordshire HP2 7DP
Tel: 01442 346776
Website: www.corian.co.uk
(kitchen countertops)

The Craft Depot
Tel: 01458 274727 (mail order)
*(fridge decorations, e.g. stick-on
foam and magnets)*

Cucina Direct
Tel: 020 8246 4300 (mail order)
Website: www.cucinadirect.co.uk
(synthetic bone-handled knives)

Dart Valley Services
Unit 1&2, Alders Way
Yalberton Industrial Estate
Paignton
Devon TQ4 7QN
Tel: 01803 529021
Website:
www.dartvalleysystems.co.uk
(automatic taps)

Divertimenti
See **Cucina Direct**

Facets
Tel: 020 8520 3392
(blue glass liners for silver salt cellars or mustard pots)

Falcon Products
8 Three Point Business Park
Charles Lane
Haslingdon
Rossendale
Lancs BB4 5EH
Tel: 01706 224790
(anti-slip material)

Fired Earth
For details: See **Walls and ceilings**
(adhesives for sticking worktop tiles)

Fridge Art
Magnetic Media
Saxley Hill Barn
Meath Green Lane
Horley
Surrey RH6 8JA
Tel: 01293 820861
(magnetic posters for fridges)

GEC Anderson
Oakengrove
Shire Lane
Hastoe, Tring
Herts HP23 6LY
Tel: 01442 826999
Website: www.gecanderson.co.uk
(stainless steel sinks/baths/toilets)

The General Trading Company
144 Sloane St
London SW1X 9BL
Tel: 020 7730 0411
Website: www.general-trading.co.uk
(table mats)

The Great Little Trading Company
Tel: 0990 673009
(magnetised photo frames especially designed for fridges)

A & J Gummers
Unit H, Redfern Parkway
Tyseley
Birmingham B11 2DN
Tel: 0121 706 2241
Website: www.gummers.co.uk
(automatic taps)

Hafele
Swift Valley Industrial Estate
Rugby
Warwickshire CV21 1RD
Tel: 01788 542020
Website: www.hafele.co.uk
(components for all kinds of shelving and kitchen units)

Home Hardware
Tel: 01271 326222 for nearest retailer
(grouting products)

Hot and Cold
13 Golbourne Road
London W10 5NY
Tel: 020 8960 1200
(free standing, eye-level grill gas ovens)

Hotpoint
Tel: 08709 077077
(supply kitchenware)

Liberon
For details: See **Walls and ceilings**
(finishing oil for pine wood)

kitchens

263

Luxcrete
Premier House
Disraeli Road
London NW10 7BT
Tel: 020 8965 7292
(supplier of glass bricks)

MICA
Atlas Trading Centre
Oldham Road
Sawmills, Waterloo
Ashton Under Lyme
Lancashire OL7 9AZ
Tel: 0161 339 2011
(grouting products)

**Museums and Galleries
Commission**
16 Queen Anne's Gate
London SW1H 9AA
Tel: 020 7273 1444
(list of ceramics restorers)

Nickel Blanks
6 Smithfield
Sheffield S3 7AR
Tel: 01142 725792
(make up replica pieces of cutlery)

Pisani
Unit 12, Transport Avenue
Great West Road
Brentford
Middlesex TW8 9HF
Tel: 020 8568 5001
Website: www.pisani.co.uk
(granite worktops)

Plasti-Kote
PO Box 867, Pampisford
Cambridge CB2 4XP
Tel: 01223 836400
Website: www.spraypaint.co.uk
*(anti-rust primer, e.g. for
dishwashers)*

Portmeirion Group
London Road
Staffordshire ST4 7QQ
Tel: 01782 744721
Website: www.portmeirion.co.uk
(kitchenware)

Sala
Sparrow Works
Martock
Somerset TA12 6LG
Tel: 01935 827050
Website: www.sala.uk.com
(unusual homewares)

TableWhere
4 Queens Parade Close
London N11 3SY
Tel: 020 8361 6111
Website: www.tableware.co.uk
*(find out of date china and buy
unwanted old china)*

Top Knobs Ltd
Brunel Buildings
Brunel Road
Newton Abbott
Devon TQ12 4DB
Tel: 01626 363388
(wide range of furniture knobs)

UP
Tel: 020 7278 6971
(designs for tea towels)

**Watchet Products of
Somerset**
The Mill
Anchor St
Watchet
Somerset TA23 0AZ
Tel: 01984 631207
*(tableware, coasters etc in floral
patterns)*

Whittards
Tel: 0800 525092 (mail order)
Website: www.whittard.com
(bone china)

bathrooms

Architectural Salvage Index
For details: See **Furniture**
(salvaged bathroom fittings)

The Bath Doctor
34 London Road
Faversham
Kent ME13 8RX
Tel: 01233 740532
Website: www.bathdoctor.com
(recolour bathroom suites in situ)

Colourwash
165 Chamberlayne Road
London NW10 3NU
Tel: 020 8459 8918
Website: www.colourwash.co.uk
(anything for bathrooms)

Croydex Group plc
Central Way
Walworth Industrial Estate
Andover
Hants SP10 5AW
Tel: 01264 365881
(shower curtains, rods and rails)

Curious Pedestrians
Lewiston Mill
Toadsmoor Road
Stroud
Gloucestershire GL5 2TB
Tel: 01453 886482
Website: www.bogseats.co.uk
(toilet seats)

Martin Edwards
Unit 7
Cuerden Industrial Estate
Holme Road
Bamber Bridge
Preston
Tel: 01772 334868
(architectural salvage)

CP Hart
Newnham Terrace
Hercules Road
London SE1 7DR
Tel: 020 7902 1000
Website: www.cphart.co.uk
(bathroom fittings)

Insitu
Talbot Mill
44 Ellesmere St
Manchester M15 4JY
Tel: 0161 839 5525
(architectural salvage)

Jendico
1 Cork Lane
Glen Parva
Leicester LE2 9JR
Tel: 0116 277 0474
Website: www.jendico.co.uk
sales@jendico.co.uk
(shower curtains and flexible shower curtain rails)

bathrooms

The Lab
16-18 Lonsdale Road
London NW6 6RD
Tel: 020 7372 2973 for nearest
bathroom refurbishers

Selecta
Dodgson St
Rochdale OL16 5SJ
Tel: 01706 869988
Website: www.selectasp.co.uk
(shower cubicles)

Showeristic Ltd
Unit 10
Manor Industrial Estate
Flint
Flintshire CH6 5UY
Tel: 01352 735381
*(made-to-measure shower trays and
cubicles)*

Ware Bathroom Centre
4 Star Street
Ware SG12 7AA
Tel: 01920 468664
*(circular shower rails, fittings for
ceiling)*

Zinsser
For details: See **Walls and ceilings**
(mildew bathroom paint)

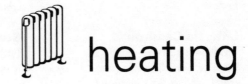 heating

Austroflamm Stoves
Tel: 01392 474060 (mail order)
(wood-burning stoves)

Cachet
Chartwell Road
Lancing Business Park, Lancing
West Sussex BN15 8TU
Tel: 01903 756534
(metal radiator covers)

Centre for Alternative Technology
Machynlleth
Powys SY20 NAZ
Tel: 01654 702400
Website: www.cat.org.uk
(solar panels)

Chesney's
194-202 Battersea Park Road
London SW11 4ND
Tel: 020 7627 1410
Website: www.chesneys.co.uk
(marble fireplaces)

Classic Radiator Cover Co
Unit 2, Mountain Ash Ind. Estate
Cardiff Road, Mountain Ash
Mid Glamorgan
Tel: 01443 477824
(radiator covers)

Clearview Stoves
More Work
Bishops Castle
Shropshire SY9 5HH
Tel: 01588 650401
Website: www.clearviewstoves.com
(wood-burning stoves)

CORGI
1 Elmwood
Chineham Business Park
Crockford Lane
Basingstoke
Hampshire RG24 8WG
Tel: 01256 372300
(register of certified gas fire fitters)

Focal Point
135 Eardley Road
Streatham
London SW16 6BB
Tel: 020 8769 5497
(specialists in fireplace restoration)

FrancoBelge
Unit 1
Weston Works
Weston Lane
Tyseley
Birmingham B11 3RP
Tel: 0121 706 8266
Website: www.franco-belge.co.uk
(wood-burning stoves)

Kampmann
47 Central Avenue
West Molsey
Surrey KT8 2QZ
Tel: 020 8783 0033
Website: www.kampman.de
(underfloor heating systems)

heating

Liberon

For details: See **Walls and ceilings**
(Stone Floor Cleaner: good for stone hearths)

Lithofin/Casdron

Tel: 01962 732126
Website: www.lithofin.com
(slate sealant for fireplaces)

Myson

Eastern Avenue
Team Valley Trading Estate
Gateshead
Tyne & Wear NE11 0PG
Tel: 0345 697509
Website: www.myson.co.uk
(heating systems without radiators)

Original Club Fenders

Tel: 07000 286722 (mail order)
Website: www.clubfender.com
(hand-made fenders)

Out of the Wood

Rowan Cottage
Gascoigne Lane, Ropley
Hants SO24 0BT
Tel: 01962 773353
Website: www.ootw.clara.net
(radiator covers)

Plasti-Kote

For details: See **Soft furnishings**
(Hot Paint: for painting gas fires)

Platonic Fireplace Company

Phoenix Wharf
Eel Pie Island, Twickenham
Middlesex TW1 3DY
Tel: 020 8891 5904
(contemporary grates)

Solar Solutions Fountains

6 High St
Kington
Herefordshire HR5 3AX
Tel: 01544 230303
E-mail solarshop@aol.com

Website:
www.solarsolutionsfountains.co.uk
(solar-powered fans for conservatories)

Stovax

Tel: 01392 474000 (mail order)
(cast-iron stoves)

Strippers

For details: See **Walls and ceilings**
(paint strippers for cast-iron fireplaces)

Thermo-Floor (GB) Ltd

Unit 5
Elbridge Farm, Chichester Road
Bognor Regis
West Sussex PO21 5EF
Tel: 01243 822058
E-mail: thermofloor@aol.com
(underfloor heating)

Chris Topp

Lyndhurst
Carlton Husthwathe
Thirske
Yorkshire YO7 2BY
Tel: 01845 501415
Website: www.christopp.co.uk
(made-to-order internal air grilles)

Warmup plc

Unit 1 Rowley Industrial Park
Roslin Road
London W3 8BH
Tel: 0800 318360
E-mail: sales@warmup.co.uk
Website: www.warmup.co.uk
(underfloor heating)

Welsh Slate Company

Business Design Centre
Unit 205
52 Upper St
London N1 0QH
Tel: 020 7354 0306
Website: www.welshslate.com
(sells slate sealant for fireplaces)

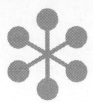

lighting

Fred Aldous
For details: See **Soft Furnishings**
(does a full range of lampshade frames)

Ann's Lighting
34 a/b Kensington Church St
London W8 4HA
Tel: 020 7937 5033
(lampshades to order)

A Touch of Brass
210 Fulham Road
London
Tel: 020 7351 2255
(brass and chrome switch fittings)

JD Beardmore
17 Pall Mall
London SW1Y 5LU
Tel: 020 7670 1000
E-mail: beardmore@beardmore.co.uk
Website: www.beardmore.co.uk
(range of light fittings)

Columbia Glass
13-16 Sunbury Workshops
Swanfield Street
London E2 7LF
Tel: 020 7613 5155
Website: www.columbia-glass.co.uk
(unusual light designs, by appointment only)

The Conran Shop
Michelin House
81 Fulham Road
London SW3 6RD
Tel: 020 7589 7401
Website: www.conran.com
(night light and glass candle holders)

Decorative Textiles of Cheltenham
7 Suffolk Parade
Cheltenham
Gloucestershire GL50 2AB
Tel: 01242 574546
(silk and beaded fringes for lampshades)

Delusions of Grandeur
1 Wine Villas
High Street
Elham
Near Canterbury CT4 7TA
Tel: 01233 750177
(chandeliers in unusual designs)

Feng Shui Catalogue
Tel: 020 8992 6607 for catalogue
(crystals to hang for their light effect)

lighting

Formatt Filters

Unit 23
Aberaman Park Industrial Estate
Aberaman
Aberdara
Mid Glamorgan CF44 6DA
Tel: 01685 870979
Website: www.formatt.co.uk
(Cocoon: softens fluorescent lighting)

Liberon

For details: See **Walls and ceilings**
(Tourmaline: gives an aged look to brass)

Lighting 2000

759-763 Finchley Road
London NW11 8DN
Tel: 020 8731 8601
(range of lights and shades)

Mathmos Direct

20-24 Old St
London EC1V 9AP
Tel: 020 7549 2700
Website: www.mathmos.com
(lava lamps and replacement parts)

Nice Irma's

For details: See **Floors**
(candles for outdoors)

Outdoor Lighting

(Louis Poulsen UK Ltd)
Surrey Business Park
Weston Road
Epsom
Surrey KT17 1JG
Tel: 01372 848 8000
Website: www.louis-poulsen.com
(lights for outdoors)

Louise Slater

27 Merthyr Terrace
London SW13 8DL
Tel: 020 8748 6918 (mail order)
(sells fairy lights and chilli lights)

Sola Lighting

1 Newton Road
Wollaston
Wellingborough NN29 7QN
Tel: 01908 585840
Website: www.solatube.com
(Solatube: a clear dome used to bring natural light into a room)

Wind & Sun Ltd

Humber Marsh
Stoke Prior
Leominster HR6 0NE
Tel: 01568 760671
Website: www.windandsun.co.uk
(solar/battery lantern)

Christopher Wray Lighting

591-593 Kings Road
London SW6 2YW
Tel: 020 7736 8434
Website: www.christopher-wray.com
(6,000 lights in a wide variety of style)

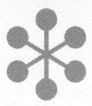

storage

Betterware
Stanley House
Park Lane
Castle Vale
Birmingham B35 6LJ
Tel: 0845 143 1010
Fax: 0121 693 1000
Website: www.betterware.co.uk
(carrier bag bin)

Chairworks
Unit 75-80
Chelsea Bridge Business Centre
326-342 Queenstown Road
London SW8 4NE
Tel: 020 7498 7611
(baskets of every sort)

The Conran Shop
For details: See **Lighting**
(magazine racks)

Crispins
Hows Street
London E2
Tel: 020 7739 0303
(storage service)

The Holding Company
184 New King Road
London SW6 4NF
Tel: 020 7610 9160
(storage products)

Keramica
Unit 9
Parkworks
Ogden Road
Hanley
Stoke-on-Trent
Staffordshire ST1 3BX
Tel: 01782 207206
*(vases with useful storage
applications)*

Lakeland Plastics
Alexandra Buildings
Windermere
Cumbria LA23 1BQ
Tel: 01539 488100
Website: www.lakeland.co.uk
(storage products)

Ocean
689 Mitcham Road
Croydon CR0 3AF
Tel: 0870 242 6283
(storage products)

Paperchase
Head Office:
12 Alfred's Place
London WC1E 7EB
Tel: 020 7467 6200
(brightly coloured storage boxes)

storage

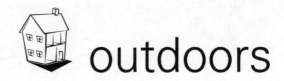

outdoors

Bartholomew Conservatories
Unit 5
Haselmere Industrial Estate
Haselmere
Surrey GU27 1DW
Tel: 01428 658771
(conservatories)

Benattar Brollies Ltd
577 High Road
Leytonstone E11 4PB
Tel: 020 8539 5967
(specialist umbrella manufacturers)

Beresford Pumps Ltd
Carlton Road
Foleshill
Coventry CV6 7FL
Tel: 02476 638484
(water garden pumps)

Broxap and Corby
Rowhurst Industrial Estate
Chesterton
Newcastle-under-Lyme
Staffs ST5 6BD
Tel: 01782 564411
Website: www.broxap.co.uk
(collapsible parking posts)

Cane Store
207 Blackstock Road
London N5 2LL
Tel: 020 7354 4210

Dorset Weathervanes
284 Bournemouth Road
Charlton Marshall
Blandford
Dorset DT11 9NG
Tel: 01258 453374
(weathervanes, e.g. witches, trains)

Elpees Entertainments
Unit C6
Laser Quay
Medway City Estate
Rochester
Kent ME2 4HU
Tel: 01634 297708
E-mail: flags@elpees.co.uk
Website: www.elpees-entertainments.co.uk
(custom-made range of flags)

Focus Do It All
Tel: 0800 436436 (mail order)
Website: www.focusdoitall.co.uk
(wide range of water features)

Fountains Direct
41 Dartnell Park Road
West Byfleet
Surrey KT14 6PR
Tel: 01932 336338
Website: www.fountains-direct.co.uk
(fountains and pond pumps)

The Garden Factory

Canon Gates Ltd
Martindale
Hawks Green, Cannock
Staffs WS11 2XT
Tel: 01543 462500
Website: www.cannockgates.co.uk
(wormeries)

GP Plastics Ltd

156 Bordesley Middleway
Stratford Street North
Birmingham B11 1BN
Tel: 0121 772 0033
Website: www.gpplastics.co.uk
(bubble tubes for vertical water displays)

Haddonstone Ltd

The Forge House
East Haddon
Northampton NN6 8DB
Tel: 01604 770711
Website: www.haddonstone.co.uk
(reconstituted stone balls for gateposts)

House of Marbles

The Old Pottery
Pottery Road
Bovey Tracey
Newton Abbot
Devon TQ13 9DS
Tel: 01626 835358
Website: www.houseofmarbles.com
(specialise in glass nuggets for your garden)

International

For details: See **Walls and ceilings**
(durable paint for garden gnomes)

Kiddie Wise

PO Box 433
Leek
Staffs ST13 7TZ
Tel: 01538 304235
(natural wood swings, slides and climbing frames)

Marc Kitchen-Smith

C5R Metropolitan Wharf
Wapping Wall
Wapping
London E1 9SS
Website: www.hiddenart.com
Tel: 020 7488 3270
(mosaic garden pots)

Mexican Hammock Company

42 Beauchamp Road
Bristol BS7 8LQ
Tel: 0117 972 4234
Website: www.hammocks.co.uk
(hammocks)

The Mosaic Workshop

Unit B
443-449 Holloway Road
London N7 6LJ
Tel: 020 7263 2997
Website: www.mosaicworkshop.com
(mosaic materials for making table tops)

Natural Collection

The Oaklands
Admeston
Telford
Shropshire TF5 0AN
Tel: 01952 254101
Website: www.gravel.co.uk
(coloured gravels)

Oxley's Furniture Restoration Services

Lapstone Farm
Westington Hill
Chipping Camden
Gloucestershire GL55 6UR
Tel: 01386 840466
(restoration of metal benches)

outdoors

Park Leisure
Unit 2
Fairview Industrial Estate
Ruckinge
Kent TN26 2PW
Tel: 01233 733782
Website: www.parkleisure.com
(recycled tiles made from shredded car tyres for use underneath children's play areas)

Plasti-Kote
For details: See **Soft furnishings**
(durable paints for garden furniture)

Potmolen Paint
For details: See **Walls and ceilings**
(durable paint for concrete areas outside)

Thomas Sanderson
Waterberry Drive
Waterlooville
Hampshire PO7 7XU
Tel: 0800 220603
Website: www.thomas-sanderson.co.uk
(awnings)

Sovereign Distribution UK Ltd
Sovereign House
34 Robeson Way
Boreham Wood WD6 5RY
Tel: 020 8954 1616
Fax: 020 8954 1313
Website: www.fiesta-heaters.com
(outdoor gas heaters)

Strippers
For details: See **Walls and ceilings**
(alkaline-based poultice for removing leaded paint)

Timber Decking Association
PO Box 99
A1 Business Park
Pontefract
West Yorkshire WF11 0YY
Tel: 01977 679812
Website: www.tda.org.uk
(advice on the best decking for your garden)

Wadham Trading Company
France House
Digbeth St
Stow-on-the-Wold GL54 1BN
Tel: 01367 850499
(numerous topiary frames including animals, e.g. penguins, frogs)

Walton Garden Buildings
EC Walton & Co. Ltd.
Sutton-on-Trent
Newark
Nottinghamshire NG23 6QN
Tel: 01636 821215
Website: www.waltons.co.uk
(children's playhouses, log cabins, sheds, etc.)

WaterDance Creations
The Old Barn
Combe Cottage
Sortford Road
Leaden Roding
Essex CM6 1RB
Tel: 01279 876055
Website: www.waterdance-creations.co.uk
(unusual garden sprinklers spraying water in different shapes)

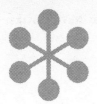

cleaning and fixing

Acanthus Architects
5 Lilymead Avenue
Bristol BS4 2BY
Tel: 0117 977 2002
(publicity and marketing for 12 architects around the country)

Association of British Picture Restorers
Station Avenue
Kew Surrey TW9 3QA
Tel: 020 8948 5644
Website: www.abpr.co.uk
(will direct you to an expert)

China Restorers
The Coach House
King Street Mews
King Street
London N2
Tel: 0208 444 3030
(have been mending china for 40 years)

Classic Rocking Horses
Green Acre
Islebeck
Thirsk
North Yorkshire YO7 3AN
Tel: 01845 5**Tel:** 01330
(sell and restore rocking horses)

Harry Berger Cleaners & Dyers
For details: See **Soft furnishings**
(cleaners and dyers of cotton velvet curtains)

Clewer Cleaning Services
4 Winifred Road
Apsley
Hemel Hempstead HP3 9DX
Tel: 01923 268139
(uses Stain-Away: the product that removes hard layers)

Easy Architectural Salvage
6 Cooper Street
Leith
Edinburgh EH6 6HH
Tel: 0131 554 7077
(Edinburgh salvage)

Foxall and James
For details: See **Walls and ceilings**
(Acorn paint roller; furniture polishes)

General Woodworking Supplies
76-80 Stoke Newington High St
London N16 7PA
Tel: 020 7254 6052
(latex-based glue: good for sticking material to wood)

cleaning and fixing

Gray & McDonnell
264-269 Poyser Street
Bethnal Green
London E2 9RF
Tel: 020 7739 4022
(glass restoration)

Jali Ltd
Albion Works
Church Lane
Barham
Canterbury
Kent CT4 6QS
Tel: 01227 831710
Website: www.jali.co.uk
(decorative MDF work, e.g. radiator covers, staircase designs)

Kensington Traders
Unit 25-27, Progress Park
Ribocorn Way
Luton LU4 9UR
Tel: 01582 491171
Website: www.spiral-staircases.co.uk
(do spiral staircase installations)

Kleeneze Homecare
Martins Road
Hanham
Bristol BS15 3DY
Tel: 0117 975 0350
kleeneze@kleeneze.co.uk
(Bar Keeper's Friend: a powder to keep your sink sparkly)

Langfords
Silver Vaults, Chancery House
53-64 Chancery Lane
London WC2A 1QU
Tel: 020 7242 5506

Le Creuset UK Ltd
4 Stephenson Close
Andover
Hampshire SP10 3RU
Tel: 0800 373792
Website: www.lecreuset.com
(pots and pans cleaner)

Liberon Waxes
Mountfield Industrial Estate
Learoyd Road
New Romney
Kent TN28 8XU
Tel: 01797 367555
Fax: 01797 367575
Website:
www.woodfinishsupply.com/uk.html
E-mail: Liberon@liberonwaxes.uk
(touch-up pens for scratch marks on furniture)

Gifford Mead/Spindlewood
The Old Bakery
8 Edward St
Bridgwater
Somerset TA6 5ET
Tel: 01278 453665
(replacement spindles and bannisters)

WR Outhwaite & Son
Town Foot
Hawes
N. Yorkshire DL8 3NT
Tel: 01969 667487
Website: www.ropemakers.co.uk
(rope for handrails)

Presents for Men
PO Box 16
Banbury
Oxfordshire OX17 1TF
Tel: 01295 750100
Website: www.presentsformen.com
(small copper-plated balls for cleaning vases, etc.)

RIBA Clients' Advisory Service
Royal Institute of British Architects
66 Portland Place
London W1B 1AD
Tel: 020 7307 3700
Fax: 020 7580 5533
Website: www.architecture.com
(help to find an architect)

Royal Institute of Chartered Surveyors
Surveyor Court
Westward Way
Coventry CV4 8JE
Website: www.rics.org.uk
Tel: 020 7222 7000
(can recommend someone locally)

Rutlands
Holly House
Rutland Square
Bakewell
Derbyshire DE45 1BZ
Tel: 01629 815518
(reconditioned nail guns from the US)

Safety Stairways
45 Owen Road Industrial Estate
Owen Road
Willenhall
West Midlands WV13 2PX
Tel: 0121 526 3133
(make spiral staircases)

St Blaise
For details: See **Furniture**
(historic house repairs)

Salvo
PO Box 333
Cornhill-on-Tweed
Northumberland TD12 4YS
Tel: 01890 820333
Website: www.salvo.co.uk
(magazine with info on reclaimed materials; help in locating items and for finding nearest reclamation yard)

Scrubs
Merchant House
Parsonage Square
Dorking RH4 1UP
Tel: 01306 743868
(polisher for cleaning stainless steel saucepans)

Southdown Abrasives
Unit 3A, Dolphin Way
Shoreham-by-Sea
West Sussex BN43 6NZ
Tel: 01273 463677
E-mail sales@saic-uk.co.uk
Website: www.saic-uk.co.uk

Stanley Tools
Woodside
Sheffield S3 9PD
Tel: 08701 650650
(Dynagrip knives: retractable blade trimming knives)

Superyachts ... Supermodels Ltd
Unit 9, Wat Tyler Country Park
Pitsea
Basildon
Essex SS16 4UH
Tel: 01268 559377
(modelmaker who makes to order and considers abandoned projects)

Verdigris London Ltd
Arch 290
Crown St
Camberwell
Tel: 020 7703 8373
(brass, copper, pewter and bronze restoration)

Wellfield Trading
2 Enterprise Centre
Cranborne Road
Potters Bar
Hertfordshire EN6 3DQ
Tel: 01707 664444
(Compact Sport multi-tool)

Wilkinson and Son
1 Grafton Street
Mayfair
London W1X 3LB
Tel: 020 7495 2477
(glass restorers)

cleaning and fixing

craft shops

Fred Aldous Ltd
For details: See **Walls and ceilings**
*(everything you might need for all
types of craft work)*

The Art Shop
26-28 Broadwick St
London W1V 1FG
Tel: 020 7734 5781
E-mail: art@cowlingandwilcox.com
Website:
www.cowlingandwilcox.com
(art and craft equipment)

The Craft Depot
For details: See **Kitchens**
*(everything from feathers and
pompoms to doll's house furniture)*

Hobby Craft
7 Enterprise Way
Aviation Park
Bournemouth International Airport
Christchurch
Dorset BH23 6HG
Tel: 0800 0272387
*(superstores with over 40,000 items
for 150 crafts)*

❋ index

index

index

index

287

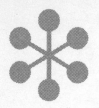

acknowledgements

My thanks to Emma Callery, Ciara Lunn and Dan Newman – a cool and collected team ... and poor Anne-Marie Hoines who had the hardest job – checking all those phone numbers!

And to Tina Moran for all her support at the outset and Allegra McCauley for her weekly enthusiasm!